Praise for **Truth with Stretch Marks**

Truth with Stretch Marks received rave reviews from seven out of the thirteen residents of Richland Township.

–Tom Katt, *Township Trustee*

This laugh out loud book is so darn funny it has been banned from the local hospital psych ward and both funeral homes.

–Doug Graves, *Pushin' Daisies Mortuary*

Truth with Stretch Marks has been consistently the number one best seller at Freddie's Flea Market for two straight days.

–Freddie Cooter Jr, *Owner Freddie's Flea Market & Beauty Parlor*

Widow Shufflebottom laughed so hard she lost her lower bridge in a six-quart Tupperware container of banana pudding.

–Chris P. Bacon, *Chat & Chew Club President*

The three-book Oskaloosa Library has placed *Truth with Stretch Marks* on their must read list.

–Rita Booke, *Head Librarian*

This book of humor is taking the county by storm. Towns as far away as Iantha, Milford, and Kenoma have been begging for one additional copy.

–Dusty Rhodes, *County Commissioner*

TRUTH WITH STRETCH MARKS

BY BEN REED

This is a work of fiction. Names, characters, businesses, places, events and incidents are either the products of the author's imagination or used in a fictitious manner. Any resemblance to actual persons, living or dead, or actual events is purely coincidental.

TRUTH WITH STRETCH MARKS

First Edition

ISBN: 978-1-4675-5428-2

All drawings by Ben Reed
Interior and cover design by Heidi Lowe

Printed by Litho Printers & Bindery
Cassville, Missouri

DEDICATION

I DEDICATE THIS BOOK to my youngest son, Brad. Cancer claimed his earthly life at age 36. I can still hear his voice. I can still hear his laughter. I miss him more than I can possibly say.

Sometimes parents and children share similar family characteristics. Then again, sometimes they are as different as night and day. One specific family trait that Brad and I seemed to share was our sense of humor. We both liked a good joke. We both liked a funny story. We both liked to laugh.

Even through his vigilant battle with cancer, Brad would continue to find humor. Finding humor when facing your own mortality could not have been easy. But Brad did. Sometimes I think he found humor more for us than he did for himself. It was his occasional wit, his joking sarcasm and his humorous story telling of hospital events that would ease the pressure and tension of a most difficult situation. Looking back, it may have been Brad's sense of humor, which provided the glue that held our family together during such a horrendous time in our lives.

David Bradley Reed
(3/15/1972 – 7/3/2010)

So what about this book? Well

over a course of several years, I had written a few humorous short stories. Brad had read some and had been after me for years to make them into a book. Even after he and his family had moved to Georgia, almost every Saturday afternoon phone call would end with, "Hey Dad! How's that book of funny stories comin' along?" Naturally I would do what only a Dad knows how to do best…I would lie. "Comin' right along," I would tell him. The truth of the matter was I didn't have the slightest clue on how to go about making a book and really didn't have any intentions on figuring out how to do so. But sometimes we have our ideas changed. Since his loss and remembering just how much Brad enjoyed a good laugh….figuring out how to make a book of funny stories seemed the very least I could do to honor his memory. So to my son I can now finally say:

Brad, believe it or not, the book is finally done. Good or bad, right or wrong, funny or not, it's done. I hope you're still smiling. I hope you're still laughing. And I was thinking of you when I finished writing the final chapters. There is not a day that goes by that something doesn't remind me of you. I miss you and I love you every single day.

-Dad

P.S. – Your kids are doing great. You would be so proud of Benton, Olivia, and Chloe. The all share the best of your favorable and maybe just a couple of your not so favorable qualities……but mostly the favorable. And yes, they make me laugh. Your life is definitely being carried on through your kids.

CONTENTS

INTRODUCTION

"TRUTH WITH STRETCH MARKS" is a collection of actual happenings of my life. As you read the stories of my life, I will plead guilty in advance to stretchin' the truth just a bit. But I will also guarantee that each chapter contains an absolute minimum of at least one percent truth in each and every story. The other ninety-nine percent could also be truth, but may have been stretched to assist in enriching the reader's imagination. Like one of America's favorite sons, Will Rogers once said, "Don't let the truth get in the way of a good story."

My humorous outlook on life didn't just happen by chance. It was caused by identity theft. On the day of my birth, some nitwit nurse got me mixed up at the hospital with some other newborn chick. In the confusion, my folks were told they were the parents of a brand spankin' new baby girl. Even though my dad said that I was the biggest, hairiest, homeliest looking baby girl he had ever laid eyes on, they accepted the nurse's announcement and would try to figure out how to learn to love me anyway. So on my very first day on earth I was faced with making a life changing decision. Just because Nurse Nimrod couldn't look at my cold shivering naked little new born body

(*See Note) and tell whether I was a Larry or a Mary, didn't mean I couldn't laugh it off and wear my new pink hospital bracelet home with pride.

My perspective of the situation in between squaws and dirty diapers was that I could grow to become a bitter old man with a sissy name or I could try to see the funny side of life. I chose to see funny. I will have to admit that I was more than pleased when all my ten little fingers and ten little toes plus one other little appendage were accounted for just in a nick of time. For certain, if things were allowed to stand as they were, I would have most definitely been the biggest, hairiest, homeliest Vickie Larue at my senior prom.....and most likely without a date.

Why humor? Why not? If not for humor, I might possibly go nuts. In my work, I have intellectual type folks above me in faraway places that have the IQ of flannel. Financially, I have monthly bills that can literally out race my paycheck to the bank. Proportionately, my truck eats more gas than I eat food. My rising health insurance premium pays for everything except my never before heard of body ailments. And just like clockwork, every mechanical device that I purchase will always shoot craps exactly one week after the warranty is up. So since there are usually more than enough somber situations to cloud up the sunniest of days, for the less stressful moments of life I would like to smile.

I have found that almost any calamity can have a twist of humor if we just stop and take the time to look for it. Everyone knows what it's like to have a bad day. So this is my thought. As you read about the perils of my life, I will not be offended if you laugh with me or even laugh at me just as long as you laugh. If just one of my life suffering

* **Note:** In my defense, there needs to be an explanation offered concerning, "my cold and shivering naked little new born body." There is actual scientific proof of what effects cold temperatures can have on little or even big boy private parts. It's called shrinkage.

mishaps brings a smile to your face or jogs a humorous memory of your own past, then my brighten your cloudy day work is done. Go ahead and smile. It will be at my expense.

MOON
BUSTER

CHAPTER 1

THE GREATEST FOURTH OF JULY SHOW EVER

THE YEAR WAS 1962. I was 10 years old. The sun was so hot, humming birds were sucking on snow cones. The humidity was so high bumble bees were doing the back stroke from flower to flower. The stench of burning sulfur could be smelled in the air. The occasional sonic boom explosion would rattle the windows of our farm house, leaving the animals in the barnyard on full shattered nerves alert. Yes, all of these signs could mean only one thing - it was the Fourth of July.

When growing up on the farm, the annual neighborhood Fourth of July celebration was a much anticipated event. The gathering of family and friends, ice cold watermelon, homemade ice cream, and most importantly for a 10 year-old boy – the fireworks – all combined to make this a very special day. Even trying to decipher the fragments of Chinese newspapers which were used to make firecrackers was part of the annual Fourth of July ritual.

The only thing wrong with our Fourth of July farm celebration was our local fireworks show just couldn't compete with the fireworks displays held in town. Area communities had towering sky rockets which would zoom into the heavens and shower the sky with millions upon millions of every color of the rainbow miniature asteroids. My miniature bottle rockets would only jump up a few feet off the ground, which more or less resembled a fire fly with a chronic cough. Sure, I could light an M-80 or cherry bomb and send a pork-and-bean can a quarter of a mile, but the colorful night show was what everyone really enjoyed. Well, I vowed this year our Fourth of July show was going to be different. No more Lady Fingers. No more of those silly Black Snakes which left scorch marks on the sidewalk until Christmas. This Fourth of July was going to be so special no one would ever forget it.

Unbeknownst to my folks, I started well in advance by saving up the necessary dollars needed for a first rate fireworks show. I collected pop bottles and stray feed sacks and turned them into cold hard cash. There would be no more of those piddley two for a nickel bottle rockets. I was going to invest in 12 of the infamous MOON BUSTERS. This show was going to be the talk of all Central Township.

After the rockets were secretly purchased at a small town general store, I began working on my 10 foot 2x6 board launch pad. First I used Dad's brace and bit to drill holes for placement of each individual rocket. Between holes I used a chisel to cut a groove to hold my ignition firecracker powder which would create a spectacular synchronized launching system. My launch pad complete, I hid my Cape Kennedy behind a rose bush and balanced it on a feed bucket, two paint cans and a Karo Syrup jar. The rockets were in place, the ignition powder was poured, and all systems for launch were go. Boy, was everyone going to be surprised when my dozen MOON BUSTERS streaked across the darkened sky.

As evening approached, our farm turned into a beehive of activity. Family and friends began arriving for the annual Independence Day celebration. Dad was in the milk barn hurrying to finish up chores. Mom was scurrying around the kitchen taking pies and cobblers out of the oven. As for me, I was killing time with my cousins by getting a little pre-fireworks practice with some Black Cat fire crackers.

Everything was going fairly well according to plan until one of my half witted cousins lit an entire 10 cent pack of firecrackers and unknowingly tossed it over the rose bush into my secret launch area. The first firecracker blast sent one of our farm cats streaking out from under the rose bush and right into the syrup jar portion of my home made launch pad. As the jar went tumbling down, so did the entire south end of my 2x6 launch board. This changed the entire elevation and trajectory of my soon to be launched MOON BUSTERS. As the fire crackers continued to bang away, one landed on the powder launch system somewhere between missile six and missile seven. Instead of having a gradual synchronized from end to end launch, I had rockets being lit in the middle and firing at will.

Rocket 6 was first to take off. It sailed into a spreading elm tree and exploded. The shower of sparks taught baby pink sparrows how to fly six weeks before they thought they could. Rocket number 7 headed straight for my uncle's new Buick and sliced a one inch permanent part on the right side of its velvety vinyl top. A professional barber could not have done better.

As the cry went out to hide the women and the children, number 8 missile went zipping across the driveway and came to rest on the front porch right under my Aunt's new stars and stripes skirt. When the rocket exploded, her skirt flew up about eye brow high and pretty much looked like Old Glory waving in the wind. If it hadn't been so dangerous, I think all of the men folk would have stood up and saluted.

MOON BUSTERS 5 and 4 more or less took off together and headed for the milk barn window. The double explosion was soon followed by a tremendous racket. Shortly after, "Hard Faucet," one of Dad's favorite milk cows came crashing through a door bucking and bawling with the stanchion still around her neck and the milking machine still attached to her milking parts.

In times of stress and frustration, my Dad could speak three different languages: English, a little German, and on rare occasions another language called Army Talk. The latter could usually be heard at the milk barn when he was trying to break a newly freshened Holstein heifer to the milking machine. Well, Dad came charging out the milk barn door in a fit of rage chanting a mixture of all three of his favorite vocabularies. However, as brave as Dad was, when rocket number 9, with its rocket's red glare, parted his hat from his hair, he used every bit of his World War II infantry training to low crawl back to the safety of the concrete milk barn bunker.

Rocket number 3 landed and ignited a dry patch of grass in the corner of the garden, which was just a few yards away from a ripened field of oats. Ducking and dodging the continuous shower of sparks, my cousins and uncles grabbed buckets and dipped water from the horse tank to put out the fast spreading fire. Missile number 10 ricocheted off the tractor muffler, bounced off a maple tree and smashed into the hen house door with a defining explosion. Mom's hens immediately went on a six week laying strike.

Rocket number 2 fired and went skipping across the yard right towards Granddad. Granddad immediately took evasive action. He tossed his cane aside, which I thought he needed just to be able to stand upright and turned into a world class sprinter and hurdler. He covered 20 yards in six steps. In one Olympic style leap, he cleared the picnic table without even knocking over the mustard. In a cloud of dust, he slid as if he were stealing second base to the safety of Mom's tractor tire flower garden. Everyone was impressed with Granddad's athletic skills.

MOON BUSTER number 11 sailed straight through the open door of a metal grain bin. It did absolutely no damage, but we heard later the echoing explosion was magnified so loud, it was heard almost 20 miles away.

Across the road, the neighbors beef cow herd was safely lined up at the fence obviously enjoying watching the fireworks display. However, when rocket number #12 whooshed across the yard, skipped across the backs of four Hereford cows, and exploded in a flash in the Angus bull's face, their sense of humor turned into terrifying panic. It was three fences, one railroad track and two corn fields later before they stopped to take their first breath.

Last, but certainly not least, my favorite MOON BUSTER number #1 ignited and zipped across the yard at mach-1speed close on the heels of our two pet dogs. The collie and cocker spaniel dove for cover under the front porch along with a dozen of their mortal enemies... the cats. Evidently a pet truce had been reached until World War III came to an end. Rocket number #1 glanced off of a porch post and accelerated straight up into the darkening sky. As I tilted my head backward to watch the magnificent ascent of my final rocket, the evening sky was suddenly filled with a beautiful red, white, and blue glitter as my MOON BUSTER exploded into the formation of a Jimmy Durante nose.

I was at the height of my ten year old glory. What a Fourth of July show it had been. Even if the few smoldering flames and columns of smoke drifting on the horizon did have great similarity to General Sherman's March to the Sea, it had been an evening to remember. In the last visible moments of the twilight hour, with MOON BUSTER number one's sparkling ash still falling all around me, I shouted, "Wasn't it the Greatest." As family, friends and farm animals crawled hesitantly from their hiding places in disbelief of what had just happened, no one uttered a sound. I suppose words alone were just not enough to express just how much they had really appreciated "The Greatest Fourth of July Show Ever."

CHAPTER 2

THANKS FOR THE TOILET RHODA

AS I LOOK AROUND today at all of the modern conveniences, I think back to the 50's when our lives weren't quite so prosperous on the farm. I'm not suggesting we were poor or anything, but I think we did have a zip code of E-I-E-I-O. Those were hard and tough times. We answered the phone by listening to the length of the Morse Code rings. I think ours was a long and two shorts. Our television took 17 minutes to warm up to get the one and only snowy station available. And, Mom didn't have one of them new fancy wringer washers, so once a week she would just take me and my brother down to the creek and beat us against a rock. This solved two chores. Not only did she get our clothes clean, but it would give her a head start on dishing out the punishment we were most likely going to deserve before the week was over.

Our family lived on a rented farm and it was a fairly typical farm of the time. No one really specialized in farming in those days. Most farms had a little bit of everything. Dad grew some wheat, oats, corn and a few soybeans. When he wasn't in the fields, there were always livestock chores to do. There were hogs in one lot, dairy cows in the pasture, and the chickens pretty well had open range. What wasn't so typical about our farm was the house. It didn't have any running water or indoor facilities. What we did have was a little hand pitcher pump in the kitchen, which gave us a nutrient enriched mixture of roof top rain water and bird poop from a cistern. Yum! Yum! Our new dairy barn, on the other hand, had to meet Grade A regulations in order to get the highest price for milk. This not only meant the milk barn was equipped with good clean running well water, but there was a hot water heater thrown in to boot. Good Grief! This meant our milk cows were actually a couple higher steps up in society than we were. And since we didn't have indoor facilities, that meant we resorted to using outdoor ones, sometimes better known as the outhouse, or privy, or thunder box, or the Sears and Roebuck library.

I'm not sure our family would have ever stepped out into the 20th century if it had not been for Rhoda. Rhoda was a Rhode Island Red chicken and not of the ordinary variety. She was the one meanest hen that ever roamed the earth. I would bet money, if her Kentucky fried genealogy could be traced, some kind of Cranky-Bird-A-Soris dinosaur ancestry would show up in her bloodline. She was like a feathered covered, snapping turtle sporting the disposition of a wounded grizzly bear with a toothache. We once had a collie dog that could whip every dog in the township, but Rhoda could put him under the porch with his tail between his legs in a heartbeat. Many a time I saw Rhoda chase a feed salesman back to his truck in a dead run. And, if anyone was ever stupid enough to reach under Rhoda to gather her eggs while she was still on the nest, well, it was just a known fact they were going to be drawing back a bloody stump of an arm. Of course, this did give me a chance to have some fun when my city cousins came out to the farm for a visit.

But for all of Rhoda's bad traits, she did lift our poverty stricken family out of a destitute state, even if it was by accident. In the spring of each year, Rhoda would just up and disappear. It would disgust her to no end to return to her nest each day and find her previous day's work was now fried, scrambled or hard boiled. So each spring, when her maternal settin' hen instincts were the greatest, she would pull a disappearing act and make her a nest in an undisclosed location. It might be in a post pile, a weed patch or a hayloft. And then as if just by magic, in about three weeks she would show up with a dozen or so fuzz ball chicks following after her.

One particular spring, Rhoda found the safest of all places to hatch her young. She somehow found a way to squeeze just underneath the back corner of the outhouse and build her nest on a small ledge of dirt. If solitude was her priority, there was no doubt that under the outhouse was most definitely the safest place to be on our entire farm. However, this is where the story gets a bit interesting. This was the day that Rhoda and my dad's paths would cross. My dad had a regimental daily routine, which you could set a clock by. Rain or shine, he would get up at five o'clock sharp every morning, put on his chore clothes, and head for the milk barn. He would finish the milking, come back to the house, and then eat a breakfast of champions. With breakfast finished, he would then tuck the latest farm magazine under his arm and walk the well worn path to the outhouse. Within a step and a half of the door, one overall suspender would already be undone. As he would open the door, Dad would do this little pivoting ballet move and enter the privy backwards. As the door closed, the overalls would be around the ankles and the first paragraph of "Corn Damage Caused By Grasshoppers" already read. This was the one moment of leisure which my dad counted on each and every day. But today, it was not to be.

Now from Rhoda's perspective, she was already in an agitated state. Of course, if I had been sitting in the same spot, in the same position for three weeks, I probably wouldn't be a happy camper either. Especially, if it was under the outhouse. I don't even want to try to imagine her view! Exactly what went through Rhoda's mind, we will probably never know for sure. Maybe she thought she needed to protect her soon to be young. Maybe she was half starved and mistakenly thought she saw manna from heaven. Who knows? But for whatever reason, she mentally snapped. She didn't cluck. She didn't ruffle her feathers. She gave no warning whatsoever. She just reached up with her beak and grabbed a hold of dad and gave him a yank. From that moment on, our lives would never be the same.

Now it hadn't been that many years since dad had been in a fox hole in Germany during World War II. His nerves were still a little on the shaky side. Unexpected loud noises would make him jump. A flash of lightening would send him diving for cover. And Oh My Gosh, you never, absolutely never, wanted to sneak up behind him, grab him and yell Gotcha. So when Rhoda did her south of the border tug of war act, Dad went absolutely berserk. I'm not sure how he did it, but he come flying out of the outhouse without even opening the door. There was lots of yelling and screaming about being snake bit by a rattler. With dad's overalls still around his ankles and his boxers not much higher, he came hopping across the yard like he was in a gunny sack race. My first thought was, how could Dad's arms be so tan and the rest of him be so snow white? There were more yells and screams with a few remnants of left over army talk thrown in about being clawed by a Louisiana Swamp Cat with rabies. When he finally made it to the house, Mom was trying to help pull his overalls up, while Dad commenced to loading up his 12 gauge shot gun.

In the next few minutes Dad gave us boys a complete reenactment of how he single handedly won the Battle of the Bulge. KABOOM! KABOOM! KABOOM! Dad began unloading his shotgun from the hip. With each blast a new hole would appear and chunks of boards would go flying in all directions. BAM! BAM! BAM! The door finally fell from its hinges and wooden shingles were sailing out into the pasture. A new box of shells provided Dad with plenty of ammo, so he just kept firing and reloading as fast as he could.

Eventually, even mean old Rhoda couldn't handle the pressure of all the buck shot whizzing overhead. From the back porch, we saw

Rhoda poke her head out from the back side of the outhouse and then scramble to safety through a tall patch of horse weeds. However, at this particular time, it didn't seem prudent to walk up behind dad and tell him we had seen his offender escape, especially when he had a loaded gun in his hands. So we just kept our mouths shut and let the bombardment continue. KERR POW! KERR POW! KERR POW! With the last shot gun blast still echoing off the hay barn and gun smoke hangin' in the air, we watched our outhouse teeter and then totter and then finally collapse into a pile of rubble.

Even though not a word was said, I know all of us were beginning to reach the same conclusion, just about the same time. Okaaaaaaay! But now what are we supposed to do when nature calls? Better yet, just how long will it be before we might be able to do it? As Dad slowly turned around, he couldn't help but notice the "we hate constipation look" we were all giving him. But not to fear. Even with his eyes still glazed, Dad went into immediate action. His fingers dialed that rotary phone like it was a Las Vegas roulette wheel. He called the landlord. He called his brothers. He called neighbors and any other casual acquaintance he could think of. I'm not so sure he didn't get a couple of wrong numbers. But that didn't really matter because Dad was pleading for help from anyone who would listen. Time was of the extreme essence.

The work began immediately. While some began digging a water line from the milk barn, others were digging a hole for the septic tank. A sense of urgency could be detected, as the dirt went flying from spades in every direction. In the meantime, the out of county landlord was on his way down with, a brand new to us, used commode. In less than 36 hours, our family was in business of doing our business. And, just in time I might add.

There was only one slight hitch to our new indoor facilities. Although the used commode worked mechanically just fine, it didn't necessarily mean business would be completed in a pain free manner. Almost invisible to the naked eye, there was a hair line crack in the wooden seat that would have never passed OHSA regulations. Unless you came in at an angle or sat hunched up side ways, the seat would pinch you until tears flowed. I'm not sure Rhoda could have inflicted any worse pain. Every time I received a pinch, I debated just how much longer I could handle this movement towards upper society. But eventually, Dad did get the seat fixed. It was kind of nice to believe, if only in our own minds, that we were now living like rich people, or at least as good as our milk cows. Who would have ever believed, a chicken, especially such a mean old chicken like Rhoda, could have single handedly elevated the social status of an entire family? All I can say is, "Thanks for the Toilet, Rhoda."

"Thanks for the Toilet, Rhoda."

SAD
CAMP

CHAPTER 3

LAZARUS....GET YOUR LAZY BUTT UP.

THANKS TO THE CULTURAL Revolution spearheaded by Dr. Sigmund Freud during the 20th century, the majority of child rearing psychologists refer to today's over active children as industrious, exceptionally motivated, high spirited or over achievers. Wow! In my day, we were known as nut buckets, out of control idiots, brainless wonders, or freaks of nature. To assist in my rearing or rear ending, my folks were firm believers in not sparing the rod or the switch or the belt or a splinter filled 2 x 4 yanked off a nearby shed in order not to spoil the child. Basically, whatever was within arm's reach would suffice as a disciplinary tool of tough love parenting…better known as pain. If I had a nickel for every time I heard the words "Believe me Son, this is gonna hurt me more than it's gonna hurt you," I would have had enough nickels to have retired at age twenty-six. The only good that ever came about of Dad not owning a copy of Dr. Freud's parenting book on how to hit a child where bruises won't show, was it was just one less weapon Dad had to inflict parental pain.

Finding out from friends that I was now old enough to go to church camp was like the folks being told they had just won the Freedom From Kids Lottery. Not only would the week long religious experience help keep a hyper active eleven year old on the straight and narrow, but would also prevent my parents from breaking the sixth commandment of Thou Shalt Not Kill. I'd never seen my folks so excited. Among their low whispers I think they were either planning a long over due second honeymoon getaway or maybe even a permanent change of address during my absence. Either way they each had these goofy little grins on their faces like they had just been granted parole from a life sentence of hard labor.

Along with a cardboard suit case I was tossed out on the church parking lot without the folks '57 farm truck even coming to a stop. It soon became obvious that this was a universal religious drop off zone for sugar saturated kids. As word spread throughout the community about the church camp dump site, moms and dads from all religious faiths began unloading their kids for the week. Parents that had never even darkened a church door except for an occasional wedding or funeral were taking advantage of this week long religious free babysitting service. This ranked right up there with getting store bought meat with a book of green stamps.

Eventually, all of us rowdy orphans for a week were corralled and herded into a convoy of station wagons to begin our journey of spiritual transformation. After a two hour long, packed like a sardine in a can car ride, we arrived at the infamous SAD (Save A Delinquent) Church Camp. The campground had been purchased with donations from parents long before today's Valium was ever marketed as a parental recreational drug. According to camp bylaws approved by parent charter members, Camp SAD was required to be constructed in a secluded wooded area that would avoid any and all contact with closely related adult civilization.

Being late arrivals, we immediately noticed hundreds of kids already milling around in the camp ground gravel parking lot. Camp counselors were busily trying to divide the campers into teams. It would have been easier to drive a herd of cats into a bread sack. As we tumbled out of the station wagon like a car load of clowns, I got to hear her before I ever saw her. "I'll take the big one" she screamed. I turned around just in time to see this big fat girl with pig tails running straight for me. That is when I first laid eyes on Wanda Jo. She was two hundred pounds of pure round. I will be the first to admit that I am certainly no prize when it comes to looks, but poor Wanda Jo was way past homely. Her face looked like a catcher's mitt that had caught one too many fast balls. And as big as she was, Wanda Jo still had not had time to grow into her Incredible Hulk size buck teeth. That girl could have eaten corn on the cob through a picket fence.

"You're mine," she hollered, as she began man handling me and dragging me off to my new team. How embarrassing! How humiliating! If I could have broken her choke hold, I would have crawled under a rock. For the first time in my life, I began missing parental corporal punishment. An elm switch whipping would have been less painful.

Wanda Jo was bigger than me. She was taller than me. She was definitely louder than me. And, I was soon to learn that she was better at all sports than me. Worst of all, she seemed to have a crush on me. At eleven years old, the least of my non hormonal worries was being bit by an oversized love bug. But did that matter to Wanda Jo? Heck no. She made it crystal clear that she wanted me for her new gal pal.

Regardless of the camp activity, swimming, softball, meal time, evening camp fire services, Wanda Jo would drag me around the camp grounds like a rag tag security blanket. Every time I tried to make a break for it, there was Wanda Jo cutting me off at the pass. If I tried to hide in the woods, she would pop out from behind a tree and ambush me like the Zodiac serial killer. During lunch, she thought it would be romantic if we shared sandwiches. Her idea of sharing meant she would eat hers, then mine. My only place of seclusion away from Wanda Jo was a small wood frame building on the back side of the campgrounds. In other words, I spent as much time as I could in the camp outhouse. But even then she would stand outside the door and yell loud enough for everyone in the southern hemisphere to hear, "Are you 'bout done in there?" Naturally that would always insure 500 pairs of strange eyes would be staring in my direction as I exited the outhouse door. It would have been better to have been constipated for the entire week.

At the beginning of the week, teams were given names and would compete in a variety of camp activities. Each team had to choose a name that would relate to a book of the Bible in some fashion or another. There was the Kings and Queens. There was the We Have Your Numbers. There was the Mighty Galatians. And since we had an equal number of boys and girls, we were known as the She and Hebrews. Not only was there an open competition among teams, but I had made the decision to enter into a personal little competition between Wanda Jo and myself. I would show her who the real boss was.

While the She and Hebrews Team was holding its own among the team competition, my private Wanda Jo rivalry was not going as well. She was beating the socks off me in every event. In softball, if I hit a stand up triple, Wanda Jo would clear the bases with an over the cow pasture fence home run. In the memory verse competition, while most kids chose a single Bible verse, I stood up and delivered the 23rd Psalm word for word. Wanda Jo then bounced up and recited the entire book of Genesis and then asked if she could say it backwards in Latin. The mid week competition was comprised of a bunch of Sadie Hawkins type outdoor events. Wanda Jo was the Rock of Gibraltar anchor for our team on the tug of war. When she braced herself, you couldn't have moved her with a bull dozer.......maybe with a fried pie, but not a bull dozer.

I somehow got paired up with Wanda Jo in the three legged gunny sack race. Before the start I gave her my best Johnny Unitas look and said, "You better keep up with me girl." When the whistle blew, Wanda Jo and I took off like a couple of scalded hound dog pups. Leading the pack by a good ten yards, all was going well and then it happened. I tripped over a hidden sandstone and went down in a heap. With our legs inner twined in the feed sack, Wanda Jo came crashing down on top of me like a 200 year old Sequoia. Air rushed out of me like a tree stob puncturing a tractor tire. Just before blacking out, I had the most unbelievable feeling of my spirit beginning its ascension up into the heavens. What I was actually feeling was Wanda Jo's competitive spirit. She had jumped up, put both her legs into the burlap bag, threw me across her shoulder and single handedly or footedly hopped us to a first place finish. The word "mortification" does not even begin to do justice to my humiliated male ego. I would have preferred to have been publicly flogged.

By the end of the week, thanks to Wanda Jo's wonder woman heroics, the She and Hebrews found themselves in a neck and neck championship race with the Here Comes the Judges team. The final team competition would be a reenactment of some scene from the Bible and would in all likelihood determine the overall winner. One team chose Moses and the burning bush and about three acres of a nearby farmer's pasture was lost to a get away fire. Another team spread out about thirty bed sheets over several rolled up sleeping bags in order to symbolize the swells of the Red Sea. However, before Moses could part the sea, a wind came up and blew most of the bed sheet water into a barb wire fence. One by one we saw Daniel not get eaten by lions, Noah nearly drowning by falling off an ark that wouldn't float in the camp swimming pool and Adam and Eve dressed in catalpa leaf skirts chomping down on some freshly picked worm riddled apples.

It was a make or break time for the She and Hebrews. For our academy award winning performance, we selected the scene of raising Lazarus from the dead. A kid named Dennis was tall and lanky so he got to be Jesus even though Wanda Jo wanted the part. For what our production had in mind, it was important that our Lazarus be a light weight. Stanley was short and skinny and border line wormy.

He was a natural for the dead Lazarus role. Doris and Mona, a couple of girls from Arkansas, got to be Lazarus's sisters, Mary and Martha. Most of the other team members got assigned to be part of the wailing crowd. Although I didn't get cast for any of the leading stage roles, at least that show off Wanda Jo didn't either. Our important talents were needed else where.

Our reenactment was going to take place on the stage of the tin barn /church camp chapel. To dazzle the judges and out score our opponents, we decided to sensationalize the Bible story by taking a few creative liberties with props and scripts. Since we didn't have a tomb for Lazarus to walk out of, we decided it would be extremely dramatic for Lazarus (Stanley) to be lowered from the ceiling down to Dennis (Jesus) to be raised from the dead. To do this we needed some kind of a make shift stretcher. We found an old wooden door which happened to fit perfectly between the barn rafters. Holes were then drilled and ropes attached to each corner to make the perfect Lazarus lowering gurney. The only decision left was what kind of mechanism would be needed for the lowering. This is when I learned of my important contribution to the production. Just my luck, I once again found myself teamed up with my wannabe girlfriend, Wanda Jo. Being the strongest on the team, it was up to Wanda Jo and me to be the human winches to lower the emaciated looking Lazarus (Stanley) down to the healing floor.

Every spare moment we were practicing our skit. With his natural look of death, Stanley was a dead ringer for Lazarus and didn't need much rehearsal. As luck would have it, Dennis already had a fairly deep booming Jesus voice. This was basically because he had spent too many years in the fourth grade. It was evident that Doris and Mona were very emotional, had plenty of experience in crying and whining, and made perfect wailing mourners. As for me and Wanda Jo, we both had George Foreman biceps and got where we could lower the Lazarus back to life door slick as a whistle. We practiced and practiced and practiced for our big day. First place was going to be a cinch for our She and Hebrews team.

To avoid any other team from snitching our great bringing Lazarus back to life idea, we practiced mostly at night behind closed doors. What hadn't been thought about was that our actual production would be taking place in the middle of the afternoon. Forgetting about that one little tidbit of information turned out to be our Achilles' heel. On show day, the up in the rafters August afternoon heat easily surpassed 120 degrees. Shortly before curtain time, from a hidden ladder Wanda Jo, little wormy Stanley, and I climbed up to our suffocating rafter perches. The unbearable heat from the sheet metal was only inches from our heads. As our narrator began preparing the audience for our production, I gave a quick glance towards Wand Jo to see if she was ready for our rope lowering debut. Holy! Moly! I had never seen a fat girl sweat like that before. She was all red faced, her pig tails had gone limp and she was about to baptize poor dead Stanley with the rivers of sweat pouring off of her face. She was beginning to pant and her entire body was quivering like a bowl of strawberry Jell-O. Just my luck, Wanda Jo could even sweat better than I could.

Our cue to lower Stanley was when Dennis (Jesus) said, "Bring your dead brother unto me." Then there it was. Dennis (Jesus) spoke. As Doris and Mona wailed away and tried their best to dodge Wanda Jo's showers of sweat, we began our descent of the lifeless Stanley. About eight feet from the concrete floor, I saw something happen that could have revised the King James Version of the Bible. What I saw was Wanda Jo begin losing the grip on her ropes. What a rush. This was my chance. After a week long of being outshined by a fat girl, I finally had found something I could do better. If there was one thing I could do and do quite well, it was hang on. I don't know if it was years of fighting for and holding on to the last Sunday dinner chicken leg or hanging on to my dad's overall suspender when he tried to teach me how to swim by throwing me into the creek.

For whatever reason, my grip was every bit as good of a hound dog hanging on to a soup bone.

With Wanda Jo's ropes slipping through her sweaty palms and me showing off my vice like grip, Stanley's wood door stretcher was quickly turning into a city park slide. While I held tight to Lazarus's feet end of the stretcher, Stanley began his head first backwards eight foot free fall from Wanda Jo's end. I'll have to hand it to Stanley. He stayed right in character. He didn't open one eye or omit any girlish screams on the way down. He hit the concrete floor Kerr Smack with his head and his Lazarus body never quivered once. Caught somewhat off guard and since Wanda Jo had already dropped her end of the door, there was really no point for me to hang on to my end of the door any longer? Wham! Bam! If Lazarus had any life left in him after the rafters to the floor fall, the wood door to the chest definitely finished him off. Dennis (Jesus) was really going to have his work cut out for him. Lazarus never moved a muscle, while his mourning sisters pulled the door off of him. Not realizing that Lazarus was out cold, Dennis (Jesus) kept to the original script, "Lazarus…arise and walk." After about the fourth, "Lazarus arise and walk" with no response and thinking Stanley was just clowning around, Dennis finally got ticked and changed Jesus's words to "Lazarus get your lazy butt up." I am reasonably confident that those are some red lettered words that will never end up being printed in a revised version of the Bible.

Drenched in our own sweat, Wanda Jo and I climbed down to check on Stanley. A camp preacher was on stand by just in case last rites were needed. The camp nurse had a wet cloth on his forehead and was breaking a truth serum capsule under his nose. The good news was Stanley could moan or maybe was trying to speak in tongues. He didn't remember who he was or where he was, but that wasn't a for sure fact even before his accidental fall. Stanley never was the sharpest tack in the box whacked on the head or not.

When Stanley's eyes finally unrolled from the back his head, we packed him over to a chair. Since Dennis (Jesus) was totally disgusted with the entire performance, he had already cut out for a dip in the pool. It was obvious the judges weren't buying the dragging of Stanley to a chair as part of the reviving Lazarus part of the show. To add insult to injury, the words "lazy butt" seemed to have crossed the church camp creative liberties line. Our team score fell faster than the Black Friday stock market crash. We went from first place all the way down to the cellar in a matter of mere seconds.

As the years have gone by, I have lost track of most of my 1960's fellow church campers. I sometimes think back to those simpler times of the good old days. I often wonder what became of Dennis, Stanley and even big ole' Wanda Jo. I am sure they have all married, raised a houseful of kids and lived successful lives. But if they are anything like me, I wonder if they ever think back to the times when a bunch of country kids almost rewrote the Bible with the words "Lazarus, get your lazy butt up."

23

CHAPTER 4

FRIDAY NIGHT FOOTBALL OFFERS LEADERSHIP

NONE OF US EVER know when we may be called upon to lead. Leadership can range from being picked first on a school yard play ground or elected by voters to a political office. Being a leader is like walking an emotional tight rope. Emotions can range from disappointment to "Yee Haw" with lots of frustrations thrown in between for good measure.

There are times when leadership isn't always what it's cracked up to be. I often think back to the days of high school football when my leadership abilities were first put to a test. Each football season has one game, which is designated as a homecoming game. Teams always try to pick an opponent they can beat, to insure there would be a homecoming winning experience. Of course my senior year, the easiest team in the conference to beat.... just happened to be us. I saw more hay wagon floats in one year than would normally be seen in the Rose Bowl Parade. In short, we were the conference chumps. We had been beaten so many times we were in the basement of the conference dog house. Other schools were so excited about playing us that if they couldn't get us scheduled for their own all important homecoming game, they would try to move their own homecoming activities to our school. To our chagrin, conference officials over ruled our own attempt to schedule ourselves as our own home coming game opponent for the season.

More by default than by democratic process, I was elected captain of our team for our next home game. Of course, the next home game just happened to be our own dreaded homecoming game. Since we had just lost our sixth homecoming game of the season, unbearable coffee shop pressure was being applied for either a team win or a team forfeit. With the Friday night homecoming game only days away, I was given the job of taking the bull by the horns and trying to figure out a winning team strategy. We needed spirit. We needed support. What we really needed was Divine Intervention. With lots of student help, home coming posters and banners started popping up in town businesses. Soap victory messages began appearing on many of the car and truck windows parked around the town square. The cheerleaders somehow got the art class nerds to paint a tiger's head on a huge break away banner. Even the band came up with a couple of new "go fight win" tunes. The entire community was hungry for a win. What better game for our very first victory of the season than our very own homecoming game? The team was getting pumped.

Game night finally arrived. The bleachers were packed. Alumni had traveled for miles to see the new and improved fighting tigers. Our team was gathered under our goal posts waiting to be introduced in the pre-game ceremonies. On cue, as team captain I was supposed to run through a pre-marked spot on the backside of our new tiger banner. The idea was to funnel the entire team through the roaring mouth of our tiger mascot banner. Jumpin' through a piece of paper wasn't exactly rocket science. But to ensure perfection, our team had practiced the tiger entrance move more in the past week than we had our offensive ground attack. Two of our beefiest cheerleaders were holding on to two wooden poles, which stretched the tiger banner tight. The crowd was yelling. The remaining cheerleaders were milling around and cheering on the opposite side of the banner pumping up the Tiger fans. The band was playing. Excitement filled the air. There was little doubt that our team was more than ready....at least for the pre-game ceremonies.

My cue from the cheerleaders to explode through the tiger's mouth was the word "GO." In our jumping up and down, one over exuberant player accidentally cleated another player's foot and the kid yelled "Get off my TOE." In my defense, in the midst of lots of yelling, the word toe pretty much sounded like go. Off I shot with the rest of the team close on my heels. However, unbeknownst to me the cheerleaders in an effort to keep the paper banner from tearing prematurely had attached an almost invisible quarter inch booby trap close line rope at the bottom of the two posts. Tripping on the rope, I began stumbling and made my grand entrance through the hairy part of the tiger's chest. To make matters worse, when I fell I just absolutely slobber knocked five of the seven unsuspecting cheerleaders on the other side. It was probably the best hit of my entire football career.

Well Crapola with a capital CRAP. I was about as good a leader as General George Armstrong Custer. To add further salt to the wound, the rest of the team was following like lambs going to slaughter. My team mates kept right on piling in to each other like a chain reaction multi-car interstate pile up. For what seemed like eternity, the tiger mouth just kept on regurgitating one football player after another. Even three coaches tumbled into the mixture of arms and legs and helmets and cheerleader skirts before it was over.

There were moans and groans and an occasional cuss word, which I believe to be coming from one of the cheerleaders being squashed on the bottom of the pile. It took game officials 15 minutes to untangle the mess. Three of the more seriously hurt players were carried back to the locker room, while others limped their way to the sideline bench for treatment. Our team sustained numerous injuries and we hadn't even had the coin toss for kick off yet.

As the other team cheered for us from across the field, several of the less injured players threw off their football gear and tried melting in with the student body. Others made a break for it looking for any unguarded exits. However, the announcer called for a complete football stadium lock down to thwart any ball player escapee break out. The coaching staff posse began nabbing several of us football fleeing felons. Eventually enough healthy bodies were rounded up and forced to play the annual homecoming game.

Hoping to vindicate ourselves from such a non-auspicious beginning, our team fought with a renewed energized team spirit. By the end of the first quarter we were only down 21 to 0. Battered and bruised our team regrouped and vowed to stop their Mr. Fancy Foot Running Back if it was the last thing we did. It was the last thing we did. At half time our opponents held a slim 40 to 0 lead. During the half time break, our coaches tried motivating us by telling us what a bunch of miserable no account losers we were. Gee Whiz! That really seemed to perk us up. We got the usual "football is a game of life" speech. "How you play the rest of this game is how you will live the rest of your life." What a dismal outlook on life. People we didn't even know would be running right over the top of us for the rest of our lives.

Our choices were clear. We could try hanging ourselves with our jock straps or we could go out the second half and show the other team what we were really made of. We began the second half with a kick off and a rekindled spirit. The other team responded with an 85 yard touchdown return. As if on cue, the band, the cheer leaders, the entire current and alumni student body began exiting the stands. Even our parents were headed for the gates in hopes they still had time to get home to see the #1 rated "Carol Burnett Show." Not only our parents, but our varsity opponents also headed for the sidelines. Of course they were replaced with a JV team that still ran the final score up to a depressing 64 to 0 shellacking.

Like I said, "Sometimes leadership isn't always what it's cracked up to be." Many times leadership can be about more than just the win or the loss column. Leadership can be all about perspective. It is all in the way we look at something. Another word which interacts well with perspective is spin. There is a good side and a bad side to almost everything. The downside was, yes, we lost another game. We could have walked off that field feeling down and out because we had not just lost another game; we had lost our final senior homecoming game. But, on the other hand, maybe we could put on a spin that would emphasize the pluses and minimize the minuses. That is what a leader does to rally the troops and that is exactly what I did. School history was made that chilly November evening and we were part of it. We weren't losers. We had accomplished a feat that no other past or present Tiger team has been able to do in the history of our school. We were the new record holders. To this day our senior class still holds the Big Ten Conference distinction for having the most consecutive homecoming game losses (7) in a single season. A record is a record and sometimes that's all that counts. Now that is what I call leadership.

CHUCK

CHAPTER 5

FOR BETTER OR WORSE..... I WILL ALWAYS LIKE CHUCK

CHUCK AND I ARE just pretty darn tight. He has his own special spot at my place. We go to work at the same time. He takes me hunting and fishing. We actually go on a lot of fun trips together. Yep! Chuck and I spend a lot of time together and I'm not afraid to say it…I like Chuck. In fact, I have liked Chuck to the tune of $373.72 each and every month for the past 60 months. Chuck is my truck.

I tend to give nick names to those people, animals, or objects that I become attached to. I once had a three legged dog named Tripod. Slick was my twice removed cousin who always wiped his runny nose on his shirt sleeve. And as for Chuck….Well, Chuck is a Ford Ranger. Chuck Norris was a famous Texas Ranger. Since they are both rangers….Walla…my truck Chuck.

Although I would never intentionally jeopardize our friendship, I have to admit I have begun noticing some subtle changes in Chuck's demeanor. Now that Chuck is no longer restricted to warranty work, he is starting to show some almost human like characteristics that are spooking the dickens out of me. Has automotive technology advanced to the point that trucks can now actually think for themselves? Is it possible for a truck to actually have mood swings? It's as if Chuck's computer chip has developed a bipolar Jekyll and Hyde personality like a girl I once dated.

A while back, I was west bound on an interstate, which was jammed packed with big rigs. As Chuck and I crested a hill, there must have been 15 or 20 18 wheelers all lined up bumper to bumper in the slow lane ahead of us. A quick glance in the rear view mirror revealed a half dozen big rigs coming up fast in the passing lane. Not wanting to get trapped in the slow lane, Chuck jumped into the passing lane with all the spirit of a straight off the show room floor model and made a run for the roses. With a Peterbuilt and a couple of Kenworths hot on his tail, Chuck started passing the long line of trucks like it was a slow movin' camel train. Then just as he pulled even with the lead slow lane truck, with absolutely no warning and for no other reason than to remind me of my irregular arrhythmia flare ups, Chuck went on strike. Every mechanical, electrical, and chemical function about Chuck just went DOA. At 75 plus mph, going code blue in the passin' lane is not necessarily a good thing. With horns blarin', brakes screamin' and black smoke boilin', our Indianapolis 500 big rig passin' lane buddies were taking all sorts of evasive action to keep from making me and Chuck their hood ornaments. Since the slow lane was already bumper to bumper, the only option left for Chuck and me was to coast. We kept going slower and slower and slower. Glaciers have been known to move faster. Chuck was down to 5 mph in the passin' lane when the final slow lane truck went cruising by with the toot of his horn. By now, even the fast lane trucks had moved over into the slow lane and were noticeably very uncordial as they too began passing us by. Before I was able to coast over into the slow lane and off to the shoulder, I learned an interesting fact about truck drivers. To a driver, they looked to be about nine parts muscle and one part mouth. And, no lip reading qualifications were needed to understand what they were yellin'. But if I happened to have been hard of hearing, I'm sure the international brotherhood of trucker's one-finger sign language still would have conveyed their message of displeasure to me.

More recently, Chuck as developed a cantankerous dislike for being wet. He doesn't like mud puddles. He loathes thunderstorms, and absolutely despises the carwash. Every time he comes in contact with water, weird stuff starts happening. One under belly mud hole splash and the dome light might pop on. A half dozen stray raindrops and the check engine light or the door a jar ding donger will sound off. Worse yet, right after a carwash bath the lightest tap on the brakes might result in a face in the windshield four wheel skid, not to mention the air bag to the kisser deployment.

I was on a homeward bound three-hour road trip one off and on rainy afternoon when Chuck found a new way to dislike wetness. Somctimes to pass the time on a trip, I tune in a radio talk show on the A.M frequency. There is usually some Dr. Quackola explaining how his concoction of eye of a toad, wing of a fly, and hair of a bat can help fat people lose weight. Well Duh!! One sip of that brew, I'd probably never want to eat again myself. Or better yet, I always enjoy listening to a female psyhco-cologist condemning all men for not being sensitive enough to women's ever changing emotions. Just as I was learning why most men are considered to be members of the swine family, Chuck's intermittent wipers kicked on. But simultaneously as the wipers kicked on, the radio changed stations. I was now listening to a deep throated southern Mississippi radio evangelist getting down to business about the shortcomings of sinners. "Sinners are liars and cheats and are the putrid bile of the earth."

Wow! It was one of those, scratch your head how did Chuck make that happen kind of moments. All I knew for sure, I was definitely more comfortable in being considered a common pig than being thought of as putrid bile of the earth. But like most swine, I didn't want to miss out on how men could better deal with the 371ST known female ever changing emotion, so I tentatively retrieved my Dr.Von

Hilda Man-hater station. It was less than a quarter of a mile when Chuck's wipers kicked back on and once again I heard the screaming baritone words, "Listen up fool, I said you sinners are going to die and burn forever." I'm here to tell you, those were definitely some of the most attention getting slow down and snap your seat belt kind of words I had ever heard in my life. If someone would have shoved a collection plate in the window, I would have emptied all my pockets. At 45 mph and listening to at least 30 different sermons, it took Chuck, me, and Reverend Hell Fire and Damnation almost an extra two hours to get home that day. This putrid bile wasn't taking any chances on not gettin' home in one piece.

Not long ago, Chuck thought it might be fun to check out my reaction time to a pure panic situation. One evening as Chuck took me home from work, my mind was off on one of my many imaginary vacations. On this particular little get away, I was at a faraway tropical paradise island, sipping milk straight from a coconut watching a beautiful sunset. Just as I was getting to the hula hula girl good part of my trip, Chuck was making his final approach to a railroad crossing near the local grain elevator. This is a railroad crossing we have crossed together twice a day, five days a week, for the past 20 years. Suddenly from out of nowhere blared a train engine horn so close that it blew the fruit right off my looms. As my heart clawed its way out of my chest, I slammed the brake pedal down with both feet. With box cars on a siding blocking my view, I only got a glimpse of the Doom of Death head light baring down on me. I knew it would be mere seconds until a Kansas City Southern ground me into a batch of southern fried grits if Chuck didn't get stopped in time. As Chuck's off road mud grip tires dug into the asphalt, I tried to remember if I had changed my "just in case I was ever in an accident" underwear. OOOPs ! Too late. Now I know what Chuck's "lube and go" must feel like.

With horn blaring and head light now in full view, I guestimated my short term life expectancy to be that of a Teetsie Fly. Wondering how many folks would take the time to attend my rest in peace services, I bravely braced myself for the impact. In other words, I shut my eyes and whimpered like an abandoned kitten. With only a few feet to spare, Chuck miraculously screeched to a stop with literally inches to spare. Re-swallowing my heart and wondering why my lungs had forgotten how to suck oxygen, I watched as the lone runaway engine shot out from behind the parked box cars at a supersonic speed of bottom of the bottle catsup. A snail with a limp could have out run him. With my hands still frozen to the steering wheel, I hoped above all hopes there had been no witnesses to my act of stupidity. No such luck. Four cars and two grain trucks across the tracks, three vehicles behind and two kids on bicycles all had front row seats to see the dork of the day. They stared as if they had just spotted the kidnapper of the Lindberg baby. Hoping to conceal my identity, I slid as low in the seat as I could to avoid possible recognition.

I did glance into my rear view mirror just in time to see a lady in a following car put up both hands to her cheeks as if she was about to witness a beheading. Good Grief! Her concern seemed to be a delayed reaction. I had gotten stopped. No train was going to be grinding me up into a sausage patty. The red lights across the tracks were flashing. The crossing bells were dinging and the far side cross arm was starting down. So what was this lady's problem?

As my light bulb of a brain started flickering, in a flash it came to me. If the cross arm was going down on the other side, Chuck was about one second away from being tommy-hawked by the railroad crossing arm on this side. With an opera like scream, I slammed Chuck into reverse and we now laid a reverse rubber trail over our previous trying to stop skid marks. Move Chuck Move! In just a nick of time and with only the slightest bump on Chuck's cab and one big Kerr Twang of his radio antenna, we miraculously made it out of harm's way. Chuck somehow came to rest right in front of the previously concerned lady that now had her hands covering her eyes.

Naturally the rail road crossing crowd had now increased in size by a lady walking her weenie dog, two joggers and a city maintenance worker driving a backhoe. From the looks on their faces, I had now been appropriately promoted to geek of the week. If a shovel had been handy, I would have dug a hole big enough for both Chuck and me to crawl in. Nerves shattered and totally humiliated, all I could think of was, how close was the tallest bridge and the deepest river? I would have gladly taken the plunge.

As the slow moving locomotive controlled by an engineer with one very perplexed look on his face was exiting the crossing, Chuck and I made the decision to get the heck out of Dodge just as soon as the gettin' was good. With the crossing arm halfway up, Chuck roared to life and we made a break for it. Kerr!!! Smack!!!! I would have bet good money I had remembered to take Chuck out of reverse. Not expecting a backward motion, the steering wheel once again reared up and smacked me in the face. Wow! That goose egg was really going to leave a mark. Chuck's tail gate looking bigger and bigger gave Mrs. Hands to the Cheeks and Eyes something really to worry about now. Chuck's tires nearly worn down to almost pure air pressure, once again locked up his brakes to avoid the fast approaching disaster. Incredibly, Chuck was up to the challenge and was able to come to another screechin' halt no more than a gnat's eyelash from the lady's front bumper.

Well, now let's size this little debacle up. I have already been christened Dork of the Day and Geek of the Week, so why not shoot for Moron of the Month? All I wanted to do was to click my heels together three times and wish that Chuck and I were back in Kansas with Toto. However, being completely drained of all self-esteem, Chuck and I with hood and head held high resumed our trip home as if it was an everyday normal occurrence. Remarkably though, not one car or truck, not one bicycle, not even the dog walker's weenie dog made a move until they were sure Chuck was going to either go forward, backward, sideways or maybe do an inverted two and a half double twisting backward somersault.

In all fairness, I really think Chuck is good for me. He seems to keep me young and old at the same time. Sure he might lock the doors and keep his keys in the ignition when I am in WalMart. Or maybe roll off the garage concrete pad backwards when he is not put into park and wedge himself between a Chinese Elm tree and a propane tank. But all in all, Chuck and I have shared many good times and have made lots of lasting memories. So for whatever it's worth.... for better or worse, I will always like Chuck.

CHAPTER 6

ME AND MY UNCLE MOSES

PEOPLE HAVE THIS UNCANNY desire to know where they come from. Family genealogy is becoming one of the fastest growing American hobbies. Tracing the family heritage back from the newest branches to the oldest possible roots can reveal some very exciting information about famous ancestors. It is not uncommon to uncover a war hero, inventor, or president in the family linage. On the other hand, the skeletons could really come rattling out of the closet when you find out great great great Uncle Bob wasn't just a horse rancher, but was hung for being a horse thief.

Well, last winter the genealogy bug kind of bit me and I started wondering just how far back my own Reed family limbs might reach back. Carefully following each family generation in reverse, I dug for hours hoping to find some type of Reed royalty in my blood line. It was somewhat of a disappointment to find that my family blood was not blue, but just the average run of the mill red like the rest of the world. Sometimes it wasn't even red, but barely had a pink cast. But just as I was about to throw in the towel of locating any famous Reed relative, it happened. After an all day exhausting research and almost totally by luck, I stumbled on to the famous relative mother lode. People can have their Davy Crocketts and their Martha Washingtons, because I am here to tell you it was a real kick learning that I'm related to Uncle Moses. Not just any Moses. That's right. The one and only stone tablet carrying, water to blood changing, Red Sea parting Moses.

I always subconsciously felt I might possibly have come from good stock. Naturally over time, the purity of my Uncle Moses bloodline may have been contaminated with a few minor imperfections from some of our less than perfect family members. But as watered down as my veins may be, I have always had this little gnawing inner feeling that there was greatness within me. Finally, after some exhausting long hours of difficult Dick Tracy detective work, I can now back up my suspicions with some cold hard facts that my family roots almost saw the Promised Land.

My first clue was the strong family resemblance. It is common for family traits to be passed down from one generation to another. It may be physical stature, facial features or the color of hair. According to Charlton Heston in the Ten Commandments, my Uncle Moses came down from the mountain top with a beard and flowing masses of snow white hair. Although most of my roof top hair didn't take time to turn color.....it just turned loose..... I am proud to say that on occasions I have sported a quite fashionable white mustache.

Further evidence linking Uncle Moses to the Reed clan is that we are a family of farmers. It is a known fact that Moses tended his flocks of sheep in the dessert. I too have raised cattle, hogs, and yes, even a few sheep during some pretty dry years. All of us know about Uncle Moses and the burning bush, which may have been the very first ever controlled burn. I too have experienced in lighting fires. I have burned bushes, along with my neighbor's hay field, my own jeans while still wearing them, and the right side of my mustache once when trying to light a faulty gas hot water heater pilot light. My pyromania notoriety has become so well known throughout our community that 911 calls me if smoke is spotted in the direction of my farm.

As farmers, both of us experienced some tough times on the

farm, sometimes referred to as plagues. Remember when Moses saw the Pharaoh's cattle die? I too lost three cows last winter. Sure it might have been because they were old as Methuselah, and had no teeth. But, they died all the same. How about the plague of lice? My cows rubbed off enough hair on fences this past winter that by spring the barbed wire looked like an Angus cow curling iron. Moses dealt with hail, and yes, this past year my soybeans received hail the size of eggs that would have made a settin' hen proud. Fortunately it wasn't a total wipe out or there wouldn't have been enough soybeans left for the swarms of summer grasshoppers to munch on. Uncle Moses referred to them as locusts.

It is a known fact that Moses and his friends were asked to leave Egypt through a parted Red Sea. There were walls of water on both sides of them as they made their way to safety. I too on occasions have been shown the door. It may be coincidental, but just recently after a fourth trip to an all you can eat pizza buffet, my lightweight buddies and I were also asked to leave? A sea may have not divided for our pizza palace departure, but there was a whale of a storm delivering rain by the bucket fulls as we left. That's pretty darn close.

One of the best things I have going for me in this new Moses connection is thank goodness I am not a first born. Whew! That was a stroke of luck. I suppose on some occasions there are some benefits to being the so called daddy's little accident. But, on the downside, if I had the short term outlook of my older brother I'm not sure that I would even be buying any green bananas.

In most cases, the lack of proper family record keeping has prevented people from going back very many generations. Many family trees look more like a brush hogged ragweed. I suppose the Reed family was just really fortunate to find out about Uncle Moses. I have certainly watched enough Law and Order reruns to understand that much of my circumstantial evidence may be considered flimsy at best. But there is one irrefutable, proof positive piece of evidence to back up my Uncle Moses Reed claim. Is there anyone that would challenge the supreme authority of the Bible? I would certainly hope not. I don't know why it took me so long to find out this information because it has been right in front of me for years. I'm surprised my church going neighbors hadn't mentioned it to me sooner. Right there in black and white in the book of Exodus it says my Uncle Moses was found among the "REEDS." Well there you go…absolute proof.

Whether you want to believe this "Believe It Or Not" Reed family tale is not important. What does matter is that this Me and My Uncle Moses story is now officially documented into the Reed family genealogy. And that's my story and I'm stickin' to it.

ME AND MY UNCLE MOSES

BATTERED
BOWEL
RANCH

CHAPTER 7

I DON'T WANT TO BE A COWBOY ANYMORE

I DON'T KNOW WHY every time I get around a horse, I immediately revert back to my childhood years. The 1950's were a special time in my life. Growing up on a farm with milk cows, pigs, and chickens, all I ever dreamed of was growing up and being a cowboy. All of my TV heroes were cowboys. And what was even better, all of my heroes owned a big, beautiful, fast, creek jumpin', rattlesnake stompin', outlaw catchin', good looking girl savin', partner for life, wonder horse. Roy Rogers had Trigger. Gene Autry had Champion. And the Lone Ranger had "Hi Ho SILVER Away". What better life could there be than growing up to be a cowboy riding his trusted steed into the setting sun? However, on Crabgrass Acres my only riding choices were Ada the Ayrshire, Wilbur the pig, or Hinny Penny. It's hard to be very cowboyish when you don't have a horse to ride.

Being a horse back ridin' cowboy was my youthful dream. The adult reality is that a horse ride on a cantankerous old nag can be about as much fun as a three fingered prostrate exam. If not careful, a middle aged horse ride can change your productive life different than as you once knew it. When men get old, crawling on the back of a horse is just a bone crunching, ear biting, snot snorting, shin kicking, sideways jumping, four legged accident waiting to happen. Regardless of how bad the want to be cowboy itch maybe, don't scratch it. It is just a good way to make use of your insurance deductible.

My only adult horsemanship experience was limited primarily to one horse owned by my father-in-law. He was a magnificently brown and white paint horse named Lucky. I am not for sure how Lucky obtained his name. It may have occurred when after each exhilarating life threatening ride, the rider would breathe a sigh of relief as he climbed out of saddle saying, "Good gosh all mighty, am I lucky to be alive." For whatever the reason, the name Lucky stuck.

Lucky was a horse well ahead of his own time. He had been into ear biting long before Mike Tyson ever thought of it as a boxing technique. While some horses like to nuzzle their riders, Lucky liked to permanently notch unsuspecting victims with teeth marks, much like a gun slinger would notch his six guns. Lucky could have also been involved in space aeronautics. He could have single-handedly saved the space program millions of dollars by sending astronauts into orbit without the assistance of booster rockets. More than once did good ole' Lucky launch me towards the four moons of Saturn.

Lucky was the only horse I knew which rarely felt the urge to gitty up when kicked in the ribs, slapped on the rump, or whipped with the reins across the neck. On the other hand, if a sparrow happened to tweet or a grasshopper sneezed unexpectedly, he was like a Ferrari going from 0 to 180 m.p.h. in directions unknown. In an instant, my head would snap back and the G-forces would pull my chubby cheeks even with my ears. And, that was just across the barn lot. In total fear, I would hang on for dear life and listen to my heart beat match Lucky's hoof beat. If a barn lot gate happened to be open, he would try his Kentucky Derby best to break every equestrian speed record possible to escape his barn lot prison.

As for a smooth ride, I never did have one on Lucky. His favorite gait was sort of a bone jarring frog hop, which was real similar to riding a banana seat bicycle with two flat tires down a railroad track. And this hop along gait was always at break neck speed. Unfortunately, it was usually my neck breaking that was in question. To make matters worse, neither Lucky nor I had very good horse running to riding rhythm. Unusual sound effects would normally accompany our cow chasin' pasture rides. My backside going down would meet his saddle coming up and would make this continuous rapid fire whop whop whop whop noise. Pretty much like the sound a flat tire on the car makes when you're trying to beat the Baptists out of Sunday Morning Services to the only fried chicken restaurant in town.

The only equivalent to Lucky's jet propulsion acceleration was his four hoofed anti-lock braking system. In most cases a simple "whoa" could start the down shifting procedure which gave a whole new meaning to curvature of the spine. However, a "whoa" was not always required. Lucky was unique in his ability that he could be running faster than the wind and still stop on a dime when spotting a single blade of grass in bad need of munchin'. Of course this would send me sailing from Lucky's launch pad, sometimes referred to in cowboy jargon as a saddle. And who ever invented the saddle neuter horn must have had one sick, demented sense of humor.

Even if Lucky was a bad runner, he was most definitely a worse jumper. Lucky had this little quirk about jumping across a ditch. For some reason he would have a panic attack whenever he approached a crevice. We're not talking about a Grand Canyon. A shallow road ditch, a caved in mole run or even a dry weather crack in the ground could send him into a horse seizure. In most cases those seizures would occur when he was on a dead run and without one ounce of warning. Many times I have picked up my grassed stained Wranglers off the ground in a semi-conscious state and tried to pleasantly reassure Lucky that there was no evil horse spirits on the other side of the crack in the earth.

The last time I tried to convince Lucky that ditch jumping was a natural function for horses, he gave me a lesson on how cowboys got to be bow legged. I rode Lucky across a prairie hay field and slowly approached a minimal sized road ditch. I dismounted and pulled by hand all of the grasses and weeds to make sure Lucky had a clear jump path. Then I got down on my hands and knees and pretended to be a horse excited about getting to step across a ditch. As Lucky stood there cock eyed observing this unusual occurrence, I half crawled and half hopped back and forth across the ditch several times showing him how much fun it could be. I needed to prove to him there was absolutely nothing to fear. I did get a couple of bewildered looks from the rural mail carrier and a neighbor disking a field across the road. But for whatever reason, neither one stopped to ask if I needed help or if I was once again ran out of my hearing voices in the head medication.

Anyway, after telling Lucky what a brave and courageous horse he would be to cross this ditch, I remounted and said, "Do it for me big fellow." With a slight nudge and one gigantic rodeo yell, Lucky made a jump which would have made NASA proud. I have never seen a horse gain altitude so fast, but with little to no forward motion. In mid-air his fears must have got the better of him and he tried to reverse course. He was like a cat falling from a tree trying his best to land on his feet. All four legs were flailing in four different directions. Of course, it would have been much better for me if Lucky had been a cat, because in one spastic awkward motion, he landed on his back in the bottom of the ditch with me still on board. Naturally, this was the first and only time I couldn't seem to fall out of the saddle. Upside down and on top of me, Lucky floundered back and forth from one side of the ditch to the other trying to somehow get his feet back under him. I was beginning to feel like a Thanksgiving turkey wishbone. I had always wondered how cowboys got bow legs. Now I know. This scene would have undoubtedly answered William Shakespeare's famous cowboy question. After seeing his first bow legged cowboy, he asked, "Tally ho I say, What men are these, Who wear their Wranglers, In Parentheseezes?" After a ten minute rolling around in the ditch, Lucky finally regained his footing and stood up. Then I fell off.

Even when I was not attempting to ride Lucky, he had ways of gaining my attention. At one point in time, Lucky got grass foundered and it became my job to deliver him to a world renowned horse doctor located some 25 miles away. I didn't have access to a cattle trailer, let alone a horse trailer. My only means of horse transportation was a two wheel portable cattle loading chute. With a lot of pushing, shoving, and dragging I tried to convince Lucky that going to the doctor was going to be fun. I finally had to promise him my one good left ear to chew on before he would agree to be loaded.

As I pulled into the famous horse doctor's parking lot, I soon realized I was out of my horse element. There were huge bright silvery mobile horse homes parked everywhere. Every horse in line to see the doctor was wearing a bright colorful pup tent on its back along with a color coordinated mask. And, the more fashionable horses had their tails tied up in a bow. What caught my attention most of all was every horse was being held by a horse woman. These were not the typical run of the mill farm gals either. These women wore pants that stuck out three feet on each side of them for no apparent reason. They were all fitted with tall black leathery boots which went halfway up their thighs. Their heads were not adorned with the typical western cowboy hats either. Instead they wore these tiny little yellow and orange short billed helmets, which wouldn't keep the sun out of their eyes even on a cloudy day. As I dragged Lucky out of the portable chute and we took our place in the sick horse line, I am sure I heard the horse whispers say, "Humph!! Another poor excuse for a cowboy."

When it finally came our time to see the doctor, Lucky wouldn't budge. I pulled. I pushed. I shoved. Lucky wouldn't move a muscle towards the get well "horsepital" barn. It was then I heard an "Excuse me. Let me show you how to do that." With a rub on the nose and a whisper to the ear, Lucky trotted off with one of those strange looking women as if he was entering the Belmont Stakes. Thanks a lot, Luck. I always look forward to embarrassment, especially in front of the opposite sex.

The doctor made his examination and confirmed the diagnosis of grass founder. He prepared a delightful smelling creosote dip with Tuna Helper drench, which should lead to Lucky's full recovery. I was asked to assist in the horse drenching procedure. My job was to stand in front of Lucky and hold his head perfectly still as the doctor inserted the ten foot long PVC plastic lateral line down his throat. For some reason, Lucky became somewhat apprehensive about having his plumbing works being retrofitted with schedule 40 plastic pipe. His eyes were wide. His nostrils were flaring. His muscles were taunt and slightly quivering. I felt I was witnessing a calm right before a storm. In all my years of being around horses, I was always cautioned to be aware when walking behind a horse. Why? Because horses, cows and almost all hoofed beasts are well known for kicking backwards? Lucky was no exception. He had a really mean back left hoof. I felt definitely fortunate to be in such a safe frontal position. Standing eye to eye with Lucky, I'm sure he winked just before he demonstrated his right knee lift to the groin trick. I didn't know a horse was capable of doing a Karate Kid high knee lift. His knee exploded into an area only a bow legged cowboy could appreciate. As my internal organs tried to crawl out through my throat and the last bit of oxygen rushed out of my lungs, I wondered why no one had ever taken the time to warn me about the danger of a horse's front leg maneuver. But then I stopped wondering, because I was OUT.

The inside of the barn was soon encompassed into total darkness as my eyes rapidly rolled back into my head. Within minutes or maybe hours, I can't really remember, the light slowly began to reappear. My first recollection was I thought I saw a beautiful yellow and orange sunflower speaking to me. It took a few minutes to realize I was on the barn floor surrounded by no less than a dozen of those yellow and orange capped horse women, bent over looking at me. Although I lacked the ability to utter a word, I began to hear conversations like, “Look what color he is now.” “Is he still breathing?” “This would make a great episode for ER.” “Drag him out of the way. It's my horse's turn.” When I finally regained my ability to speak, the vet asked if there was anything he could do for me. With a raspy voice, I requested two bullets, one for me and one for the Lucky. I didn't care which one of us went first, just as long as it was swift and merciful.

I would like to urge all adult males past 30, who may be heading towards a mid-life "I WANT TO BE A COWBOY" crisis, to resist the Roy Rogers mentality that horse riding is nothing but Happy Trails. If you really need a Champion, the Wheaties cereal boxes are full of them. If you sincerely treasure the ability to walk up right, trade in those horse ideals of the Lone Ranger and buy yourself a silver Ford Ranger. It took me 37 years of ripening on the vine to finally overcome my boyhood wannabe a cowboy dreams. But I now know for sure, I DON"T WANT TO BE A COWBOY ANY MORE.

CHAPTER 8

I'LL TAKE MY HUNTIN' BUDDY EVERY TIME

THERE HE STOOD. He was poised magnificently on the bank of a dry ravine ready to spring into action. For nearly an hour, he had left no blade of grass or broken twig go unturned as he tracked our wounded prey to this isolated briar infested gulley. With muscles tensed and eyes fixated, he remained absolutely motionless waiting for the perfect moment to launch his attack. As his eyes widened and nostrils began to quiver ever so slightly, I knew his wild game conquering moment was close at hand. It is every hunter's dream to witness the conclusion of a successful hunting drama unfold right before their eyes.

Suddenly without warning, he unleashed his lethal attack by diving head first into the thorn piercing briars. The fight was on. This wasn't the first time he had taken on a long bearded tom turkey for me and there was little doubt who the eventual victor would be. I immediately recognized a familiar pain induced scream. After nearly 40 years of hunting together, I have become well acquainted with the terrorized screams of my huntin' buddy, Kent. "Hang in there, Buddy. You got him now," I coached from the safety of the sidelines. Since I knew my huntin' buddy was going to be tied up for the next few minutes, I sat down at the base of an oak tree and began reflecting on some of our more memorable hunting adventures.

In all honesty, I don't know why hunters think they need a trained hunting dog. My experience has been the benefits of a good huntin' buddy can far outweigh what a huntin' dog has to offer. You take my huntin' buddy Kent, for instance. I don't feel obligated to have him vaccinated for heart worms. I don't have to feed him…..much. And best of all, I don't have to scrape the dog doo doo out his pen every evening. How many huntin' dog owners can make that claim? Better yet, a good….and I mean a really good huntin' buddy can be a pointer, retriever, and blood hound all rolled up into one. I would like to meet a hunter who has one dog, which can do all of that.

"Ouch! Ouch!"............"Stick with him, Kent. You almost had him that time."

I remember one miserably cold December morning when we shot a mallard duck and it landed about 30 yards out in the water. Now I knew it was cold because of the snot cycles forming on my huntin' buddy's mustache. We drew straws ten straight times to see who would be wading the frigid water to fetch our feathered prize. It soon became painfully obvious to my buddy that regardless of how many short straws I drew, I wasn't going wading. He never said a whole lot; he just mumbled a couple of very colorful adjectives and began his duck retrieving striptease. When he began his polar bear plunge, I have never heard noises like that ever come from a living or dying human being. It was kind of like a high pitched weenie dog with his tail caught in the screen door sound. And, it only took about 30 seconds for his body to reach the color of an over ripe eggplant. But did he complain? No siree Bob! He just waded right on out into the arm pit deep water, went into slight convulsions, latched onto the two pound chunk of feathered liver and then headed back to our blind. However, before he could shiver his way back to shore, I spotted some more ducks sailing in on the horizon. I did what came natural. I hollered for him to take cover. I think my exact word was, "Duck!" Unsure of whether I saw a duck or he needed to duck, he did the only thing a well trained good huntin' buddy could do. He held my dead duck on his head, pinched his nose, crossed his eyes, and sank like a rock. Kerr!! Pow!!....Yee Haw! Another dead duck splash down. Man, did that ever work out good. Thanks to my buddy's quick reaction, he was able to bring both ducks back to me on the same trip. Now how many retrievers are that intelligent?

"Yeow!!!!!!"......... "Hold on, Buddy. You're wearing him down."

For years, my huntin' buddy and I would head out in November on a marathon walk to chase bobwhite quail. During those years, our hunting arsenal would always include a birddog of some foreign descent. It may be an English pointer, an Irish setter, or a German shorthair. But when it came to finding dead birds in a patch of multi-flora rose bushes, it didn't matter what international language we would scream, English, Irish, German or occasionally some back alley blue colored talk, our dogs simply refused to be butchered by the briary bushes. This is when Kent's dog training skills really shined. To prove to a dog it could be done, he would get down on his hands and knees and actually demonstrate the art of finding dead birds in thorny bushes. Of course this was perfectly all right with the other bird dogs as long as they didn't have to go into the concertina wire torture chamber themselves. Sniffing the ground like he was on scent, Kent would strategically maneuver his way through the maze of thorny slice and dice bloodletting bushes. In a matter of moments he looked as if he had single handedly led the Normandy D-Day invasion. To his credit, he not only found both my dead birds, but pointed a couple of live ones on the way back. And bless his little bird finding heart, he held those birds on point long enough for me to get into a briar free comfortable position for a good clear shot. I was so proud of him, I promised him a new tick collar when we got back to town.

"Yee.....ikes!!!! He's spurring me in my never never land"......... "Come on, Kent. Quit your horsin' around and finish the job."

Most of our spring turkey hunts are never picture perfect like written about in Field and Stream. Between the two of us, we are the prime example and maybe the actual definition of Murphy's Law. If something is going to go wrong, it's going to find us. Sometimes our guns go click when they're supposed to go boom. We have had a coyote sneak in and grab one of our $29.95 decoys for a midmorning brunch. We have fallen asleep and woke up just in time to discover a dozen long bearded trophies being driven away by a herd of Angus cows. Even with the Murphy's Turkey Curse Law hanging over our heads, we somehow do manage to accidently get a turkey every once in a while.

This years' turkey hunt was one of our typical malfunctioning hunting adventures. At 6:00 AM we were sitting beside our favorite tree listening to the gobbles coming from the nearby woods. At 6:01 AM lightening flashed, thunder rolled, and rain began to pour. No problem. This was a turkey hunt. A little wet never bothered us. After setting there long enough to grow web feet and a set of gills, and still not seeing any turkeys, we decided to go on the offensive. We always use our offensive strategy when it's too wet and miserable to lie down and take a nap.

Leaving all of our turkey enticing equipment behind, except for the guns, we took off on a turkey locating stroll. Just as we were concluding our mile long cross country exercise, Kent grabbed me and said "freeze." I was sure I was about to stumble into a rattlesnake convention. No. Through the underbrush, he had spotted a turkey head in an open pasture dead ahead. Kent is a turkey seeing Cyclops when it comes to spottin' a turkey. For 20 minutes, he made me play statue, fearing the turkey would spot us first. Every joint and muscle I had was begging for mercy. Finally Kent gave me the all clear sign to slowly get down. I toppled over faster than a statue of Saddam. As it turned out, there was not one turkey in the field, but four great big granddaddy toms having their mid-morning brunch. We looked at each other and just got giddy. Getting giddy is not easy to do when you're cold, soaking wet, and more importantly over 50 years old. Of course the turkeys were still about 300 plus yards away, but that's closer than we had been to one all week.

After yards of belly crawling through briars and mud, we got as close as we dared. Still we were 200 yards or more away, when Kent gave one of his most seductive come hither calls. The toms immediately broke into a run in the opposite direction. I suggested further turkey calling might not be in our best interest. For two hours we watched the quartet of long bearded birds just wander back and forth across the field, feeding at their leisure.

Finally by accident, the turkeys' path of feeding was going to take them directly in front of our ambush site. They still weren't close, but it was going to be one of those now or never choices a turkey hunter sometimes has to make. As they wandered in front of us, I whispered to Kent to give them a call so they would stop and raise their heads. He purred. He cackled. He clucked. He even gave them a watch your butt putt call. The ever wary birds gave every indication of now being hearing impaired. Not a head came up. But when I hollered, "Hey turkey! Get your head up," that seemed to do the trick. Sometimes $20 turkey calls can be over rated.

Our gun barrels began to smoke. Lead began to fly by the bucket full. Kent picked out one and fired and watched him run away. I chose one standing proud and tall directly in front of me and let loose on him. I swear he took a step back and smiled. So I let him have it again. This time he winked. In the meantime, Kent fired at another turkey, which took off flying in another direction. Even with all the banging and booming and scattering turkeys, my turkey was holding his ground like the Rock of Gibraltar. Okay Mr. Turkey, take this.....KERR WHAM! This time I swear I heard him giggle. It was right about now the fourth turkey came running straight for me. At 20 yards he was going to be mine. Click! Great! I was out of ammo. I yelled for Kent to get him. Just as he fired, the turkey did one of those stage right things and ran right into the trunk of an oak tree. I'm sure he knocked himself silly, because our guns weren't having much effect on them. Regardless, Kent jumped on him before he could regain consciousness. Yee Haw! We had us a turkey.

As the smoke began to clear, I noticed my turkey had finally taken flight and flew across the field into a brushy little gulley. Feeling a little jealous of Kent showing off his prize, I tried redeeming myself with some really make myself feel better talk. Words like, "Man, I think that turkey of mine is hurt really bad." "Boy, he landed really hard over there." "I don't know what kept him on his feet." To ease my misery, Kent suggested we walk across the pasture and take a look in the gully, although neither one of us really believed we would even find a feather.

We were half way across the field when we realized we had left almost our entire arsenal back at our favorite hunting tree a mile behind us. We had gone days, almost entire hunting seasons without ever firing a shot, so what were the odds of us both running out of shells? More by accident than forethought, Kent scrounged up a couple of last year's leftover shells in one of his coverall pockets. Handing me one and him chambering the other, we began flanking the landing site of my so called wounded turkey.

As Kent circled in from the left and me from the right, I had to stifle a scream when the turkey popped his head out of the gully and squawked at me. At a distance of 10 foot, I instinctively pulled the trigger in pure self defense. It was a clean miss, but I did manage to shoot one strand of the barbed wire fence in two. Still laughing, Mr. Sure Shot shoved me aside to show the proper way on how to finish off a turkey hunt. Evidently, one stray pellet of one of my earlier shots must have grazed Mr. Red Head enough to cause a migraine headache. The turkey's head was bobbing from side to side like one of those slinky poodles dogs found in the back dash of a '57 Chevy. In his demonstration of expert marksmanship, Dead Eye fired right just as the turkey bobbed his head left. Great! Now all of our fire power was gone. We tossed our guns aside and grabbed up some sticks to use for war clubs. Kent vaulted the fence, but by this time my turkey had trotted up the little brushy ravine out of harm's way.

All bets were off now. No turkey was going to beat us out of a half a box of shells. With our turkey tomahawks in hand, we systematically made our way slowly between trees and proceeded up the ditch beating on any bush or briar patch that could possibly hide a turkey. As we poked and prodded our way through the underbrush, I am sure we resembled one of those Merlin Perkins Wild Kingdom African safari jungle drives. Just when I thought all hope was lost, Kent froze above the last possible turkey hiding briar patch.

And that brings us to now. It's really really quiet, almost too quiet. Come to think of it, I haven't heard any screams or squawks for some time. Well, I suppose I should at least get up and see if Kent needs a drink of water or maybe my belt for a tourniquet. Just as I picked myself up to go investigate, my huntin' buddy came crawling out of the briar infested ditch with my turkey in hand. "Hey! What took so long?" I asked. I got a look that would have cured a ham. As he tossed me my 22 pound feathered trophy, I made a good will gesture and offered to help him through the barbed wire fence. I figured it was the least I could do for tracking down my Tom Terrific.

Breathing like he had just completed a Fear Factor competition, he sneered back at me, "Could you give me just a couple of minutes? I've been through kind of an ordeal here." Gee! Whiz! My huntin' buddy seems to be getting a little persnickety in his old age.

Even so, with all things considered I ask all hunters this. When it comes to retrieving ducks, finding dead quail or doing battle with a wilily old tom turkey, would you rather have a pen full of disease catchin', feed consumin', pen messin', all night barkin' one occasion hunting dogs or just one good for all seasons huntin' buddy? As for me, even though father time may have slowed him down a step or two and he does seem to whine a tad bit more than he used to, I'll still take my huntin' buddy Kent every time.

CHAPTER 9

ARE DOGS REALLY MAN'S BEST FRIEND?

LASSIE.....OH LASSSSSSIE!!! IN AN obedient answer to her master's call, one of the most beautiful collie dogs that one can imagine comes bounding across a beautiful wild flower meadow. As Lassie slides to a grinding halt without one hair of her glistening coat out of place, her ears perk up as she hears, "Help! Help me, Lassie." It seems Little Timmy, her beloved master has fallen into an abandoned well and needs to be rescued. Lassie races off to find help so Little Timmy can be saved for the next Saturday morning episode. What I want to know is, out of all the dogs which have shared my residence over the past thirty years, why couldn't just one of them been a television type wonder hound like Lassie?

When I need the help of a dog, I have to go through an entire "Come Here" begging routine. Here Boy! Here Boy!! (Clap Clap -- That's the we're going to play and have lots of fun sound). (Whistle Whistle -- That's the come and get it... free food call). (Smooch Smooch ...on my knees -- That's the come get your pat on the head sound). Even with all the clapping, whistling, and smoochin', the odds are still not in my favor of me getting a dog to come if I really need one. With my luck, I could have a heart attack, fall unconscious face first into the dog pan, lay in a six week coma, and still most likely go unnoticed by any of my past or present man's best friends. My farm seems to be the foster home for the entire unwanted dog population of the county. The chances are slim to none that very few of these unwanted mutts will ever show up with a maternal or paternal pedigree that can be traced back to any intelligent canine ancestry. But you would think if nothing more than just by accident, at least one dog would show up with an I.Q sharper than a ham bone.

It has always been my custom to name a dog after something I can readily associate them with. It might be by the color, size, personality or some cute little peculiar act they could perform. As long as I put out food and water, a majority of my transient canine guests will stay forever. Others just used my farm for a brief Bed and Breakfast Resort before moving on to greener pastures or possibly better table scraps.

One of my more memorable wayward guests was a three legged English Sheep dog, which I appropriately named Tripod. As long as Tripod was on the move, he got along reasonably well. It was when he came to a stop that he had trouble keeping his balance. Oh! And he did present a fairly comical sight when he would hobble up to a tree to do what most boy dogs instinctively enjoy doing. However, when poor Tripod picked out a tree to water, he would just stand there for a brief moment with a confused look on his face. It wouldn't be long before he would lose his balance and end up leaning against his favorite handicap accessible doggie pee tree. I considered renaming him Eileen, but the name just didn't seem appropriate for a guy dog.

Then there was Backhoe. Everyone knows it is common for almost all dogs to carry off a chicken bone and bury it for a late afternoon snack. But Backhoe must have had an insatiable appetite. I guess his reasoning was why have a happy meal now when he could have a full meal deal later? He would scour the neighborhood for any decaying livestock carcass, gnaw off a rotting hind quarter, drag it home, and proceed to bury it in the front yard. Backhoe moved so much dirt in our yard one summer, neighbors began the rumor that we were putting in an Olympic size in ground swimming pool.

One of the greatest advantages of living on the farm is the many freedoms it has to offer. One of these farmer freedoms is night time weather checking. When it is the middle of a hot August drought, it is a well known fact most farmers will step out onto their porch right before bed time in hopes of spotting any signs of lightning on the western horizon. I might add that this evening ritual is usually performed in BVD's. This is where Frosty comes in. Frosty was a coal black Heinz 57 something or other and had the uncanny ability of sneaking up behind you without making a sound. Frosty received his name for his always frigid ice cold nose. With one little touch of his Arctic Circle snout in a well placed BVD back side area, Frosty could send goose bumps the size of hen eggs racing up my spine.

Now Listerine was a friendly sort of dog, but he had breath that could peel the paint off an out house floor. We never did find out what Listerine ate or licked to make his breath so rotten. Some things are just better off not knowing.

Collector was definitely a retriever. He would find and bring home every cow bone in the community. Of course Collector would pursue this hobby in earnest the day the banker was scheduled to stop by for the yearly farm asset inventory. It was always a plus if the live cattle inventory matched up with the all important financial statement. There's nothing like a yard full of dead cow bones to impress the banker.

I never did know what breed of dog Whizzer was. In fact, I'm not sure he even was a dog. He was more like a hairy four legged bladder with teeth. When I would drive in the driveway, Whizzer could wake up from a nap with a hind leg cocked, circle my truck in a dead run, pee on all four of my pickup tires and on a good day even hit the spare, and be back to snoring before my pick up could even coast to a stop.

Terminator was a German Police dog. He kind of had a Barney Fife mentality. He would bark his brains out if a butterfly fluttered across the yard, but never raise an eyebrow if a convicted felon was attempting to steal my truck.

I once had a cocker spaniel named Velcro. He could run through a soybean field, collect every cocklebur in 40 acres and bring all of them home in his ears. As good as he was at ridding a field of cockleburs, I probably should have named him herbicide.

Avon was just plain nasty. He was rude, crude, and ill mannered. Invariably he would always feel inclined to jump up on the porch, stretch out on his back and proceed to lick himself from top to bottom every time the Avon lady came calling. He would only stop long enough to give me a wink and smile. Talk about an embarrassing situation. All I could do was maintain good eye to eye contact, order about $300 worth of after shave and hope the lady didn't notice his disgusting act. I could always kick Avon later.

I never saw FeFe, the wayward French poodle, when she wasn't in a family way. She had lots of boyfriends and seemed to be the most popular hotty naughty dog in our neighborhood. It just amazed me, that out of all the years that I raised hogs, an eight pig litter average was the best I could ever hope to achieve under ideal conditions. On the other hand, FeFe could crawl under a dirty building, give unassisted birth to a dozen multi-colored, multi-cultured, multi-daddy off spring and raise each and every one of them. Not only that, she could do it twice a year just like clockwork. She was the ultimate puppy making machine. Thanks to FeFe, I had a free puppy sign in my front yard for years.

Surprise was a pointer bird dog. Every time he went on point it was going to be a surprise on what he had found. Sometimes it might even be quail. But then again, it might be a rabbit, or a 'possum or even better yet a skunk. On more than one occasion, thanks to Surprise, I have waded into a patch of weeds expecting to find a covey of quail only to find Pepe Le Pew standing at attention with his tail in the I salute you position.

His bark is much worse than his bite. Baloney!!! Whoever spouted off that famous line had never met Chainsaw. There is not a doubt in my mind, if there was a top ten most wanted list of dog assassins, Chainsaw would be public enemy number one. He was a mass murderer. He was a serial killer. Chainsaw's teeth were equal to that of JAWS. He loved to inflict pain, especially on me. Chainsaw had only one mood and that mood was "ticked off." Even if I reached out in a gesture of friendship, chances were in Chainsaw's favor that I would only bring back two of my five fingers. I never did like that chiwawa very much.

Banker was the name of the stray Great Dane, who spent a short vacation with us. We called him banker because he would leave these gigantic deposits in our yard the size of Mt. Everest. When I would hit one of these colossal monuments just right, I could actually do a wheelie with the lawn mower.

I have found dogs are extremely blessed with a multitude of communication talents. They seem to have a different bark for different occasions. There is the "I'm meaner than you are" bark. There is the "I'm scared of the dark" bark. There is the "I like to hear myself bark" bark. There is the "I'm sooooo hungry again" bark. And my all time favorite is, "I know you are in there trying to sleep, but can you still hear me bark" bark.

If dogs really want to be our best friends, why do they love to roll in something dead and then beg to be petted? If dogs want to ride around in the truck with us, why do they believe it is fashionable to carry around ticks the size of concord grapes behind their ears? If dogs want to be our faithful companions, why do they love stretching out in a mud puddle and then get up and shake like crazy just as we're leaving the house dressed in our best church going clothes? I suppose dogs may be man's best friend, but when you think about it, they can sure find a variety of ways to test that friendship.

E
F P
T O Z
L M Q R
T W I K V
C O B U C K O Y

CHAPTER 10

HUNTING IS MAN'S DESTINY

FROM THE BEGINNING OF time it has been the destiny of man to hunt. Man would take to the woods and prairies where the buffalo roamed and the deer and antelope played to hunt for animals. For the most part, their primitive weapons consisted of stones or clubs. More sophisticated weapons became available with the opening of Wal-Mart stores in local neighborhoods.

It was first thought man hunted out of necessity for food, animal skins for warmth or bones for tools. But then it was discovered that man roamed around the earth looking for other stuff, even female companionship. A more scientific study suggests man hunts because of a genetic chromosome imbalance. It doesn't have to be wildlife or women. It can be anything. Man has the ability to put something down and in milliseconds have no earthly memory of where he just placed it. Car keys, socks, or the ever elusive TV remote have all been victims of a hunt. There was actually a report of a man driving away and leaving his wife stranded in a shopping mall parking lot. That particular incident is still being questioned as to accidental or premeditated.

Anyway, since the instinct to hunt has been passed on to me through generations of my manly hunting ancestors, I finally got the fever to go deer hunting. Having never chased the wondering white tail before, I relied on the advice and experience of my fellow deer hunting brethren. Every guy has his own specific ideas and opinions on how to bag the granddaddy of all daddy deer. Most of the suggestions given required a tremendous time commitment. Time was one thing I was almost always short of. Because of work, I had little to no time to prepare for the upcoming season. There was no preseason scouting. There was no glamorous tree stand from which to hunt. In fact, most of my preparation consisted of digging through one of my son's closets hoping to find something orange to wear. Luck was with me because I found an orange stocking cap and vest from one of my kid's previous deer hunting escapades. I also found some expired doe scent in a can that was guaranteed to make me absolutely charming and irresistible to any fun loving buck in the woods. It just kept getting better and better when I found a grunt call and a handful of bullets for my lever action Winchester. Grabbing my fire power off the rack, I did my Lucas McCain Rifleman imitation a couple of times and I was set for my next day hunting adventure.

Before heading off to nighty night land, I listened to my favorite weatherman, Lying Lou, for his opening day deer season forecast. According to his prediction, there should be a slight temperature drop from today's beautiful 65 degrees, calm winds, and of course, absolutely no chance of precipitation. After having a restless night's sleep, I got up early and opened up the back door to a 14 degree bone chilling temperature, a 40 mile per hour howling straight out of the north wind, and a quarter inch of frozen sleet on the ground. Way to go, Lou. Your lousy weather forecasting record is still intact.

Without a constructed deer stand, there was a need for me to improvise. On my way to my wooded ambush site, I stopped by the machine shed and grabbed an empty plastic hydraulic oil bucket to sit on. The bucket happened to be orange in color and I couldn't help but think to myself, "How cool is that? Now all of my important body parts will be protected by orange." As I crossed the cow pasture in the early morning light, my cows suddenly appeared thinking my bucket contained feed. I'll admit there was a lot I didn't know about deer hunting. But I felt reasonably certain that traveling with a 60 mooing cow entourage was not particularly the best way to sneak up on deer. After shooing them in my loudest cow shooing whisper and throwing a multitude of frozen cow muffins in their direction, they finally got the message and pulled up stakes for better feed opportunities. They all left except for the bull. Baby Maker persisted in staying hot on my trail. Shooing him not only didn't stop him, it didn't even slow him down. The closer he got the more excited he became. With his nose glued to the ground, he was picking up speed and closing ground fast. I was now in a full trot and about 100 yards from the pasture fence line. It finally dawned on me that Baby Maker wasn't interested in feed. His low "wait for me" bellowing sounds made it clear that he had pure unadulterated passion on his mind. I guess that doe scent really works. I had two choices, run for my life or brace myself. I immediately became an Olympic sprinter, hurdler, and high jumper. It is amazing how the fear of being romanced by a 2000 lbs. bull can turn a natural born slacker in to an instantaneous over achiever.

Although somewhat winded, but safely on the other side of the barbed wire fence, I sought out the best deer shooting spot. I placed my bucket at the base of a huge oak tree and faced the direction I believed the deer would most likely be traveling. The direction was north. The same direction as the -9 wind chill, tree bending, life sucking, gale force winds were blowing from. In a matter moments my eyes watered and then froze into a permanent glassy stare. I was afraid to blink in fear the white part of my eyeballs might crack. The cold converged upon my body and gave me a greater appreciation for the old saying of, "must have ice water in his veins." Beginning with my extremities of toes and fingers, the cold met in the middle collapsing my entire nervous system. I was so cold I was trying to think of three good reasons why I shouldn't just shoot myself instead of waiting for a deer. I was only able to think of two before the thought processing part of my brain went numb. But through the shivering and shaking, I persisted with my hunt because down deep I knew it was the destiny of man to become the hunter.

And then it happened. Out of the corner of my frozen cornea I spotted movement. A doe! Then another doe! But no rise in blood pressure for me, because I am a man hunter and I will not settle for a girl deer. I am after a great horned buck. Cold or not I will wait. Then as if almost by power of persuasion, there he was. From behind a fallen tree stepped out a looking great on my wall Mr. 12 Point buck. He was a magnificent specimen with a rack as wide as a Harley Davidson's handle bars. As I raised my rifle, I tried to spot the deer through my scope zeroed in at a 150 yards. The only problem was the buck was standing only about 15 yards away. His nostrils were so big in the scope they looked like steaming coal mines in the frosty morning air. Here I was with the buck of all bucks standing in front of me and he was too close for me to find him in my sites. Now I know why my forefathers chose clubs and stones for weapons.

Shaking not from buck fever, but from body temperature dropping hyperthermia, I tried to control my deer alerting convulsions. On the other hand, since my shaking was causing me to aim at everything in the western hemisphere, I probably should have pulled the trigger. Odds were I would have most likely hit him sooner or later before I ran out of ammo. As the Grand Daddy of all bucks moved a little further away I pivoted slightly on my plastic bucket to hopefully improve my soon to be trophy winning shot. And then CA.....RACK!!!!! The sound echoed through the timbered hillside. The sound a hunter lives for. The sound which says I have conquered and prevailed because I am a man that hunts. It is also the same sound a frozen brittle plastic bucket makes when shattering under too much twisting weight stress.

Numb and disbelieving, I began picking myself up from the frozen tundra. I stood and watched the biggest buck of the woods and his harem of two does bound off to safer parts unknown. Oh well, Mr. Buck, luck was with you today, but I will see you at first light tomorrow because I am man and hunting is man's destiny.

HUBBA
HUBBA

CHAPTER 11

HANK YOU HANDSOME HUNTIN' HOUND

ARE YOU KIDDIN' ME? This was like having Christmas, my birthday, and an Uncle Sam tax refund all rolled up into one. I had just been one week on my new town job when my boss approached me for a favor. I have always been somewhat leery of those asking for favors. The office was a soil and water conservation district office. In conjunction with an office staff, the district had an elected board made up of local county farmers. One of these farmers loved hob knobbing with politicians and almost anyone of prominent importance. It seems each year he would invite a couple of muckity muck lawyer types from the Kansas City Chapter of Quails Unlimited to his 900 plus acre farm to go quail hunting. Being up in arthritic years, he would normally ask the district conservationist, my new boss, to act as their hunting guide.

Now for the favor. Tomorrow, the day of the scheduled hunt, my boss had been notified of an unexpected regional "attendance mandatory" meeting. Almost apologetically, he wanted to know if I would mind going hunting in his place. Oh! Oh! There's got to be a catch somewhere. His next sentence began with "Since this is a work day".... There we go...here comes the catch... "And since these Kansas City hunting chaps were conservation minded, this hunting trip would be considered an on the clock conservation job," he continued.

Again, you have got to be kiddin' me. I love quail hunting. I would rather quail hunt than eat cream filled Ding Dongs, and I have fantasies of being stranded on a deserted island and surviving on nothing else but cream filled Ding Dongs. I could hardly wait to tell my huntin' pals that I was actually getting paid to go quail huntin'. They would be moldy green with jealousy. My Gosh! I might become the next Harold Ensley. Who knows? This could be the first step of me starring in my very own, Sportsman's Friend Huntin' and Fishin' Show.

The next morning I was up at the crack of dawn. I pulled on my favorite briar torn huntin' pants, grabbed my beat up old Betsy (Remington pump shotgun) and headed out to load up ole' Hank. Hank was my pointer bird dog. I think. What he lacked in hunting style, he lacked even more in looks. He had one badly split ear from a fight with a coyote, one brown and one gray eye and a peculiar marking on his forehead closely resembling the birthmark of Gorbachev of Russia. Hank was a multi-taskin' dog. He played with the kids. He didn't mind chasin' rabbits or even treein' a squirrel. And he could put an escapee cow back through hole in a fence faster than I could yell, "I'm going to haul your mangy carcass off to McDonalds."

If those talents weren't enough, Hank was what you might call the Don Won of Wonder Dogs in our neighborhood. Every female canine within a two-mile radius had been courted by Hank in what you might call a puppy love manner. I have lost count of the unhappy neighbor phone calls I've received for me to come pick up my Handsome Hank. Hank truly lived up to the scripture of "To Go Forth and Multiply." Each time I would pick him up from one of his wayward courtship escapades, I would scold him while tossing him in the back of the truck. He would just give me this quirky little smile that said, "Thanks for the ride home boss, because I'm too blame tuckered out to walk." No matter how hard I chastised him for his Romeo-ing around the neighborhood, Hank believed he had a macho "top of the mound hound" reputation he needed to live up to. Maybe that is why there are so many collie, shepherd and even spaniel puppies around the community sporting long slick bird dog pointer type tails.

Regardless of his good or not so good romantic characteristics, above all else, Hank was a darned good quail dog. There was something magical about the month of November. Hank could just sense when it was time to put all other fun things aside and get ready to hunt those elusive bobwhite birds. He could smell a covey of birds one hundred yards away. He could sniff out a single bird no matter how hard it tried to hide. He could find a dead bird even if it had fallen and sunk in the middle of a creek. There was no doubt that Hank was born for one intended purpose and that was to be a bird dog. Everything else he did was just extra icing on the cake.

Since I didn't own a dog box carrier, Hank usually just jumped in the back of the pickup bed and rode along until we reached our bird hunting areas. However, today was a special day and I was sparing no expense. Wanting to impress the Kansas City gents that I had sufficient bird hunting experience, I tied Hank's collar to the pickup spare tire with a piece of baling wire. Arriving at work a few minutes early, I was anxious to meet my hunting partners. I didn't have long to wait. I was almost blinded by the chrome deluxe candy apple red Ford truck as it came rolling to a stop. Being pulled behind was a silver chrome trailer that had six plush dog compartments. The illegal alien trailer park behind our office had much worst living conditions. As the Quail Unlimited dudes stepped out of their mobile hunting lodge, they looked like mannequins from the Bass Pro Shop clothing department. Their shirts still had iron creases. Their hunting pants did not have one snag. Their hunting boots still had the just off the rack shine. One introduced himself as Bartols Elliot and the other was James Steele. Wow! Bartols and James! Kind of like the wine. They might even be owners of the company. After giving me the once over, as if I might be a parolee on a work release program, they hesitantly agreed to follow Hank and me to the hopeful quail haven.

Upon reaching our hunting grounds, the first major decision was which dogs to use first. I immediately learned all of the dogs that would be hunted today had mile long pedigrees. Their ancestral canine root papers could be traced back to hunting royalty ownership of European kings and queens. Better yet, not only would I be hunting over dogs that were national grand champion field trial winners, their individual worth would most likely exceed the value of my entire farm. Wow! Was my heart pumpin'. I had never been around fine quality huntin' dogs. First out was Lord Lancelot. Good Grief! He was huge. I didn't know whether to pat his head or throw a saddle on him. I've seen horses that were smaller. With head held high and tail curving in a high arc over his back, the Lord majestically scanned the horizon. Quicker than a Dream of Jeanie wiggle of the nose, Lord Lancelot became Lord Lope-A-Lot. He broke out into a Seattle Slew run for the roses. Immediately Bartols and James began blowing their sterling silver "come back here" whistles. In less than two minutes the Lord had crossed a 50 acre picked corn field, scattered a heard of angus cows and their babies in an adjacent pasture, and had caused the rural delivery mailman to slam on his brakes to avoid a gravel road head on collision. Lancelot wasn't the slightest bit winded as he trotted up to his masters. Bartols and James, on the other hand, had heaving sides from the non-stop whistle blowing.

Next to hit the ground was Prince Valiant. He was a German Shorthair that was built just as solid as a WWII German Panzer Tank. Man, was he ever ripped! Valiant looked as if he could have invaded Poland all by himself. He was the first dog I had ever seen with a six-packed chest. The Prince had bulging muscles in places I didn't know dogs were supposed to have muscles. If there was ever a dog that could have produced his own TV workout video, it would have been Valiant. If Lord Lancelot was known for his extensive range, I was told Valiant was known for his close in work. In fact, once Prince had left the dog trailer and his feet had felt earth, he had not actually taken a step. He was as motionless as a stationary concrete yard ornament. Finally with a gigantic sigh and an "I'm already tuckered out" yawn, the show was over. The Prince lay down as if to warn all that watched to be sure and count him out of any upcoming programs that might include physical exertion.

To go along with the two big bow-wow bouncers, Bartols finally settled on his sweet little female setter companion, the Duchess of Montego Bay. Wow! She certainly was fine. In guy talk, she was a Marilyn Monroe, a Kristy Brinkley and a Pamela Anderson all wrapped up into one fine coat of dog hair. I'm pretty sure that if I had a tail I would have been waggin' it myself. In pooch talk, she was a hotty naughty Lassie and for sure Lord Lancelot and Prince Valiant's tails were waggin'. After teasing each of the big brutes with a couple of flirtatious "catch me if you can" circles, the duchess scampered off to check out a patch of Black-Eyed Susans. Either too well trained or too stupid to know what to do with the Duchess's come hither yelps, Lancelot and Valiant resumed their statuesque positions and waited for their master's hunt commands. Almost forgetting, Hank reminded me with a "please let me go" whine that he was ready to be unwired from his spare tire anchor. With a couple of counter clockwise unwire twists he was free. Over the side of the truck he jumped to take a whiz on all four tires of Bartol's fancy hunting mobile.

With the dogs ready, all we needed were our guns and a vest pocket full of shells. Bartols uncased a fancy French model shotgun that looked as if it had never been exposed to outdoor oxygen. James pulled out an Italian double barrel that had massive silver etchings equivalent to that of the ceiling of the Sistine Chapel. My poor Betsey was decorated with barbed wire fence scratches on the stock and rust pit marks up and down the barrel. But each scratch and every pit mark was like a tally on a score card for a multitude of good hunts. Okay! Guns are ready. Hunters are ready. Dogs are ready. Yee Haw! Here we go. But Wait!!!!

Only Lord Lancelot and Prince Valiant were at the ready. Where was the Princess? Hank wasn't around either, but that wasn't unusual. He was probably half way down a fencerow by now looking for his favorite Bob White buddies. After all it was the month of November. For several minutes Bartols and James huffed and puffed on their whistles trying to lure their blessed Princess back to their sides. With no response from the whistles, they began hollering all kinds of sweet promises for Princess to please please come home. Still there was no sight of the future majesty to be. Fear and near panic was beginning to set in. Did she fall into an abandoned well? Had she been bitten by a snake and was now too weak to walk back to her masters? Was a dog nabber on the loose and the Princess was now half way to Mexico? As a last resort, a search party was organized to find the missing Princess. We spread out and Bartols and James vowed not to give up until her Highness was found. The search didn't take quite as long as one might think.

It was Lancelot and Valiant that first spotted movement in the patch of Black-Eyed Susans. They stood like statutes as if not knowing what to do. Bartols was first to actually spot the princess and he knew exactly what to do. He screamed. It seems the priceless Princess was no match for Handsome Hank's seductive charms. Hank had long since made it past first base, rounded second, trotted past third, and was now in the process of scoring a home run of passionate love with the Princess. With Bartols yelling and screaming and hopping around like he had just walked bare foot over a bed of hot coals, James and I came on a dead run expecting the worst. Bartols kept yelling, "What's he doing? What's he doing?" Hank had one of those cross-eyed caught in the act grins on face that said he was pretty sure he knew exactly what he was doing. As James consoled his buddy Bartols, I reached down and grabbed Hank by the collar putting an end to his royalty conquest. Giving him the toe of my boot, I sent him off for a doggy time out to think about what he had done. Still grinning, I'm pretty sure Hank didn't really need a time out to think about what he had just done. Bartols picked up Princess and carried her back to the truck as if she had just been violated by the Boston Strangler. I tried to apologize for Hank's vulgar behavior. However, hearing nothing except under the breath worthless, good for nothing, lop eared mutt, comments, I don't think my apology was accepted.

Choking down a handful of Tylenol with a couple of swigs from a bottle underneath the truck seat, Bartols finally regained his composure. Still not wanting to expose any of their other priceless pooches to the barbaric tactics of Hank, they decided to use only Lancelot and Valiant for the hunt. I whispered to Hank that it would probably be a good idea to stay out of gun range for the first few minutes of the hunt. But within fifty yards Hank was making amends. While Lord Lope A Lot was making tracks across a field and Valiant was trotting around biting at invisible nothings in the air, Hank was on a rock solid point finding the first covey of the day. With a whir of wings, the covey rose and Bartols and James each dropped a couple of big fat birds. Hank immediately proceeded to find and retrieve each of the four downed birds. In fact, on his way back with the last dead bird in his mouth, Hank whirled and froze on clump of sage grass. James calmly walked up and shot a single quail as it tried to escape. And so the rest of the afternoon went like this. In less than three hours, Hank found four more coveys, pointed at least fifteen to twenty singles, and had found each and every dead bird that was shot. Hank was a one-hound huntin' show. He flawlessly displayed his bird hunting talents while the two pedigreed pooches of pomp and circumstance bounced around like they had been snorting crack cocaine. Sometimes their heads would jerk from side to side biting at the air as if trying to ward off invisible evil spirits. Other times they would just stop and stare at passing clouds as if hoping to spot one in the shape of a pork chop. Every time a gun would go off they would freeze, fearful that the next shot might be in their general direction.

After making a full circle of the hunting property and nearing our parked trucks, James asked if Hank might happen to be registered. I told him I didn't think so because he had just showed up at my farm a couple years ago and decided to call it home. Shaking his head, James said, "Bartols if Princess comes up with a litter of pups, I think you're going to owe this young man a stud fee." They didn't say as much, but I got the feeling if a litter of pups did show up, the long lost papers of Handsome Hank might mysteriously show up out of nowhere. Wouldn't that be something if Handsome Hank's real name turned out to be Handsome King Henry VIII of Houndland?

Hank You Handsome
Huntin' Hound

CHAPTER 12

BUILDING FENCES – A COMMUNITY BETTERMENT PROJECT

I AM SO EXCITED!!!! I have just been unanimously elected the chairman of the rapidly formed Richland Township Community Betterment Program. This year's theme is "Good Fences Makes Good neighbors." The first order of business is to be a fence building project on my farm. I am honored that a new cow holding fence on my pasture was a unanimous request by the entire neighborhood.

For some reason my cows have trouble staying home. I don't know why. Maybe they don't recognize two old rusty barbed wires propped up by elm sprouts and an occasional horse weed as being much of deterrence for reaching greener pastures. Totally on their own initiative, my cows have developed a very unique grazing system. Monday is soybean day. Either my field or one of the neighbors will qualify. Tuesday is my neighbor's corn field smorgasbord. Nothing is better than juicy succulent corn right off the cob. Wednesday is a day for munching on the flowers and vegetables of my new straight from the city neighbors. Not understanding my open range policy, they have my cattle out number on speed dial. Thursday and Friday are vacation days to parts unknown until the sheriff's department gives a call. Saturday night is a wild and woolly free for all on state owned government land. Sunday is a day of rest, which is usually in the middle of a road blocking church going traffic.

Being convinced by irritable neighbors that dodging my cows on the road was not their idea of a Neighborhood Watch Program, a bi-partisan unanimous decision was reached that a new fence was my only viable alternative. It was the first time I remember the local Republicans and Democrats agreeing on anything. I needed to either keep my cattle corralled or the entire neighborhood was going to be invited to a community-wide bovine barbecue. And it was going to be my four legged fence jumpers that would be providing the menu.

Armed with a spade, pick, pry bar and a nuclear war headed sledge hammer, I began digging the new corner post holes. As if possessed with super natural strength I attacked. Hammer…Pick…Shovel!!! Hammer…Pick…Shovel!!! More Hammer…Pick…Shovel!!! With dirt flying, rock chips sailing and sandstone dust swirling, I was nothing but a blur. In short, I was a one man post hole digging machine.

To prove to all my rich neighbors that a hernia operation is cheaper than owning a tractor and loader, I decided to single handedly man handle the 500 pound corner posts into the freshly dug holes. Having rolled one end of the Roman Coliseum post into position just over the post hole rim, I assumed the sumo-wrestling squat position at the other end and began the old heave ho. I don't know what I lack most, the heave or the ho. With bulging eyes, I got to experience what the peripheral vision of a hoot owl must be like. But with one final burst of energy and a scream three octaves higher than that of one of Jack the Ripper's victims, the post found its forever new home. A repeat of this procedure gave me solid fence holding anchors at both ends. According to local legend, if the small end of a hedge tree corner post is placed in the hole first, the post will last for an even 100 years. If the big end goes in the hole first, it will turn to stone and last forever.

Now that the corners were set, the old fence had to be removed before the new fence construction could begin. Since most of the steeples were long gone, the wire was being held together primarily by pure rust and a majority of the posts were already rotted off at ground level, the fence removal went rather well. During the course of the afternoon fence demolition, I did have one ongoing battle with a Volkswagen size horse fly. This was the first horse fly I had ever seen that was actually wearing a saddle. I have no idea what happened to his rider. Some folks say these gigantic hairy legged creatures are carryovers from prehistoric days. The old timers in our neighborhood remember one particular dry year when Pettis Creek horse flies got so big that they were known to carry off dogs and cats and on occasions unattended small children. Children in our area didn't grow up fearing the boogey man, they grew up scared to death of the galloping horse fly.

Anyway, I spent almost the entire quarter of a mile flailing my arms and hands around my head trying to discourage the painful bites of my horse fly attacker. By about the third excruciating bite, I felt certain he must be packing his own hypodermic syringe. Finally, enough was enough. It was my turn to declare war. As I was prying out one of the last steeples with my hammer, I felt the wretched blood sucking critter do a Kamikaze landing just above my right ear. Without considering consequences, I went into attack mode. In one swift motion and a kung-fu yell I went for the kill. KEEYAH! Take that! Kerr Plunk!!!! Looking back, it would have been a much greater chance for success if I had remembered to drop my hammer first. A few moments later as my pupils began to recognize light, I had this unbelievable throbbing sensation on the side of my head. The pain could best be described as having a root canal performed by a well digger without the benefit of Novocain, an epidural, or even a shot of white lightening. It is amazing just how far a knot on your head can stick out and still not fall off. I'm not for sure just how long I had been stretched out knocked cold in my cow pasture, but as my eyes began to refocus, I noticed three circling turkey buzzards sizing me up for brunch.

With the old fence now gone and new fence construction about to begin, it was time to put my all time favorite fence building technique into action. This technique consists primarily of pouring a heart wrenching guilt trip over one or both of my sons. It begins with a persuasive phone reminding of all the Dad things I had done for them so they could have a better life than their poor worn to the bone father. I only had to mention my high blood pressure and bad back no more than three times before the eldest reluctantly volunteered to come help dear old Dad with his fence building project. There was also the mention of my having to sell the farm and maybe moving in with him if I couldn't get this fence project done. It is amazing how a guilt trip combined with out and out right fear can bring about a speedy resolution to an issue.

The next morning number one son showed up bright and early and we begin pounding fence posts until we were nearly stroke victims. We pulled and stretched wires so tight that meadow larks were landing on the fence just to play Name That Tune. Our backs bent over so many times putting on wire holding clips, that by day's end either one of us could have had starring roles in the Hunchback of Notre Dame. Remarkably, after a 14 hour day and a few gallons of sweat, the Ragreed Ranch was sporting a quite spiffy brand new fence improvement. Tuh Duhhh! The very first Richland Township Community Betterment Project was now complete and it was completed on one of my cow grazing pastures.

I tried to really lay on the sugar coated thank yous to my son for all of his help. "Just remember Son, this is all going to be yours someday," I told him.

I heard him scoff back as he sped down the driveway, "Don't be doing me any favors." I'm pretty tight with my sons, but there needs to be some significant clarification in the meaning of their words addressing my senior years. I hear contradicting phrases that can give me cause to worry. Phrases such as, "Dad, we'll take care of you" or

"Dad, we'll have you taken care of." It's kind of like raise and raze. They sound a lot alike, but I'm pretty sure they have totally different meanings.

Before calling it a day I had to take one last look at my day's work. With the sun slowly setting in the west, I stepped on to the front porch for yet one more admiring look of my new fence. It was not only a proud moment for me, but for all my neighbors that had been providing free cow meals to my herd as well. There is nothing like the feeling of pride in accomplishment. Burrrrrrring! And once again there is nothing like the ring of the blasted telephone to interrupt one of my few and far between special moments. "Hello." It was my neighbor on the back side of my place. He just wanted to remind me it was Tuesday night and my cows were already in his corn field. Humm! I wonder if my youngest son would be up to helping me build another Community Betterment Project next weekend.

CONGRESS

CHAPTER 13

ALMOST EVERYTHING IS BETTER WITH A LITTLE BIT OF CHOCOLATE ON IT

I LIKE FOOD. IN fact, I adore food. Since food is at the top of my all time favorite pastime list, I sometimes tend to look at favorite foods in a philosophical manner. For instance, take chocolate for an example. Life is like chocolate. Life can be totally good and then again sometimes not so good. An example comparable to chocolate would be; kind of like taking a bite of that mouth watering delectable sweet milk chocolate and then having to taste that mouth revolting eye twitching bitter dark chocolate. Then there are those memorable moments of life that are in the teeter totter chocolate category. They start out good, switch to bad, and then finish kind of all right. I would put an Almond Joy bar in this middle of the road chocolate category. It starts out with a great chocolaty taste, gets interrupted with all that noxious weed coconut junk and then ends up with a sweet syrupy mixture covering a nut. Personally, the bar would have had more than enough Joy in it for me if they would have just stopped with the chocolate.

Even still, with the exception of coconut, almost anything can be made better with just a little bit of chocolate on it. There is chocolate pudding and chocolate milk and chocolate ice cream. Candy bars, Bon Bons, Ho Hos and cupcakes are all covered with chocolate. A raisin or a nut or a cherry can all be chocolate dipped for flavor enhancement. For the most part, chocolate can break up the tedium of boring foods as long as it is the right chocolate. Bitter has trouble making something better.

As I compare my life to chocolate, I can't help but think back to one of those memorable bitter sweet chocolaty moments. More by default than popularity, I somehow got roped into one of those uncomfortable positions of representing other folks. In other words I drew the short straw and was elected president of an employee's association. One of the primary roles of this position was the ability to go begging for dollars. With no health insurance and no retirement and drawing a ditch digger's wage, employees were being turned over faster than one of Grandma's griddle cakes. To slow this annual loss of man power, we set about tackling the problem of locating funds for benefits, primarily health insurance.

Short of standing in front of Wal-Mart with a tin cup, we decided to make our case for money to the uppity ups at the Senate Appropriations Hearing Committee. Maybe....just maybe we could strike a nerve of sympathy and they would toss a few dollars our way for a bottle of Aleve and band aids. The first step was to find out when the appropriation committee met. Completely green about the process of government, I knew I had to find the proper "who knows something person" to help me out. Late one afternoon I picked up the phone and started making random calls to the state capitol. After being passed around from one "didn't have a clue" person to another, I finally struck pay dirt. A lady told me that yes indeed, there was going to be a Senate committee hearing. In fact, it was going to meet at 8:00 AM sharp tomorrow morning and would I like my name on the agenda to testify. Before I could slap myself silly, I whimpered out a feeble "yes." Good grief! What was I thinkin'? Except for watching old Perry Mason reruns, I didn't know anything about testifying. What if I got confused? What if I got rattled? What if I confessed to a crime I didn't commit? Would they give me Martha Stewart's old prison cell for telling a fib? Should I water the house plants just in case I was issued an orange jump suit? I hung up and speed dialed every brainy-ack person I could think of who might be willing to take my place. If they had an I.Q. of flannel, they would be better than me. I made call after call and got...Nine...Nada...Zilch....No Way! It was as if every intelligent being had slid off the face of the earth. Several of the troops did rally and agreed to back me up in body and spirit, just not in words.

Time was of the essence. I spent the evening at home throwing together some impressive need for health insurance sounding phrases. My time would have been better spent if I could have consolidated one or two of those phrases into at least one coherent sentence. This was a one shot deal and I was getting as nervous as a pig in a bacon factory.

Normally, I have this built in rise and shine sense and have no need for an alarm clock. However, since it would be a three hour road trip to the Capitol, I thought it better to be safe than sorry for making my early morning testimony. I dug out my old turkey huntin' alarm clock and set it for the pre-cock-a-doodle-do hour of 3:00 AM. This would allow me plenty of shining up time and more than enough time for travel. I was somewhat surprised how the tick tock of the old clock seemed to act as a sedative. I was in Rip Van Winkle land before I knew what happened. Sometime during the night I awoke to the Mr. Sand Man ticking of the old clock and decided to see how many more hours I had in slumber land. I was certainly glad the old clock still had a pleasant tick tock, because evidently the ding dongers were gone from its bell ringer. The blood drained from my eyes as I made out 4:00AM. I had over slept an hour.

I flew out of the sack and made the bathroom in two jumps. I brushed my teeth and hair with the same brush. My razor shaved some parts of my body, but I am not sure what parts. I threw on my favorite all around wedding/funeral tan slacks blue blazer outfit. I grabbed up my unrehearsed speech and made a jump for the truck. Being frigid February, I set my truck heater on parboil, my compass on north, and began my three hour Capitol Hill trip. In my mind I began rehearsing my all important presentation. After 75 miles, even my own words started to bore me. The heater was taking its toll and my eyelids started to roll down like awnings on the sunny side of the porch. Since I didn't have any health insurance, I couldn't afford an accident, so I pulled over at an all night gas and go to get a wake me up. A cup of coffee and a giant "everyone's favorite" Snickers candy bar seem to fit the bill. There is nothing better than caffeine with a side order of chocolate to perk you up on a cold winter morning. With very little extra time to spare, I jumped back in my pick-up and decided to partake of my nourishment on the go. With my heater still on fry daddy, I was slurpin' my coffee out of one hand and nibblin' on my Snicker's bar with the other. Steering around curves with knees was not all that easy. On occasions when down shifting was needed, I would sometimes place my cup of coffee into my portable between the legs crotch cup holder to free up my shifting hand. Although my little Ford Ranger has many minuses, like cramped seats, poor gas mileage or not enough engine to pass a terrapin turtle going downhill, it makes up for it in heater BTU's (Burned Through Unmentionables). The faster I went the hotter it got. I began feeling like a heat stroke victim passing from this world by means of a four wheel coal oil furnace. Feeling faint, I cracked the window to let in some fresh North Pole air. Still slurping the coffee and munching on my Snickers bar, the final miles began to click off.

With the play clock running down and just when I thought all was lost, I crested a hill and spotted our state capitol. The early morning light shining on the capitol dome presented a majestic and much welcomed site. More importantly, it was obvious that I had made up some precious alarm clock failure time. I zoomed up the capitol street and like a buzzard searching for a piece of rotting flesh, I circled the capitol three times before finding the last available parking space. Jumping from the truck, I took one last swig of my coffee, wiped away any leftover Snickers chocolate from my mouth, and reached for a handful of coins to feed the meter. I dashed across the frozen capitol lawn like an Olympic sprinter and made for the closest door. I could hear the capitol clock begin gonging out the all important 8:00 o'clock morning hour as I bounded up three flights of stairs. This was going to be close. Just as I cleared the third story step, a hearing room door opened and a lady began calling out. "Ben Reed to testify. Ben Reed to testify!" With my heart pounding and lungs burning, I squeaked out a barely audible, "That's Me." Holding my chest and sucking for air, unknowingly I had just transformed myself into the perfect poster child for health insurance.

The hearing room was crowded with some very stern and serious minded looking elected officials. They looked down from their gallery at me as if I was a death row inmate and they were the firing squad. Their intimidating stares were reducing my spine to a rubber tie down tarp strap. With sides heaving and in full body perspiration, I hesitantly made my way to a very small podium. Since my rehearsed speech was long since forgotten, I stalled for time by explaining that I was a little bit nervous in speaking to such an esteem body. Just as I placed my folder on the podium, my nerves must have gotten the best of me. All of my paper work slipped off the podium and scattered around me in the shape of a horse shoe. Totally embarrassed and humiliated, I excused myself and began bending over to gather up my scattered script. I could hear a collective air sucking noise from the Senate gallery and audience as I proceeded to collect one paper after another.

Gathering strength in my rubbery knees, I stood back up half expecting and somewhat hoping to be shown the door. But a funny thing happened. The stern faces were gone. Even though the legislators had scooted well back from their desks, they seemed to have a sincere interest and appreciation in me as a person. As I expressed the need for having good health insurance, nods of sympathy began coming my way. With more and more nods of approval being directed my way, my own self confidence began to build. In a matter of minutes, my timid straight from the farm shyness transformed me into a cross between Clarence Darrow and Billy Graham. With papers in hand, I would stroll from the podium and approach the legislative gallery with confidence. I couldn't tell if I was delivering a sermon or a summation. When I returned to the podium I saw faces filled with genuine understanding for the urgency of employee health care. They seemed to be so totally convinced of my funding need argument, I think they would have signed on the dotted line right then and there if I would have asked them to do so. I concluded my presentation, thanked them for their consideration, and exited the hearing room.

In the hallway I was greeted with plenty of "that a boy pats on the back" from fellow health insurance hopefuls. I was getting pretty well caught up in the back slappin' moment when a friend stepped up beside me and helped bring me back down to earth. "HEY, GREAT JOB", he said. "And by the way, you got a little something on your pants." Realizing my go to meetin' truck, which also doubles as a farm truck, usually is filthy from doing farm chores. I began trying to wipe away any dust or hay from the front of my slacks. He said, "No. You don't understand. You really have something on the back of your pants." Since I didn't have the neck of an ostrich to look behind me, I basically had to bend over and look up between my legs. Uggg! On my thermo heated mad dash to the capitol, a small flake of chocolate from my all time favorite Snickers candy bar must have fallen and melted in the crotch of my tan slacks. I'm sure the nuclear heated cup of coffee had something to do with enhancing the chocolate melt down. It is amazing how one small piece of chocolate, less than half the size of a chigger's eyelash can melt into16 square inches on the backside of tan slacks. From cheek to cheek it looked as if I had failed Potty Training 101 for the 40th consecutive year.

Wow!! My chocolate decorative art work began explaining a lot of things. No wonder when I bent over to pick up my dropped papers the Senators tried to scatter like a flock of mallards on opening day of duck season. No wonder when I mentioned the urgent need for health care, cell phones were making 911 calls for paramedics. No wonder when I said we are depending on them, they were actually wishing that I had worn some Depends. No wonder when they saw a stain the size of a 9 by 13 chocolate fudge sheet cake on the seat of my britches they were willing to sign a blank check just to get me out the door. Will chocolate wonders never cease?

So this brings me back full circle to my original chocolate philosophy of life. We all know life is never going to be easy. We will always have those bitter sweet day to day moments to contend with, but sometimes you just have to step up to the plate and take one for the team. The bottom line is, my chocolate covered bottom helped to seal the deal for people getting health insurance. So that just goes to prove that regardless of how difficult the task may be, almost everything is better with a little bit of chocolate on it.

CHAPTER 14

LET ME BE BEE

IN THE LOCAL FARM pasture mowing society circles, the buzz word this summer is Bees. Not just any bee, but the miserable, homicidal Bumble Bee. The pastures seem to be full of them. If there is any one insect on this earth which deserves to be placed on the extermination species list, I say, "Let it be the Bumble Bee." I don't care how many vegetable blooms would miss getting their blooms pollinated. If it means the difference between me getting to eat a cucumber or getting a bee stung bumpy head like a Star Trek Klingon, I'll go cucumberless.

Besides the pollination process, just what do bumble bees do anyway? I'm not for sure they even realize they are a bee. Unlike their cousins the honey bee, they don't even know how to turn common bee spit into honey. They don't live in a hive like normal bees, but rather live underground where they partake in the underground dark side of life activities. A good portion of their time is spent just hangin' around down in their lair of darkness waiting to be provoked. Once disturbed, they launch a surprise attack in mass on their unsuspecting victim, which is usually me driving a pasture mowin' tractor. Regardless of how many of these little buzz bombs I fight off, there is always at least one which sneaks in from underneath the tractor seat and ends up stinging me right on the A of my WRANGLERS.

Bumble bees have many favorite body stinging locations. Their first and foremost target is usually the back of the neck, right about the hair line. They like having just enough hair for their hind legs to grip, because it gives them that little extra leverage for deep stinger penetration. However, if the neck is not available, bees are willing to go to plan B to sting other vulnerable locations. On more than one occasion, when stung on the eyelid I have looked like I was the loser in a 15 round Iron Mike Tyson boxing match. But, at least the bees didn't gnaw on my ears. Screaming is a major part of bee fighting. However, I have also found it nearly next to impossible to pronounce any words beginning with a W after being stung on the tongue. And whether stung or not, I can do a great Richard Simmons "Sweatin' To The Oldies" aerobic workout when a bumble bee buzzes his way up inside one of my pant legs. That bee just has to be stopped before he makes it to the big boy park.

Once stung by a bumble bee, I become completely paranoid to anything unexpectedly touching me. In other words, I am as goosy has a Chiquita banana in a tree full of monkeys. With nerves on edge, the slightest touch of any leaf, any flying weed seed, or any piece of grass tossed forward by the brush cutter will transform me into what looks like a tractor riding Karate Kid. My arms and legs go to flailing around like an ADHD flamingo having a Ritalin with drawl. And the feed salesman who just happens to be driving by at the time, thinks I'm trying to flag him down to place a gigantic feed order.

Immediately following one of my many bee sting biopsies, my peripheral vision also becomes magnified to that of Superman. Always on constant visual alert, any fly, mosquito, or gnat which comes fluttering by will turn me into a herky jerky ninja warrior combatant. Sometimes a speck on my glasses can cause the same bee hallucinating reaction. I'll be mowing across the pasture and my eyes will sometimes play tricks on me. Once I looked down and got a glimpse of a bee in a well drilling position ready to bury his drill bit into the fat part of my arm. I immediately went into my anti-bee self-defense mode, "panic". I continuously beat that bee senseless until my arm resembled a piece of tenderized round steak. It was only painfully later I discovered when the bee wouldn't leave, that it wasn't really a bee at all. It was only a grease spot from the morning's tractor greasing.

I have discovered while mowing pastures this summer, bees are in an unbelievable grumpy mood this year. If I get as close as fifty yards to a bee, they seem to take it personally. Me and old Rocky, my 10 foot brush cutter or sandstone grinder depending on which pasture I happen to be in at the time, will be bouncing along minding our own business, when for no apparent reason I become a bee magnet. Basically I have a low tolerance for pain. Okay I'll admit it. I am a wuss. I'm a panty waste. I'm a chicken livered little wimp, when it comes to pain. For some reason, I don't ever remember really enjoying hitting my thumb with a hammer, dropping a tractor weight on my toe, or being kicked by a soon to become steer. My life seems to be so much more pleasant and enjoyable when it is pain free. So when I see the buzz end of a bumble bee diving for a bumble bee tattoo on my forehead, I begin to freak out. Because where there is a bee there is a bucket full of pain soon to follow.

I have found that attacking bumble bees can change the entire demeanor of my usual happy go lucky personality. Although 99 percent of the time I'm basically a non-confrontational person, better defined as a "yellow bellied mamma's boy." But a swarm of attacking bumble bees can turn me into a raving Son of Sam serial killer. When push comes to shove or in this case when sting comes to pain, hide the women and the children because I'll be turning into a tractor riding Rambo. I have found my ordinarily stationary body parts can become very mobile when it becomes necessary to avoid the pain of a bumble bee sting. A contortionist couldn't have made some of the bee dodging moves I've made from a moving tractor.

Old timers tell me that "A bee won't bother you if you don't bother them." And they also usually share this little gem of wisdom. "Whatever you do, never fight a bee. If you don't fight them, they will never sting you." Well, to that I say bull hockey. A person would have to be a complete moron with an I.Q. of a crawdad mound to just ignore a bumble bee that is armed with a nuclear war head stinger. How in the world do I just disregard one of those poison dart tipped critters, which has just coasted in for a landing between the lens of my glasses and my eye ball? I find it virtually impossible to believe a person cannot feel a bee harpoon being driven into the back of their neck and not recognize it as pain. Maybe old timers are no longer on bumble bee menus. Maybe old guys just don't taste good to bees. Maybe their skin is as tough as a leather saddle and bee stingers break off before they can penetrate. Maybe old timer's memories are just so far gone they have forgotten what bee sting pain feels like. Or just maybe this is just their sick sense of humor in initiating all of us new comers to the real terrors of pasture mowing.

If you are a perfectionist and pride yourself in driving straight rows, forget it. It is next to impossible to do a neat job of mowing while fighting off killer packs of head huntin' bumble bees. Mowing in a straight path or just holding on to the tractor steering wheel can become a low priority when both hands are needed to apply a variety of hand to hand bee fighting techniques. I'm sure the immediate assumption of any passer by noticing my mowing skills would be that I was either chasing snakes or more likely had one too many nips at the local soak and suds.

My last 20 minute, hat swingin', Kung Fu choppin', blue colored word enhancin', bumble bee fight lasted for nearly a quarter of a mile. When this particular Kamikaze bee buzzed in to deliver his pay load, I was able to smack him with my hog feed farm cap right before he could stab me with his paralyzing juices. However, my cap swingin' blow didn't kill him. It just sent him sailing off his flight course plan. And worse yet, since my blow wasn't fatal, all it did was just seemed to thoroughly tick him off. The only thing I can compare to a ticked off bumble bee is a wounded grizzly with an impacted wisdom tooth that can fly. From the front, from the back, and from each side, this bumble bee unleashed a relentless attack. He seemed to be crossed between a bulldog and a backhoe and was more than ever determined to implant a Mt. Kilimanjaro welt somewhere on my body.

Time and time again I fought off the attacks of this angel of death with carefully aimed and accurate smacks of my cap. I fought him tooth and nail from every vantage point of my tractor. At one point I had done a 180 degree maneuver over the steering wheel and was now straddling the tractor hood backwards like rodeo bucking bronc out of shoot number two. With my back slowly turning into a crispy fried corn fritter because of being firmly planted against the scalding tractor muffler, I still was able to fend off all his lethal attacks with my cap. Huffing and puffing and lathered up like an old Burma Shave commercial, I was quickly reaching total exhaustion. I knew I only had one last good swat left in me and I had better make it count. As this Dr. Kevorkian bee was preparing his final bombing run, I raised and cocked my 357 magnum Purina Feed cap and allowing for windage and elevation took careful aim at the fast approaching tomahawk bee missile. At the last possible moment, I pulled the trigger and delivered a vicious cap blow which must have sent my black and yellow assassin into honey heaven. The bee was no more.

I had won. I did a careful reconnaissance of the horizon and seeing no other bee comrades in sight, I slowly reached down and turned off the key to my still bouncing tractor. Confident that the battle was over and the hard fought victory was mine, I slowly climbed back across the steering wheel, retrieved my glasses from the foot platform, and gave a few words of grateful thanks. After regaining my wind and composure, I restarted my tractor and carefully replaced my battle weary cap on my head. BAM!!!! BAM!!!! BAM!!!! OUCH!!!! OUCH!!!! OUCH!!!! That little miserable lowest form of insect life had latched on to the inside of my cap and had waited for just the right sneak attack moment to drive his 16 penny stinger into my skull. Within minutes, the top of my bald head took the form of a prehistoric top knotted Myheadasoreas Rex dinosaur.

Oh!!! Is there any wonder why I dislike bumble bees? Not only do bumble bees make a not so pleasant pasture mowing job even less appealing, they do not have the common courtesy or common decency to crawl off and die after they sting me. They are completely satisfied to just lay in wait until I come back around the field and try to pump me full of bee venom again. I don't ask for much out of this life. My wants are few. All I ask for is this. When I'm mowing my pasture..... PLEASE.......just let me be bee.

Let Me Be Bee

Chapter 15

I HAVE RESERVATIONS ABOUT MY HOTEL

THE PAST FEW YEARS with my work I have had the opportunity to stay in a variety of hotels. Each and every one of these sleepovers was unique in what it had to offer its overnight guests. Some were outstanding five star shiny accommodations, while others scored about a negative eight and were about as shiny as a fire fly's rear end. Some of the substandard services I have experienced have caused me to have reservations about certain hotels.

When I call for a reservation and hear a foreign language on the other end, the potential for problems has just increased three fold. I don't want to hear "Goodt Morgan" or "Bon Joure" or "Olga." I don't need some New Delhi fella named Ahbieb trying to explain what a continental breakfast is to me. I am from this continent. I know what a two day old donut is. If by chance someone does answer the phone in English, I automatically presume that it is most likely an F.B.I. team checking out a crime scene.

I know I don't get around much, but just getting into a room is not a simple task any more. Many hotels have done away with the old fashioned brass keys and have replaced them with plastic computerized secret coded cards that slide into a metal gizmo attached to the outside of the door. Once the card is inserted, a green light flashes, the dead bolt slides open, and the door knob is ready to be turned. If you are at the wrong door, a red light will flash sometimes accompanied by a tornado siren, then followed by a scream from the other side of the door yelling, "Get out of here you pervert." The first time I was given one of the new room key cards turned out to be rather a traumatic experience for both me and the fat lady walking out of the bathroom with a bath towel wrapped around most of her body. She screamed. I screamed. We both screamed. I don't know what happened. I had a green light.

A few older lodging facilities still do give out metal keys to maintain the character and mystique of historical hotels. The keys no longer have engraved room numbers on them for security reasons. The room number is written down on a piece paper size of a postage stamp that is lost long before the room is ever found. If the key doesn't work in the first door, you just keep trying doors until one opens. Recently I checked into a room and had just kicked off my shoes to relax when I noticed the door knob slowly turning back and forth. Thinkin' it was friends pulling a prank, I thought it would be fun to beat them to the practical joke punch. I decided to jerk the door open and yell "Surprise!" The hotel maid was most definitely surprised. She dropped like a rock. I'm sure if she had spoken better English I would have had a much better understanding of her Hispanic swear words.

Hotel phones are fun too. The last time I tried to make a collect call home from a hotel room by following the computerized number pushing sequences, I messed up by one digit and ended up getting a Russian operator. "What part of a Russia are you calling?" She asked in a comrade..ish type voice.

"I'm not trying to call any part of Russia," I replied.

"Yes you are," she said.

"The heck I am," I answered back.

"Well, you called me. I didn't call you…you…you American swine," she countered. She had a point there. I was the one that dialed the phone.

Calming down, I tried to prevent another international cold war incident. "Listen up, Natasha. I'm just trying to make a collect call to my home in southwest Missouri. Can you please help me out?" CLICK!!!! BUZZ!!!! "Southwestern Belle Operator…Can I help you?" Humm! Maybe I should become a diplomat. Moscow and I seem to have a pretty good working relationship.

Hotel services and information are important if I can understand them. But trying to break the language barrier of hotel employees is sometimes nearly impossible. I don't know how to ask which way to the pool in Portuguese. I don't know how to ask for ice in the language of a Zulu Tribe. And as for the pre-sunrise wake up calls, I don't mind them as long as I request them. An unexpected Liechtenstein good morning accent at 4:00 AM does not get my day off to a very good start.

One of the most crucial parts of the hotel room is the bed. After all that is where ninety-nine percent of the $150 a night will be spent. Some beds are feather bed soft, while others are firm as bridge planks. Some pillows prop your head up like concrete blocks, and others are made of that foam rubber stuff that tends to promote night time suffocation. Plus, I have never figured out how a house keeping staff can stretch bed sheets as tight as a trampoline. I have crawled out of bed some mornings so pigeon toed it would have made a ballerina jealous.

I also don't understand why hotel thermostats are so difficult to regulate. Is normal body heat comfort too much to ask? I've stayed in refrigerated rooms cold enough to hang beef carcasses. Other times I have awakened gasping for air feeling as if I was a rump roast being par boiled in a crock pot. It only seems reasonable that for rooms priced well over $100, you should get a room temperature midway between hypothermia and first degree burns.

Equally important as the bed, is the bathroom facilities. I don't ask for a lot, but I do prefer a commode secured firmly to the floor. I don't care much for toilet recliners. If I wanted to be part of a balancing act, I would have joined a circus. And I certainly would like to meet the sick, twisted demonic son of Satan that developed the spring loaded trip release toilet seat. The seat and lid is like a booby trap bear trap. It can change a baritone into a member of Father Flannigan's Boys Town Choir in a blink of an eye. And I would still like to flush my own toilet thank you. I have dropped a comb on the bathroom floor and when I bent over to retrieve it, the automatic toilet almost sucked the whiskers right off my face.

I had a room one time that had a shower with a flat domed shaped bell at one end of the tiled wall. Out of the metal object was a fishing like string with a metal hook attached to the end. I had an inquiring mind so I pulled on the line to see what happened. Nothing happened. After several quick pulls, there was now twice the amount of string needed to reach the opposite shower wall. So was this some kind of device to meet hotel OSHA shower safety standards? Maybe if I were to slip and fall, I could make a grab for the string to let the front desk know, "Help I've fallen and I can't get soaped." Could it be the bell was programmed to ding a ling if someone was caught lathering too long. I found out later the string was for drying delicates. At 250 plus pounds, I don't think I own any delicates. But be warned. Every so often the string when pulled out and not attached to the opposing wall security ring will not always retract immediately. It is programed with a time delay. Sometimes it just lays in wait on the bottom of the tub in a perfect attack position waiting to be activated. Right when I was in full lather and just as I straddled the zip line of pain….KERR ZING!!! Right up between my own personal continental divide. Yeeee!!! Ikes!!!! It was definitely an unexpected thrill, especially when the metal hook traveling at jet propulsion speed snagged my unmentionables. I guess I do own delicates.

The last but certainly not the least important hotel room necessity is the TV. I like big city TVs. They have multiple channels with a variety of enjoyable entertainment shows. There are sports channels, old movie channels, western channels or on the edge of your seat local drama channels for watching local city council members debating new pet leash law policies. There is a home shopping network, great outdoor killing deer shows and reruns of Gilligan's Island. Some hotels have a pay for TV naughty network. Fairly graphic movies are available for those willing to pay a nominal fee at checkout time. This channel usually likes to tempt potential customers with a few minutes of free teaser X-rated movie watching and then scrambles the picture so you can no longer tell what, when, where, or to who it is happening. Being the cheap skate that I am, I found that if I put my head at a full tilt 45 degree angle and shook it up and down vigorously, I could still tell pretty much tell what kind of naughtiness was going on and didn't have to pay one red cent to watch it. If it wasn't for the next morning stiff neck and migraine headache, I would have felt pretty good about cheatin' the hotel out of their three buck charge.

There have been a few occasions when I have never turned the TV on. The walls are usually so thin that my next door neighbors provide me with more than enough entertainment. There is nothing more entertaining than having a room next to a drunk, a family with eight kids, or newlyweds. In each case I try to be quiet as a church mouse. I'm afraid the drunk might want me to come over for a party, the kids might want to come over to play, or the newlyweds might stop doing what they are doing.

It is important to plan hotel stays well in advance. Be sure and try to select only hotels that use stars for ratings. Stay away from the ones using guns, meat cleavers or hypodermic needles for rating markers. Make sure your hotel reservations are made well in advance of your expected arrival. Check, double check, triple check, your reservations before your anticipated arrival time. The quickest way for me to get reservations about my hotel is to be pooped out from driving all day, walk up to the front desk to check in and hear those wonderful words in a far far eastern dialect "So sawee, Sir. Dees hotel has no konfuremation of your weservation." UGG!!! There have been times I should have just camped out by the side of the road.

Chapter 16

G.W. WAS RIGHT. IT PAYS TO NOT TELL A LIE

OKAY CHUCK! LET'S SHOW'EM what we're made of. Chuck is my truck. For the last 10 miles, two cars have been right on my exhaust pipe. If I speed up, they tag right along as if I'm pulling them with a tow rope. If I slow down to let them pass, they settle into their lethargic mode comfort zone and are more than willing to play follow the leader with me always being the leader. It is like I am the scout for their wagon train and they want to keep me in the lookout position.

So here I am all dressed up in my favorite go to wedding/funeral/important meeting dark blue blazer with white shirt and tie on the way to a meeting. I wouldn't normally be driving my mud hole jumpin', cow feedin', all around farm truck, Chuck, but on this day he was the only set of four wheels available. The only reason I am on this lonely country back road is that I knew it would be virtually deserted. Since I am running late as usual, an out of the way cross-country black top road like this is usually free of Smokey Bears and a great place to make up time. But right now, I'm tired of this cat and mouse game and it is time for my driving disciple followers to put up or shut up. Chuck and I mean business and we are feeling the urge to create some space between us and our two unwanted tag-a-longs.

It's pedal to the metal and here we go. Varoom!!!! Away we went.

50.... 60.... 70..... 80 mph. Way to go, Chuck! You definitely got quick like a bunny rabbit fever today. We're sure showing them Tony Stewart wannabe's how a real race driver can make tracks. Someone should have warned them, that if they're all bark and no bite, they really shouldn't be messin' with us big dogs. A quick glance in the mirror showed the cars were struggling to keep up with our new NASCAR record setting pace. With one eye on the road and the other eye on the rear view mirror, I crested a hill just in time to meet a back road crusin' highway patrolman Oh! Oh! The patrol car's brake lights came on immediately.

I'm sure this is what it looked like to the officer. A speeding truck had just passed two totally innocent correct speed limit traveling vehicles going up a hill in a no passing zone. What else could he think? Well, I suppose he could have also thought that I wasn't just a speeder, but possibly a serious criminal element on the run from Dawg the Bounty Hunter. Whatever it looked like, I'm sure I wasn't going to be looking good for me. As Chuck coasted down the hill, I hoped against all hopes that maybe the officer had decided to give me a break so that he wouldn't miss his daily Daylight Donut appointment. Flashing lights cresting the hill behind me immediately dismissed that hopeful notion.

As the patrol car began closing ground, I noticed I didn't have my seat belt on. Great! Just Great! I could visualize the dollar amount of my fine increasing by the minute. But....not a little but..... but a big but...if I could somehow get my seatbelt hooked before coming to a stop, I would most likely shave some major bucks off my inevitable financial contribution to the policeman's ball.

Nonchalantly as possible, I tried to steer with one hand and indiscreetly as possible slide my hand up across my chest to reach for my unattached seat belt. To not give away my plan, I kept my head and eyes straight forward. This was not going to be easy. I wasn't in a car, I was driving Chuck. Chuck is my farm truck and I don't normally wear a seat belt when driving down the dirt roads to go feed the cows. In fact, I had used the shoulder strap so little I wasn't for sure where it was even located. However, lady luck was with me. Eureka! On the third try I finally snagged it with my trigger finger. I slowly pulled the seat belt strap and metal clip down across my go to meeting blazer trying my best not to raise any suspicions of the pursuing patrolman. The rub came when I couldn't snap the metal clip into the seat belt clasp. The clasp was somewhere under the right side of my breadbasket, but it was virtually impossible to find it without looking down. However with the cop closing in fast, I had to give the best performance of my life that the belt had been attached from the get go. Frustration really began to set in with every repeated seatbelt snapping failure. I finally gave in and turned my head just enough in hopes of spotting the hide and seek clasp. But every time I would look down, I would invariably pull the steering wheel to the right. Bump! Bump! Bump! Gravel would fly in all directions when the passenger side tires would drop off the blacktop and on to the narrow road ditch shoulder. Instinctively I would whip the steering wheel back to the left jerking Chuck back on to the highway. After about three or four swerving off and back on to the road episodes, I'm sure a whole new list of charges were going through the mind of the officer giving chase. I was no longer just a speeding fugitive. I was now a three sheets in the wind drunk driver.

I wasn't ready to give up on my seatbelt ticket saving idea quite yet, but with sirens blaring and flashing lights now right on my tail, I was needing a new plan fast. I have watched enough of America's Most Wanted to know it is important to keep both hands in plain view, so I was hesitant about reaching down to lock the belt in place. Coasting to the side of the road, I finally had the Einstein idea of just sitting on the end of the belt. It still went across my chest and maybe he wouldn't notice that it wasn't legitimately snapped and just stuck underneath the fatty part of my right thigh.

Looking in my rearview mirror, I could tell by the extra handful of ticket pads the officer was carrying that he had plans for me meeting his entire monthly law breaking violations quota. As I sat there waiting for the officer to come up and present me with his good driving awards, I was beginning to have second thoughts about my belt under the butt cheek idea. If he looked inside the window at all, he wouldn't have to have all five points on his star to see my belt was not actually hooked to anything. It was about this time that I had my second idea of shear brilliance. I would open the door, pretend to undo my seat belt and step out to greet the approaching officer. I'm sure officers are reluctant to give high dollar tickets to super friendly folks.

As I lifted the handle to open the door, I leaned slightly to the left preparing to step out with my good will gesture of friendship. I was totally unprepared for the consequences of that single little insignificant motion. That little lean to the left removed some serious hold down fat pressure from my right fat leg side. Zing!!! The seat belt recoiled faster than a spring on a grizzly bear trap. Kerr!! Smack!! As the metal clasp flew up at mach-1 speed, it hit me right under the nose and then proceeded to snap my glasses into two separate monocles. Nothing brings tears faster to a fat boy's eyes than a good wrap on the end of the nose. I fell out of the truck like a sack of potatoes. The officer didn't seem as glad to see me as I thought he might. He acted as if I was the Unabomber. With his hand on his peace maker, he kept yelling for me to get back into the truck. Down on one knee, I could hear him, but my nose hurt so bad I couldn't answer him. All I could do was SNIFF! And SNIFF! And SNIFF! So now I have just created a third law breaking profile. I have watery eyes. I am sniffing continuously. And I am having difficulty in following verbal commands. Great! I'm higher than a kite. In less than three minutes I had graduated from an everyday run of the mill breaker of speed limits, to an all over the road drunk driver, to now a druggy most likely hooked on speed. This had all been accomplished in an effort to avoid a click it or ticket $10 fine.

The officer cautiously approached my driver side window. I'm sure he anticipated either finding America's #1 fugitive from justice or at the bare minimum an escaped felon on the F.B.I.'s top ten most wanted list. Sniffing back the tears, I complied with his request for my license and proof of insurance. Noticing my tears, he wanted to know why I was crying. Since I didn't feel comfortable in sharing my seat belt story, I quickly pointed out that this was allergy season. Telling an out and out bald face lie didn't come easy to me. However, I am not above stretching the truth until right before the elastic breaks. In this instance, I didn't specifically tell the officer that I personally had any allergies. I just pointed out that it was allergy season.

The officer seemed to spend hours in his patrol car giving me a thorough criminal back ground check. Just about the time my tears had dried up the County Mountie came striding up to my window to ask me a few more questions. Where did I live? I told him. Where was my destination? I told him. What was my reason for travelling? I was attending a meeting. My navy blue sport coat and tie should have been a dead giveaway that I was on my way to a meeting. And then the correctional officer of speed hit me with that all important make or break question. Do I normally wear my seat belt?

Wow! To lie or not to lie that was the question. What would George Washington do? Riding this "truth or lie" fence was giving me the ultimate right thing/wrong thing to do wedgie. I finally hedged my bets and said, "Well Sir, I try to always wear my seat belt, but I can't say that I remember to wear it every single time." Giving me one long last look over, I was told that I would not be getting a ticket but only a warning, if I would promise to hold down my speed. Hold down my speed? Was he kiddin'? I would have promised him a life time Krispy Kreme gift certificate to have gotten out of this ticket. Am I good or what? How often do we get to brag about getting to pull the wool over the eyes of the strong arm of the law?

Just before leaving, the officer took the time to make a couple of helpful points. Point Number One: Seat belts saves lives and it is extremely important for me to always wear my belt while operating a motorized vehicle. I shook my head in total agreement. Point Number Two: I might want to check my jacket before I walked into my meeting. It seems that it had been so long since my dusty chore truck seat belt had been used that it left a perfect three inch diagonal dust sash across my dark blue jacket. It looked as if I had just won the Mr. Missouri Liar of the Year Contest. I'm not sure a hefty ticket wouldn't have been less humiliating. I am reasonably certain the officer may have known I may have been shading the truth all the way to the edge of night. However, since he had the goods on me, but I had not actually crossed the Martha Stewart line of deception with an outright lie, he decided to give me a ticket pass. Oh well, I guess G W was right. It really does pay to not tell a lie. Plus it was just going to be too weird to see a grown fat man break down in tears again.

G.W. Was Right.
It Pays To Not Tell A Lie

Chapter 17

LET'S TALK TURKEY

I CAME TO A stage in my life where I needed an enjoyable hobby, something that would relax stress and relieve tension headaches.... Something that could dissolve work related frustrations....Something that would not require a second mortgage for purchasing a bass boat or a country club membership. On the advice of a friend, make that former friend, the hobby I chose was turkey hunting. For the past four years I have been releasing my frustrations and relaxing my mind while chasing the elusive wild turkey. It might have been even less stressful if my friend had suggested a bottle of Wild Turkey.

It is not possible for a person to wake up one day and decide to become a turkey hunter. Becoming a turkey hunter is a process. Turkey hunters have to prepare for this adventure and be willing to turn loose of a few bucks of the kid's college fund as well. What do beginner turkey hunters need? Turkey hunting magazines and videos need to be purchased. A call for each of the 38 different sounds a turkey makes needs to be secured. Camouflage, camouflage, and more camouflage is a must. There just can never be too much camouflage. The clothes, the boots, the hat, the gun, the shells, the calls, the hands, the face, the eyeballs all need to be camouflaged with earth tones. In other words, you better look like a multi-flora rose bush with poison ivy for ears when you crawl into that pick up truck at 4:30 in the morning. After about the third day of the season I kind of look like a bundle of briars whether I'm turkey hunting or not.

I have never hunted such a Simple Simon critter that was so dumb 50 weeks out of the year and then would acquire an unbelievable feathered Einstein I Q the other two hunting season weeks. Most of the year, I try to dodge them with my truck on the gravel roads and shoo them out of the way of my tractor when doing field work. The other hunting season two weeks, they become two legged schizophrenics afraid of their own shadows. They have superman eye sight and even better hearing. If they could smell, they would be impossible to track down all together. For those that have never turkey hunted and may have the desire to do so, let me give you a play by play description of just one of my many turkey hunting adventures. It may just be the nudge you have needed for taking up a new hobby.

10:00 PM	Night before… lay out all turkey hunting equipment, watch the predicted perfect weather forecast, set alarm for 4:30 AM, go to bed.
1:30 AM	Wake up, check the alarm to make sure it is set, accidently disturb sleeping wife. Waking up a sleeping wife….not a smart move.
3:30 AM	Re-check the alarm clock, walked around bed so as to not disturb the wife, learned my lesson last time.
4:45 AM	Messed with the clock so much the alarm failed to go off. I've over slept. Fly out of bed in a state of panic. A startled sleeping wife turns into a fighting Ninja.
4:47 AM	Jump in favorite huntin' truck with most of my clothes on and head for the woods at top notch speed.
5:05 AM	Arrive at favorite hunting spot with all my turkey hunting equipment. Everything except gun.
5:06 AM	Head back to house at break neck speed.

5:10 AM	Back at spot. Begin running across muddy field to get to favorite turkey killing zone.
5:11 AM	Can't see…can't breathe…stop for oxygen. Doctor's morbid obese chart was correct.
5:20 AM	Stagger on, hear thunder, feel rain, feel wet. When it comes to honesty, weather forecasters rank right up there with politicians.
5:30 AM	Arrive close to my turkey fortress vicinity, but not for sure because clouds and rain make it too dark to tell for sure.
5:35 AM	Turn round and round in circles trying to figure out where I'm at.
5:36 AM	Lightning bolt strikes close…..really really close. Lightening flash lit up the woods but blinded me in the process. Still can't figure out where I am.
5:40 AM	All weather flashlight soaked, won't work. Eyes dilated like a cat but still too dark to see where I'm at.
5:45 AM	Decide to go left
5:46 AM	Tripped! Found old barb wire fence next to creek bank. Kerr Splash!…also found creek. Now I know where I'm at. Should have turned right.
5:55 AM	Grab log and float down stream to shallow water. Cold water gave me the shakes.
5:58 AM	Climb up muddy bank to hear first turkey gobble. Gobble came from tree right above me.
6:00 AM	Low crawl through mud, water, and face ripping briars to set up come hither turkey hen decoys. Crawl back to base of tree and pull some leafy vines around me to conceal my ambush site. Too dark to recognize vines were poison ivy.
6:10 AM	The running, falling and crawling had me puffin' like a steam engine. Body heat foggin' up my glasses. Glasses

so steamed I can't even see the dark anymore. Hope the morning monsoon will wash off my lenses.

6:15 AM Hear second gobble, reach for wooden box call that has swollen three times the size of a sweet potato because of the creek water baptismal. Attempt to make a Yelp call. Sounds more like YAKKA YAKKA. Gobbler is in need of love because he answers.

6:20 AM Hair on the back of my neck stands up as Mr. Long Beard above me sounds off again. I try to answer, but box call is now reduced to a sponge. Reach for brand new guaranteed to work in all weather rubber diaphragm call. In the dark, not sure which is front or back but put in mouth and hope for the best.

6:21 AM Take deep breath....Gag gag cough gag cough – do a Heimlich Maneuver on myself trying to cough up little rubber strangle yourself turkey call. The Thunder Chicken takes off on a non-stop flight to Cuba.

6:30 AM Almost through gagging, rain slows and wind switches to the North Pole express. Body trying to generate internal friction heat by shivering and shaking uncontrollably.

6:40 AM Wonder if it would be possible to call Mr. Tom Turkey back. Used an all weather slate call. Squeak! Squawk! Squeak! Hear hens fly away in every direction except towards me.

6:41 AM Insect repellant washed off. Squadron of Mosquitoes spot me from 30,000 feet and proceed to attack in dive bombing formation. I have given less blood at the Red Cross blood drive.

8:00 AM Rain stopped, sun peeking through clouds, I'm still making turkey clucking sounds.

8:30 AM	Give my best yet "come and get it" turkey hen call. Three geese honk as they fly over.
9:00 AM	Smack! Killed my 300th mosquito. My forehead feels like a relief map of Argentina.
9:30 AM	Notice I have no feelings left in my legs. The last time my legs were this numb was when I read one too many turkey hunting articles while taking care of business in my porcelain oval office.
9:40 AM	Rearrange legs to restart blood circulation. Comfortable now. A quick snooze might be nice.
12:58 PM	Enjoying nap. Having dream. Dreaming I'm being attacked by a long beard. I can almost hear him gobble.
12:59 PM	Eyes open. It's no dream. Turkeys are everywhere. My snoring must have called them in. One tom is asking my decoy out for a date.
12:59:57 PM	BAM! Only half awake, but squeeze off a quick shot anyway. Turkeys make a break for it.
12:59:58 PM	BOOM! Second shot shoots where Gobbler's head was one second earlier.
12:59:59 PM	KERR! POW! Third shot…turkey ducks and gives a smile and a wink as he trots into the woods.
1:00 PM	Click…Cuss... Click… Click… Cuss… Cuss…Turkey shooting hours are over for the day
1:30 PM	Tears almost dried up and no longer sobbing. Pick up all turkey hunting equipment and look for my unloaded shotgun thrown at runaway turkey.
1:45 PM	Walk across muddy field to truck, scratching my poison ivy rash and thinking about how much fun it is to hunt wild turkeys.

I'm certainly pleased I was encouraged to take up such a non-stressful activity such as turkey hunting. The inner peace of finding one's soul and once again being rejoined with nature is exhilarating, even if I sometimes use of some of my Dad's favorite army talk adjectives to describe the hunt. To anyone and everyone that may be looking for a new hobby, if you don't mind hypothermia, if you don't mind being a pin cushion for mosquitoes, if you don't mind contracting unknown rashes in some well know places, if you don't mind radish size tick bites, well by all means, turkey hunting may just be for you. Come on by the farm sometime and let's talk turkey.

LET'S TALK TURKEY

CHAPTER 18

MY DEEPEST CONDOLENCES FOR YOUR LOSS

Shortly after my Grandma passed away, my mom, her brother and sister met to make some decisions about Grandma's house and personal possessions. I think in most cases, Grandma had already decided who got what of her stuff. Not only did she leave specific heirlooms to each of her children, but she wanted all of the grand and great grand kids to have a special Grandma remembrance as well. Grandma wanted to give each relative something she thought we would really enjoy. The gifts did not necessarily have to be of equitable value. In her way of thinking, the sentimental value of a gift from Grandma would far outweigh any potential garage sale dollar amount of the future. For instance, one cousin got a one hundred year old family rocking chair. Another received a trunk load of quilts that must have traveled over on the Mayflower. My brother really enjoyed his four piece solid oak antique bedroom suite. And Grandma remembered a long long time ago when I had just turned two years old how I had pointed towards one of her $1.29 red bird figurines and smiled. My inconsiderate brother seemed to be really really happy for me and my red bird inheritance. To this very day, every time he sees me he smiles and winks and asks how my bird is doing. On more than one occasion I have come close to showing him how my bird was doing.

A few days after Grandma's services, her house was listed with a local realtor. The realtor explained that due to a depressed local economy not to expect any immediate action from interested buyers. It was somewhat of a surprise when a young couple fell head over heels in love with Grandma's house and signed the contract papers less than forty-eight hours after the listing. If the economy had been any more depressed, there might not have been enough time to stick the for sale sign up in the yard. The only contract stipulation was the newlyweds wanted to take possession of their new love nest as soon as possible. Since all of Grandma's stuff was still in the house, this presented somewhat of a cleaning out the house problem for the family. Well, almost all of Grandma's stuff was still in the house. As for myself, since heavy duty moving transportation was not an issue for my redbird figurine heirloom, I had already stopped earlier and picked up my inheritance.

I had kind of been kept out of the house selling loop and wasn't even aware that a "cleaning the house out race against the clock" had already begun. In fact, things had transpired so quickly no one had even told me that Grandma's house had sold. It wasn't until my mom showed up at my place of work one day, looking as if she had just gotten the worse terminal illness diagnosis possible from her doctor, that I learned the house clearing clock was ticking. With the longest barely audible sigh I have ever witnessed, mom slowly lowered herself into the chair across from my desk. "Are you okay, Mom," I asked?

With her voice weak and cracking just a little, I heard an "I guess."

Still worried, again I quizzed her, "Are you sure there is nothing the matter, Mom?"

I got back an even weaker, "No not really."

There was no doubt. Something was the matter, but I was almost afraid to keep prying as fast as she was fading. But what the heck! I've had mouth to mouth training with a rubber dummy. I got a better than fifty fifty shot of bringing her back around if I have too. With my finger on 911 speed dial, I leaned towards her and said, "What is it, Mom? Really you can tell me."

With the last bit of energy she could summon, Mom almost whispered, "Grandma's house sold."

"Well, that's great," I said. "Wow! That happened a lot faster than you thought it would. Aren't you excited?"

"I guess. But everything has to be out of the house by Friday though," she was barely able to slur the words.

"But that's tomorrow," I reminded her.

"I know," she sighed.

Oh! Oh! When the hair on the back of my neck stands straight up, it is usually a good sign lightening is about to strike. It is a for sure sign of an imminent disaster when your own mother is the only storm cloud brewing on the horizon.

"Your Uncle Roger and his kids are at the house now loading up his things." ZAP! "And, you're Aunt Joan and her girls are up there too, boxing up their stuff." WHAM! Yep! Better duck my lightening rod head because here it comes. "I don't know how I'm going to get my things out," she mumbled. KABOOM ! A direct hit.

The guilt was being poured over me like molasses over a jonnie cake. I tried to fight back against the guilt with the fastest ammunition I could think of, "Did you check with my brother, your other son, to see if he had some spare time?" I figured it was worth a shot.

"Oh, I didn't want to bother him because he's really busy with his job and I know he is usually so tired of an evening." Ouch! That one hurt. For a couple of minutes we went into a silent stare down. Although no words were spoken, I could tell Mom was prepared to wait me out. Her breathing was becoming increasingly more irregular. Her deep sighs were getting faster but fainter. She was so low in the chair she could slip out of it at any moment.

I couldn't take the pressure any longer. I blinked first. "Well maybe, if I could get one of the guys here at work……" I didn't even get a chance to finish my sentence.

"Great! I will see you there in about ten minutes." Mom shot out of the office like she had just taken a double shot from her Geritol bottle. It's amazing how fast mothers can recover when they get their way.

Supposedly there wasn't too much to load, a couple of boxes of knick knacks and some little dish cabinet. It didn't sound like it would be a much bigger deal than when I stopped by to pick up my redbird figurine. So I called in a favor from a co-worker, Milo and we took his truck to go pick up Mom's inheritance. When we went to Grandma's house there actually was just a couple of boxes of keep sakes. But the little, insignificant dish cabinet was an entirely different story. It had grown into a full sized, cover the entire north wall, dining room China hutch. It was massive and unusual. Most hutches are made of beautifully hand carved wood with some fancy etched glass doors. This hutch was ninety percent etched glass with just a smidgeon of wood to help hold it all together. The slightest bump, the slightest jar could return this china dish monstrosity into a heap of ocean beach sand. More importantly, I knew if I was the cause of destroying this family treasure, it would for sure be my gl….ass spread out on the nearest ocean beach.

Our first moving trick was to figure out how to extract a 6' 7" glass back breaking Chinese dish holder through a 6' 6" front door. By removing a portion of the top door frame and tilting it slightly to the left, we judged we would have 1/32 of an inch to spare. However, moving it from the porch to the truck parked in the street was going to require more than a wishful imagination. This Herculean feat was going to require some Grade A prime leg, arm, and lower back muscles. And muscles were one thing Milo and I was short of. However, lady luck was on Mom's side. Coming down the street was a group of high school kids going door to door selling raffle tickets for a high school band fund raiser. They eagerly volunteered to be lifters and I thought the fifty bucks worth of chances on a fruit basket was every bit of a bargain. And anyway…I kind of do like oranges.

With a hand on every possible glass corner, Milo and I and four high school kids moved the house of glass from the porch down the steps and on to the waiting truck in the street. The way Milo and I were huffin' and puffin', I'm not for sure the kids were even liftin'. Just how heavy was the hutch? To this day Milo has a noticeable speech impediment when he tries to pronounce R words and I have been plagued with a perpetual left eye twitch.

My mom was so excited in seeing her hutch loaded, she could have done a geriatric cart wheel. She said if we hurried and got her stuff moved, there might be enough time for us to come back and get my brother's prize bedroom suite. I immediately told Milo that he would be driving slow, extremely slow. If we had to run out of gas, have four flat tires, and get hit by a runaway freight train, I guaranteed him that moving a bed room suite was not going to be happening this day. After all, I didn't get any help moving my red bird figurine.

Our unloading destiny was only about 14 blocks away. However with strong winds blowing and no suitable means of securing the hutch to the truck, the only remedy for safe delivery was for me to ride in the back of the truck to be the china hutch anchor. But before the ignition was ever started, I wanted there to be a delivery plan that we (mainly Milo) clearly understood. The plan was this. We were going to be driving slow. We were going to be dodging the busiest main drag in town because we were going to be driving really slow. We were going to be extra careful when making turns at corners. Above all else, at all times we would be driving really really slow. Just to reinforce my slow speed limit plan, I gave my furniture moving buddy one last reminder. As an analogy, I pointed out that just like water, other things can and will flow downhill. Since I did have seniority in our work place, if anything was to happen to this family glass menagerie and my mother was to come down on me, he too would be facing a life sentence without parole in a very hostile work environment. Milo seemed to really get the slow driving picture.

Milo actually did better than expected. He drove with extreme caution and at the pace of a crippled snail. Who says people don't respond well to threats? Although I felt like somewhat of a spectacle on display in the back of the truck, our delivery plan was being executed to perfection. We went down one block and then made a very slow left turn and headed towards the next block. My emphasis on slow must have really made an impression upon Milo. I swear I saw a sparrow build a nest, lay her eggs and hatch them before we made the next corner.

We were half way to Mom's house when we slowly coasted up to the main drag. All we had to do was make it across without incident and we would be home free. Also in our favor, the midafternoon traffic seemed to be lighter than normal. Getting across the usually busiest street in town was now going to be a cake walk. There was a string of cars headed in our direction from the left but only one coming from the right. If the single car from the right would quit dinkin' around we should have plenty of time to navigate our crossing before the oncoming traffic picked up. In anticipation of the car from the right passing, Milo eased out into the intersection to make our hop, skip, and a jump crossing. But for no apparent reason, the car came to an unexpected stop directly in our highway crossing path. Why on this green earth would any moron feel the need to bring his bald tired, dented up, rusted out'72 Ford Galaxy to a stop in the middle of an intersection? There was instant panic.

To avoid the accident just waiting to happen, Milo yanked a hard right. In the process of turning, his foot slipped off the brake and on to the gas pedal. We went from zero to forty in 15 feet. But it was at the 16 foot mark when the gale force winds hit me and Grandma's hutch broadside. The wind and sharp turn had Mom's precious cargo teeter tottering at a 45 degree angle. I have read stories of people seeing their lives pass before their eyes. Mine was in Technicolor. More from fear than brute strength, I pushed and strained and heaved and finally saved my Mom's crystallized inheritance from landing in the middle of the suicide turn lane.

While I was busy keeping the family hutch intact, Milo was giving a gallant effort in regaining control of the traffic situation. In his successful attempt in averting the inevitable his truck T-boning car disaster, Milo had somehow merged with the oncoming left bound traffic. I still had a life and death bear hug on the hutch and found I still remembered most of the 23rd Psalm….in Latin. It happened so fast I wasn't exactly sure what had happened. The only thing I was sure of was that it must have been Milo's fault. I gave his rear view mirror every dirty look I could think of and threw in a few choice pool hall words free of charge.

The good news was that we were once again traveling at the speed of crawl. The bad news was we were right smack in the middle of a car convoy on the busiest thorough fare that we had planned to avoid. The really bad news was the wind had picked up speed and the hutch was feeling the full force of the cross wind. Speaking of feeling, I was beginning to feel the north wind where I don't normally feel wind. Of all times, why now? I was being threatened with PBPS (Plumber Butt Pant Slide) Syndrome. It was definitely not the day to be wearing my extremely relax fit Wranglers, especially without a belt. In my save the hutch wrestling match, my Wranglers had fallen faster than my mutual funds in my retirement account. My back pockets were now somewhere between my sitting part and my knee bending part, but the wind was so strong I didn't dare release my vice like grip on the hutch. Trying to hike up my wayward Wranglers in this wind was not even an option. All I could do was just grin and bare it.

The one pleasant surprise was how slow the traffic was still moving. Normally this demolition derby avenue ranks right up there with Indianapolis 500 Speedway. It was impossible to see over the hutch so I tried to sneak a peek around the side. Up ahead I could see the flashing lights of a city patrol car. Great, a fender bender up ahead! This day is just getting better and better. Here I am in the back of a truck standing tall, while at the same time my faded blues are in a free fall. Talk about feeling like the poster child for stupid. After a couple more blocks and still not seeing Andy and Barney collaring a perp (that's perpetrator for those who don't watch Law and Order), I made another quick glance to see what had happened to the wreck. There was no wreck. The police car seemed to be controlling traffic speed by leading local drivers in a slow driving safety demonstration. In fact, a rather lengthy parade had formed and was now following the flashing lights through the center of town. Behind the parade leading cop car was a black shiny car. Then there was another black shiny car. Then there was us. And then behind us there was….. You have gotten to be freakin' kiddin' me. In our earlier near car/truck collision, Milo had somehow merged us into a funeral procession. We were just not in the procession; we were helping to lead it. To be more precise, our fourth in line position placed us right behind the hearse and directly in front of the family transportation limousine. Not only were we disrespecting the grieving family's funeral processional with our furniture hauling truck, but for the last six blocks with my faded denims at half mast I had been mooning the family with a vertical smile.

I was in one miserable peep show predicament. The wind blowing across my exposed back side was now creating a whistling noise, but I didn't dare let go of my two handed grip on Mom's glass treasure. Listening intently to a Cardinal Ball game on the radio, Milo seemed clueless to our last rites ceremonial violation situation. I finally got his attention in his rear view side mirror. I tried to mouth out the words of our precarious fix, but he didn't understand a word. I guess a mirror makes words smaller than they appear, because I was yellin' some pretty darn big words. Totally confused he finally rolled down his window and yelled back, "What?" I screamed back that he gotten us into a cemetery headed caravan and he better do something pretty darn quick about getting us out of it. I never had actually seen eyes get as big as dinner plates before. Milo started looking for escape routes in all directions. The problem was, out of respect for a funeral procession, drivers had pulled over blocking every street entrance for at least two more blocks.

A two block ride was going to seem like eternity. Forget the ride. My relax fits were only hanging on by my gritting teeth and a prayer. The next gust of wind or crack in the road could send them plunging to ankle height in a heartbeat. I stared into Milo's mirror and pleaded for him to do something. He did. And I suppose Milo did the only honorable thing he could possibly do in this particular dishonorable situation. He turned on his head lights.

We finally were able to veer away from the procession and on to a side street that would eventually lead to Mom's house. My Wranglers lost a little more ground, but was able to hang on until the end of the ride. Grandma's hutch arrived intact and looks really great in Mom's house. As for me and Milo, we're no worse for the wear and tear, but we have tried to keep our heads down and lay low around town for a few days. And as for the family of the deceased, all I can offer is my sincerest apologies and my deepest condolences for your loss.

CHAPTER 19

EVERYBODY DESERVES A VACATION ... EVEN A FARMER

EVERYBODY DESERVES A FAMILY vacation, even farmers. There is nothing easy about farming and sometimes it is important to get away from farm stress, even if only for a day. One particular family outing, along with my brother's family, found us at an outdoor water theme park. Wow! There was a gigantic wave pool, with water rides and slides as far as the eye could see. I hadn't seen this much water since Muddy Creek over flowed its banks during the great flood of '73. The kids have been telling me that I really need to get out more. I guess they're right.

Since the women folks and kids were already suited up, my brother and I made our way to the men's locker room. The changing room was packed, but I finally found an obscure corner where I could suit up. When I stepped back out in my snow white Mark Spitz swim trunks, all heck broke loose. Little kids began to cry and went scrambling for their mothers screaming something about a great white shark. It seems city kids had never seen a farmer's tan before. While my neck and arms were as brown as a cowboy's saddle bag, it had probably been years since the rest of my body had seen the light of day. My brother even said he had seen a corpse with a better tan.

Something had to be done because this traumatic, ghostly experience might scar these mama's kids for life. Just by chance my brother had been at a going out of business discount store sale and had picked up a squirt bottle of instant tan. It was guaranteed to turn a snowman into a bronze god in a mere five minutes. As I was lathering my body in the tan in a can solution, my brother cautioned me to be sure and rinse the golden goop off when the five minutes was up. After my brother headed for the pool, well, I just got to thinkin'. If this miracle tanning potion could give me a bronze god look in five minutes, I'll bet in ten minutes I could pass for a California surfer hunk. At the end of the ten minute mark, I could really feel the tanning juice beginning to do its thing. When the tingling sensation moved towards a well done barbecue burning feeling, I decided to hit the showers.

When I strutted out to the pool area sporting my new bronzed body makeover, it's kind of hard to explain what happened next. A simultaneous hush fell over the entire water park. Not a word could be heard and all eyes seemed to be transfixed upon me. Even the gigantic ocean waves slowed and then were reduced to insignificant shimmering ripples. As I strolled towards our family towel area, the wife and kids scattered like a covey of quail. I got my first real glance of my Sunkist self in the window of the snow cone stand. Yikes!!!! I looked like a comet that had just burst into flames. I suppose there really were legitimate reasons for following directions on a bottle of sun goop. In five minutes I could have been a bronze god. In ten minutes I was transformed into enormous Orange Bowl parade float. Even my brand new white trunks were now a bright, cheerful florescent orange color. If I could have had a quarter for every time I heard the words "What a geek," I could have owned that entire party pond park. I thought I spotted my brother once, but he dove into a crowded area of swimmers in the deep end of the pool and headed straight for the bottom. I think he would have set a Guinness Book world record for underwater breath holding before admitting he was related to the geeky looking orange dude.

In an effort to make myself less conspicuous, I took the path of least resistance and joined a crowd headed towards an exit. Or so I thought. Without realizing it, I had unfortunately gotten in line to ride one of the tallest nose bleed water slides at the park. I believe it was called "Mount Blister Butt" or "Mount Kiss Your Butt Goodbye" or.... "Mount something like that". After a grueling twenty minute climb and enduring comment after comment like "Whoa! Dufas Ray must want to be a walkin' highway flare" or "Stay away from him kids. You might get singed," I finally neared the jumping off point of the slide. There was a young girl lifeguard on duty giving all water sliders instructions on the importance of maintaining proper sliding intervals for safety precautions. As the rider line kept inching me closer to the takeoff point, I couldn't help but notice the kids ahead of me shooting down the slide as if they were shot out of a greased Crisco cannon. Wow! If those light weight teeny boppers could move that fast, there is no telling what speed my 250 pounds of hard lard might reach. Snapping me out of my trance, I heard the life guard politely say, "Sir, have a seat and get ready to take off. And by the way, I sure like your hunter's orange tan. Ready! Set! Go!" Okay youngens,' stand back and watch Big Daddy Glow Stick do his work.

I laid back and shoved off the suicide slide seat expecting the G-forces to peel my face away from my cheek bones. Instead, my thrill ride turned into a slow refrigerated molasses slide. From the moment I shoved off, I could feel myself start to slow down. Not only had my tan in a can turned me orange, it had turned my body into a bottom of a bathtub rubberized no slip and fall mat. Even with the running water, my body was screeching like a Ford Pinto with its brakes locked up. NASA should have glued the tile on the space shuttle with this stuff. I kept going slower and slower and slower until I finally came to a skin screeching stop just after rounding the very first dead man's curve. Confused and disappointed, I tried anything and everything to get going again. I tried sitting up and paddlin'. No luck. I tried scootin'. Nothin'. I tried turning cross way in the chute hoping to dam up enough water to get washed to the bottom. Nope. Absolutely nothing I tried had any effect on propelling me on my downhill destination. What I needed was a little nudge.

Just then I heard shrieks of laughter from above and a young girl yell, "Go get'em, Mama." Oh oh! The nudge I had been hoping for seemed to be on the way. I actually heard Mama before I ever saw her. She was singing, "She'll Be Coming Around The Mountain When She Comes." When I caught my first glimpse of Mama, I thought she really was a mountain. Now I am no light weight and I have never bought a shirt that didn't have a handful of X's on the back collar, but Mama was huge. Mama was definitely on the portly side…Portland, Oregon, that is. Mama filled the entire chute. She was flat on her back with both legs up in the air and rushing at me with the force of a California mud slide. I have never been superstitious, but the phrase, "It's not over until the fat lady sings" kept poppin' into my mind. The only thing I knew for certain was that I was about to be smashed by a fat woman and she was singing. As the shadow of Mama fell over me, I figured it was all over but the selection of the pall bearers for my memorial service.

Kerr Splat! Like a June bug hitting a windshield, Mama slammed into me like a run a way locomotive and I never slowed her down a bit. My face was painfully pressed against the cold, wet fatty part of Mama's inner right thigh. It was like trying to breathe through a wet tractor tire inner tube. Every time I tried to breathe in, I made this "Snarf"sound and when I tried to breathe out, I heard this 'Blurp noise. Snarf-Snarf-Snarf……Blurp-Blurp-Blurp. I was Snarfin' and Blurpin' for all I was worth. Just then, Mama started laughing hysterically. I wasn't sure whether she was having a good time or my mustache was tickling her. The first few curves I thought I was actually going to die. I was either going to suffocate or drown. I wasn't sure which. Finally we banked off of a high curve and Momma reached down and gave me a yank up. Getting my face dislodged from her lower jiggle wiggle regions, I gulped air like a new born baby.

The good news was our combined two tons of fun was generating tremendous speed. The last time I had traveled this fast, there was a stewardess on board offering me a bag of free peanuts. Down we flew, banking waterslide curves faster and higher than water park engineers had ever imagined possible. We kept going faster and faster like a fat couple jogging to a Baskin and Robbins two for one ice cream cone sale. There was no doubt about it. Mama and I were going to shatter the water slide course record. A huge crowd gathered as we pell-melled towards the bottom. In a blaze of orange, we hit the bottom pool with a Titanic splash. A loud cheer went up as small children were splashed up on the beach like driftwood. Spitting and sputtering, I stood up and tried to help Mama to her feet. Over and over again, I tried to apologize for tagging along on her water slide ride. Still laughing, she patted me on my orange head and told me not to worry because it had been the most fun she had in ages. I wasn't exactly sure just how to take that.

Anyway, I now have a clearer understanding of stress and I think it could possibly be somewhat over rated. The next time I start to feel overwhelmed by the day to day stress of farm work, I will take a moment and certainly remember back to my relaxing stress free vacation day at the water park. And with this new perspective in mind, it might just be possible that riding a tractor from day light to dark or being drug by a roped cow through a cow pasture full of fresh manure piles could be a heck of lot less stressful than catchin' a ride with a run-a-way corn fed Mama on a gravity defying water slide.

PRIME STAR

CHAPTER 20

FROM PRIME RIB......TO PRIME STAR

YEE HAW!!!!!! "Here he comes. Here he comes," I yelled. I was just dripping with excitement. This was better than Christmas. This was better than my birthday. This was better than the Tooth Fairy coming with a handful of quarters. Why was I so excited? Because coming down the road was "THE" van. Not just any van. This was the one and only PRIME STAR Van driven by the one and only PRIME STAR Man.

A Prime Star satellite dish in the yard makes a statement. It says, "We will go without sleep, because when we turn on our TV set, we can now get more than 2000 channels of captivating television." Yes, it's absolutely thrilling to watch the sweat dripping, jell-o shimmering, king size wedgie attired bodies of live Championship Sumo wrestling. It's on the edge of your seat excitement to watch the Hilton Hills Grand National Wonder Hound Show. And, who could ever pass up those knee slapping, grab your side hilarious rerun episodes of Leave It to Beaver? More importantly, this particular satellite dish is a sign of financial status in a community. By placing the dish in a prominent place in the front yard, preferably close to the road for neighbors to see, represents the prosperity of my farming operation. The dish will publicly announce that I probably got top dollar for my beef calves at market. A dish will state that I must have made my interest payment to the bank...and on time for a change. Even though I am most likely the last one in the neighborhood to acquire this latest television technology, my Who Wants to Be a Millionaire day has finally arrived and I am going to buy the biggest satellite dish they make.

For weeks I had been stepping out on the porch just practicing for this moment. I didn't want to act too anxious. Should I nonchalantly be leaning up against the porch post with a wheat straw in my mouth like the old bald headed guy in the American Gothic painting? Should I be sitting down on the front steps pretending to be studying my 1967 tractor manual, which I no longer even own? Should I get a paint brush and simulate the act of painting my porch? As the Prime Star van entered my gravel driveway, all of my preplan posing was thrown a side. I couldn't help myself. In my excitement, I leaped off the porch, raced across the yard, hurtling two flower beds and my sound asleep cocker spaniel watch dog and came to a sliding stop right beside the Prime Star driver's door. With all the maturity of a 12 year old, which had just discovered puberty, I gave him my very best voice cracking HI.

I soon learned Prime Star Man's birth name was Darrell. I'm sure Darrell could tell I was going to be lots of help when he saw the brand new, fully equipped, tool belt I had strapped on. Every pouch, compartment and leather loop was filled with hammers, pliers, screwdrivers and an assortment of other important looking tools. In most cases, I have no earthly idea of the intended purpose of most of these tools, but they look really cool hanging from my belt. This is the same belt I always pull out of the garage when I want to impress the electricians, carpenters, and plumbers that come out to do work around the farm. My theory is, when in Rome, if you can't do as a Roman, might as well at least try to look like a Roman repairman.

To my surprise, Darrell went to the back of the van and pulled out his own brand spanking new tool belt with the same array of tools identical to the ones I had strapped on. Oh Oh!!! Darrell then told me that this was his very first day on the job. Double Oh Oh!!! Although I'm sure I looked the part, down deep I knew I didn't have the first clue about the installation of a television satellite system. But, I was sure hoping Darrell did. This confidence quickly evaporated when Darrell asked me if I had ever seen anybody else do this before.

It was evident from the beginning Darrell was destined for a management position. He immediately took charge of the situation. From the van, Darrell pulled out picks and shovels, rolls of electrical cable, steel pipe, a bag of concrete, a huge fiberglass dish and proceeded to load me down like a pack mule. Darrell carried the manual. Huffing and puffing I led Darrell to my very best neighbor noticing place for the satellite installation. Darrell carefully surveyed the area and began mumbling some scientific satellite dish jargon to himself. Doing one of those thoughtful head scratching numbers, Darrell pronounced my selected location as unsuitable. It had something to do with the orbit of Uranus possibly blocking the Prime Star satellite signal. Man! I hate it when Uranus does that. Darrell must be really smart. He began looking skyward and then looking down and began systematically wondering across my yard in search of the perfect signal receiving location. My heart sank as I heard Darrel say, "Right here's the spot." His perfect, almost totally obscure location was right behind the lilac bush and underneath the tulip tree. Disappointedly, I began to dig the hole for my soon, not ever to be noticed from the road, satellite dish. Following Darrel's specific instructions to the letter, I carefully placed the satellite stand in the hole, filled the hole with concrete, and attached the dish to the stand.

Next, I crawled under a porch to drill holes through the house foundation for the electronic cables. Darrell bragged on me and said I was doing a good job. I thought so too. Darrell then explained that I would need to crawl under the house to drag the cables to the telephone entrance box and to a spot under the floor directly below my entertainment center. After hours of burrowing under the house like an arthritic mole, I had the wires exactly where Darrell wanted them. Once again Darrell was pleased with my work. I told him thanks.

Without realizing it, the morning was gone. Darrell commented on how time flies when he's busy. I agreed. I excused myself to go wash up and grab a sandwich for lunch. I told Darrell I wouldn't be long. After washing up, I stepped into the kitchen to find Darrell sitting at the kitchen table studying a Prime Star instruction manual. It seemed only polite, since he was already sitting at the table with a napkin tucked into his shirt collar, to ask Darrell if he would like a peanut butter and jelly sandwich also. He wondered if I would by chance have any cold cuts and cheese instead. I fed Darrell.

After letting Darrel have my last little bit of Blue Bonnet ice cream for dessert, it was back to work. The only installation step left was to hook up the all important Prime Star box to my TV set. While sitting in MY recliner, Darrell coached me through the installation procedure. The red wire goes there. The blue wire snaps into that. The two black wires go over there and under here. There, it was done. With the new Prime Star remote in hand, Darrell programed it and told me to stand back. With one push of the button, my TV gave a gigantic hiss and produced snow. Not only was I not getting my new 2000 channels, I had now lost my three local network stations. Darrell asked me if I had hooked everything up right. I thought so. After two hours of adjusting the remote, Darrell finally decided to call the main office for assistance. He asked for his supervisor. "Can I speak to Darrell please?" Oh No!!! Not another Darrell.

After a lengthy consultation and adjustments on the Prime Star box and remote, Supervisor Darrell informs my Darrell that the dish is not in the right location. I heard my Darrell whisper over the phone "That was where the customer wanted it." Darrell hung up and back to the yard we went to find a new dish site. I suggested my original preference. Darrell smiled and said not according to his laser guided

Prime Star witching locator. Darrell pointed to the new location as if he just witched an underground river. Even further from front yard view, I begin to dig a new hole closer to a thorny honey locust tree. I hate digging through tree roots. I hate getting jabbed by thorns even more. While I was setting the new stand, pouring new concrete and reattaching the Prime Star dish, Darrell said I shouldn't have cut the cable so short before, because now it will have to be spliced. I should have known better. Inside the house, we tried our new dish location. We still have snow but it does seem to be somewhat darker....maybe closer to a heavy fog. My Darrell phones his Supervisor Darrell and finds out that we still are in a wrong location. Rather than move the dish, Darrell believes if I trim a couple of limbs out of the way the signal will be all right. After removing tree limbs equal to two ricks of firewood and still not improving the dish reception, Darrell suggests I take my chainsaw and a 20 foot extension ladder and mow off the entire north side of my favorite shade tree. I suggest we give the other Darrel a call before we begin our Paul Bunyan act. Once again, Supervisor Darrell suggests we need to get out from under the rain forest canopy and head for open country. Again I hear my Darrell mumble something like, he tried to tell the customer that.

As the sun began setting in the west, I was surprised but yet elated when Darrell followed his meter to my original close to the road choice for a satellite location. I started slinging dirt before Darrell could even click his meter off. Maybe it was the moan and groan sounds I was making that caused Darrell to ask me if I had the phone number of the Rapid Response Team memorized. I said no. In total night time darkness, I set another stand, poured more concrete, dug a new trench, spliced on more cable, and re-reattached the dish once again. I guess practicing all day really helped out with the final installation process. The excitement was building. I could feel it. Or else, I was having a coronary. Either way, I knew I couldn't help but be close to finally becoming a member of the multi-television channel community.

All that was left was to reprogram the Prime Star box and remote. With remote in hand, Darrell quickly found his way back to MY recliner and asked me how the foot rest worked. I showed him. While Darrell pushed and repushed a sequence of top secret code numbers and getting nothing but more snow, I decided to heat up a can of soup for supper. Just as Darrell was complimenting the smell of my vegetable soup....BAM!!!! Darrell jumped. I jumped. There was picture and sound on my TV. It was evident the way Darrell gingerly placed the remote on the lamp table, that he didn't have a clue of how he had made the picture happen. I didn't care. In my very own living room, I was having the privilege of watching the Monster Truck Road Rally Championship in Bug Tussle, Arkansas. As Darrell and I sat at the kitchen bar eating our soup and crackers, we watched the awesome monster Trucks, Big Foot, and Grave Digger run the car crushing course. WOW!!!! Life just doesn't get any better than having good friends over for supper and enjoying a fun evening of good clean wholesome television entertainment. About 11:30 PM I finished signing all the forms. Darrell and I said our good byes and after a brief hug he was gone in the night.

The next day as I was outside admiring my massive new Prime Star satellite dish, I actually kind of started missing Darrell. You just don't spend 16 hours with another person and not develop a special relationship. My Darrell thoughts were abruptly interrupted by a white shiny van pulling into my driveway. With a shake of my hand, the driver introduced himself as Larry and that he worked for DIRECTV. I wonder what the odds were of meeting a Larry and two Darrells in less than one 24 hour period. It seems almost overnight DIRECTV had bought out PRIME STAR and he was there to install my new satellite dish. In a matter of 15 minutes, Larry installed my new aluminum pie tin size dish on the back side of my roof, where it can be seen by absolutely no one unless they fly over in a plane. He then snapped two wires into place and the job was complete. In a matter of minutes, Larry had turned my entire television satellite world up side down.

As I looked up at Larry's newly installed tin can lid size satellite dish, I thought to myself, "You know what? True friendship is a bond that should last forever." I did the only thing a real friend could do. As a memorial to my new friend Darrell, even though it was totally disconnected, totally useless, I decided to let my gigantic PRIME STAR satellite dish stay put. I think Darrell would like that. Every morning I go to the front yard and polish my satellite dish to let my neighbors know Darrell the Prime Star Man was my friend. And, if they just happen to notice that I can now afford SATELLITE TV, that's just all the better.

DEAR
JOHN

CHAPTER 21

MY DEAR JOHN LETTER

EVERYONE DESERVES A GOOD day. I guess I must have drawn the long straw, because I was having one of those Yee Haw kind of days. I had just collected one of those fatter than usual soybean checks from the local grain elevator and was on my way home to brag to the Mrs. about my better than normal farming skills. This should remove all doubt that on any given year as long the astrological star alignment was in sync, I too could become a step above the average farmer.

My back had been pretty much up against a wall this farming season. For the past few years I have been under a constant interrogation not only questioning my farming credentials but my ability in general of being an adequate household provider. How come our corn doesn't look as good as our neighbor John's? How come we have weeds taller than our soybeans and John doesn't? Why are John's calves fatter than ours? Why can't we have a satellite dish and a swimming pool like John does? Blah! Blah! Blah!

I felt like I was having the Book of John being read to me from the Bible. There is nothing a man enjoys more than being compared to one of his neighbors. She had even gone so far as to suggest....make that threatened....that if we didn't make a profit this year, maybe we should consider renting our farm to someone else. Someone like our neighbor John, I suppose.

Well, my moment in time had finally arrived. I could hardly wait to see the surprised look on her face when I waived this mega bucks check in front of her. As I bounded up the back steps and into the kitchen shouting "Come take a look at this, Baby," I was disappointed to find her not at home. Oh well, I could wait a little bit longer. After all I have been waiting for nearly 20 years for a check that would at least cover the farm expenses. What's a few minutes more?

This soybean check was like receiving the farming academy award. It needed a special place of honor, a prominent place where it couldn't help but be noticed. There was no better place than where we put all of our important documents, the kitchen "safety deposit box" counter. I cleared a spot on the counter and placed the check in a prime location next to the rooster crowing cookie jar. The rooster is where we keep all of our important documents: Our wills, titles to the vehicles, the new weed whacker warranty, phone number to the casino, etc.

As I was clearing away the morning dishes so the view of the check would not be obstructed, I noticed a piece of stationary stuck underneath the grape jelly jar. Before giving it the old heave ho in the trash, I almost tripped and fell into my morning Cherri-o bowl as I began reading the unfinished and unsigned letter.

It began with "Dear John."

My gosh! This was one of them Dear John letters. I couldn't believe what my eyes were reading. I had always heard of these letters, but never in my wildest dreams did I ever believe I would actually receive one. Talk about letting the air out of your sails. Talk about raining on your parade. Talk about taking a good day and flushing it right down the toilet. One of these letters can do it in a heartbeat. I've had a better time tweezing out two year old nose hairs.

I read on. "It is just not working out. I do not want to point my finger and place blame, but I think it is time we faced reality and do the right thing. I know with your experience, you could probably do better. I suppose people seeing your truck here at the farm will be the talk of the neighborhood for a while, but I think we are both strong enough to handle it." That is where the letter ended.

As my blood pressure rose faster than a Tomahawk cruise missile, I had mental images of me having a starring role in the upcoming neighborhood soap opera scandal.

Just what the heck was she talking about? I may not be a prize, but I do have my good points. Sure I snore loud enough to wake up folks across the state line, but that's no reason to toss me aside like a wormy apple for the first traveling feed salesman that comes along. Well Baby, it takes two to Tango or make Tang or get a fishin' line untangled or any other kind of tang thing. But I will be darned if I'm going to take this sittin' down while she's out doing the "so long sucker waltz" with Mr. Twinkle Toes.

Just then I heard our (soon to be all hers) car pull into the driveway. Just how was I going to confront her with this Johnny Be Gone letter? Would there be lots of screaming and yelling? I don't have the lung capacity to ever win that battle. Maybe I should act all smug and pretend I didn't give a rat's rear end about her opinions. Maybe I should bawl like a baby to demonstrate my sensitive side. Quick! I need to make some kind of decision. Too late. The back door is opening. Carrying in a sack of groceries I got the usual cheerful, "Hi, Honey! I'm home."

Humh! What gall! What nerve! What an ice cube for a heart! Here she is getting ready to dump me like a sack of unwanted kittens in a creek and she's trying to act all bubbly like everything is all hunky dory. I have always heard the best defense is a good offense. Not waiting for her to drop her Hiroshima bomb on me first, I sprang into action. In my calmest and the most rational voice I could muster (which was pretty much like Beaver Cleaver going through puberty)

I confronted her with, "How could you? After all I've done. You can just save those doe caught in the headlight eyes, because I found your lousy Dear John Letter."

Holding her letter next to my heart like I was trying to pull out a dagger, I was expecting a guilty look which might come from someone standing in front of an unfriendly parole board. Instead I got a smile, a chuckle, and then the snorting noise she makes when she really gets tickled. "Oh I almost forgot about that," she laughed. "You were so down in the dumps this summer when it looked as if the drought was going to tank the soybean crop that I just hated seeing you that worried. I knew you were miserable and I was trying to think of a way to take the pressure off of you. I thought about putting a letter together and seeing if our neighbor John Gastel would be interested in renting our land next year. But that August rain came just in a nick of time and you did such a good job of farming this summer that there really wasn't any need to finish writing it. Not this year anyway," she added.

Wow!!! The grapefruit size knot in my throat melted away faster than M&Ms in your hand. What a relief. I guess I still got it. I'm still the man. I wasn't being dumped for another guy after all. She just wanted to rent my farm to my neighbor. Man, do I ever feel better.

I THINK.

MY DEAR JOHN LETTER

LAST
WILL

CHAPTER 22

SHE FOUND A NEW WAY TO GIVE ME THE BIRD

YESTERDAY, I ALMOST HAD one of those magical moments which dreams are made of. This was even better than a piece of Mom's warm apple pie with a dipper of Dad's homemade "Remember the Alamode" vanilla ice cream on top. In fact, this was nearly as good as having all five of your Saturday night LOTTO numbers picked. In short, the mega bucks news I received same as said that my end of the rainbow pot of gold was almost in reach. All I had to do was bend over the pot and start filling up my pockets.

My rags to riches story began one Friday evening. Returning home from work, I noticed someone had left me a message on my phone. The message was from a Kansas City attorney informing me that a long, long, very long lost elderly old maid great great never heard of before aunt of mine had passed away in a nursing home. Okay. I guess it was nice to be notified of her passing, but why? I didn't know her. I'm sure she had never heard of me. So the question was, why take the trouble to track me down? Then it hit me. This good for nothing, ambulance chasing, low life shyster was going to try stickin' me with the funeral cost. Or worse yet, an arm load of unpaid nursing home bills. Well hold the phone, Waldo. You can squeeze all you want, but there is no blood left in this turnip.

I immediately went into a self preservation defense mode. Deny! Deny! Deny! They could hang me by my thumb nails and I would deny ever knowing or even hearing of this ole' gal. Just to cover all my bases I decided to listen to the recording one more time. However, this time I heard Perry Mason mention the word "will." It was amazing how quickly all those wonderful family memories of my favorite Great Great Aunt What's Her Name came flooding back in such a rush when I heard the word will. Oh! How I missed her sweet sweet smile and those warm smothering embraces. Through uncontrollable heart wrenching sobs, I left my mailing address on Mr. End of the Rainbow's voice mail. If all went well, my pot of gold should be arriving on the next UPS delivery.

Over the next few days I started thinkin' about all the cool stuff I could get when my ship actually came sailing in. First on the list was to fix up the old truck. Every time I turned the key, the engine makes a sound like three squirrels fighting over the same nut. There was little doubt that serious shop time was needed. Wait just one cotton pickin' minute. Hold the freakin' phone Freddy. What was I thinkin'? Why am I even considering repairs when I'm about to inherit a pair of Wranglers with some exceptionally deep pockets? I'll just buy a brand spakin' straight from the show room floor new truck. Better yet, I'll get on the Ford and GM best customer VIP mailing list and buy a couple each year. It has been said that "Money can't buy happiness," but my experience has been "neither can poverty."

After several days of anticipating my new Jed Clampett status, my Who Wants To Be A Millionaire day finally arrived. Checking my mail box one evening I found a card from the post office informing that they were holding a certified package for me. Cha Ching! I defy anyone to be able to sleep when they know they are less than eight hours away from becoming a kazillionaire. The next morning my off road snow and mud grip tires were transformed into NASCAR racing slicks by the time I slid into the post office parking lot. In a single bound, I cleared the ten steps to the post office door. I tried three times to sign for my package before the postal clerk convinced me that Rockefeller really wasn't my last name. With my new found wealth firmly in hand, I staggered with buckling knees back to the truck. Before opening my treasure chest of riches, I put every uppity up who had ever done me an injustice on speed dial. I was ready to do unto others as they had done unto me. It's called rubbin' their noses in it with tact.

Taking a deep breath, I closed my eyes and paused briefly before my fingers became a human jaws of life ripping an envelope-opening machine. Yanking out the copy of my dearly departed's will, I searched for my name connected to any gigantic dollar signs. On page two I found where some poor sucker named Fred that was getting some paltry $15,000 chicken feed amount. Another trivial $12,000 was going to some woman named Ethel. Francis and Opal were each getting a measly $10,000. Some relatively unknown couple, George and Velma, received an after thought amount of $8,000. Some poor chick named Cocktail Chrissie was awarded a charity gift of $5,000. Wait a minute. Where the heck is her beloved great great nephew me listed?

It seems Great Great Aunt So and So didn't actually name me in the will. The only reason I even got to see a copy of the will was because the three old people who had actually witnessed the horse and buggy days hand written will were all dead and gone. Since there were no actual living will witnesses, as one of the ten million living direct blood descendants, I had a right to contest the will if I so chose to do so. Pisssssssssssssss........the air in my bonanza balloon was fast deflating. To add insult to injury, the estate had already been pretty much picked clean by a California nursing home. Poof! I went from rags to riches and back to rags in mere seconds. I guess my dock is going to rot off before my ship ever comes in. Whatever money might be left was being eye balled by that leach of lawyer who was executing the will. He was circling like a vulture over a fresh highway road kill with plans for buying his own new truck.

Disappointed, dismayed, disgusted, distraught, disgruntled and any other kind of dis that is possible to feel, I kept reading and re-reading Great Great Aunt Kick Me When I'm Down's Last Will and Testament hoping to find my name somewhere next to some major or even minor moola amount. Fred and Ethel sure got there windfall. But me.... a blood relative.... got zipola. Even that crazy chick Cocktail Chrissie got a quick five grand. Now what was that all about? Who was she anyway? How come she got a mention in my aunt's will and not me? Was my aunt a booze hound? Did she go out on a toot one night and meet up with some bar fly and decide to give her five big ones instead of me, her beloved nephew? Or was this Cocktail Chrissie on the black sheep side of our family that no one ever talked about? This was a puzzle that needed solvin'. Unable to take it any longer, I decided to play family blood hound detective. I found the phone number of another blood didn't get squat relative to see if he knew who this $5,000 winner was. It was obvious this relative was sharing my pain. He too was disappointed with the results of the will. He had pictured himself in a long dreamed about new bass boat. After exchanging pleasantries and discussing our family history, I finally got around to the will. "What limb of our family tree do you think that Cocktail Chrissie person sat on," I asked?

"Are you kiddin," he laughed.

"No! Not really," I told him. "I've checked every limb, branch and twig of our family tree and I can't find one relative with the last name Chrissie."

With somewhat of a sneer rather than a laugh he blurted out, "You should have checked out the limbs of a nut tree instead of the family tree. Chrissie was her pet parrot."

Great! Just absolutely great! How fitting was that? Me, a loving blood relative got beat out of $5,000 bucks by a feathered squawk box cockatoo. I'll have to hand it to Great Great Aunt Dream Buster. She removed all doubt that she was a blood relative of mine. She's exactly like the rest of my tightfisted shirttail kin. The only thing different is, she just found a more amusing way to give me the bird.

STOP
YIELD
DEAD END
DMV
TAX
INSPECTION
RENEWAL
License Bureau Office

CHAPTER 23

GETTING MY GREEN LIGHT

As I ENTERED THE door of doom, Von Hilda, the Driver's License Nazi looked up at me as if she wanted to kill me, resuscitate me, and then kill me again. I just literally dread when it is time to get my driver's license, or truck tags renewed. As luck would have it, they both happened in the same month this year. Yuck! I need an epidural for this kind of agony. Renewing an expired license is about as much fun has having a series of rabbi shots.

The waiting room was packed, but it was so quiet you could have heard a gnat whisper. Von Hilda is old and tough. Some say her birth stone is lava. Every head was bowed, lips were sealed, and all eyes were lowered hoping to dodge any direct eye to eye contact from the License Lady of Evil. As I took a seat, I started sorting through all my documents one last time to make sure I had everything needed to get a new license plate for Chuck. Chuck is my truck.

On a normal visit to the Bureau of bloodshed, I never seem to have the right anything. First and foremost is the required renewal notice with the proper vehicle VIN number. Von Hilda is a ticking time bomb. If she catches anyone with the wrong VIN number, there is an immediate lock down, a call made for back up, and the culprit is immediately surrounded by a shoot to kill DMV SWAT team. If someone wants a two year truck license... (like who in their right mind would want to go through this misery each and every year)... two previous year' tax receipts are required. I usually find my tax receipts by the preferred needle in the hay stack method, but either my needle is getting smaller or my haystack is getting bigger because finding stuff when I need it is getting harder and harder each year. Proof of insurance is another requirement. I don't know about the rest of the world, but it seems as if I pay insurance weekly. Whether it is truck, homeowners, farm liability, livestock, crop, dental, health, life, wind, fire, lightening, flood, earthquake, hurricane, or being struck by a falling meteorite, I have to be the most insurance poor human being on planet Earth. So to pull the right insurance card out of the magic hat is not all that easy. Then there is the safety inspection. I have never paid the $12 inspection fee without paying for at least $300 worth of truck repairs first. There is always a headlight or a taillight or a brake or a muffler or whatever else that could possibly cost $300 to be fixed before I can get my grubby little hands on the all important safety inspection sticker. Finally if each and every document is in order and all the planets and moons are in perfect alignment, Von Hilda might.... just might.... issue a new truck license without casting a spell on my first born child.

Peeking up to take a look around the waiting room, I couldn't help but notice that it was filled with all men. A Von Hilda buffet. Some of these guys looked as if it might have been their first trip to the License Bureau. Von Hilda devoured men like these. She was a first time man piranha. It was obvious the guy in the hot seat was as nervous as a long tail cat in a room full of rocking chairs. In fact, Von Hilda had him stuttering so badly, I don't think he could have spelled cat if you would have spotted him the c and the a. As she sorted through his papers, a snarling sneer appeared on her lips as she yelled, "Wrong! You have the wrong tax receipt. Get out. "NEXT!"

Naturally the next victim was more than willing to give up his place in line, but he was shoved ahead into the dreaded DMV firing squad position anyway. Scrutinizing his renewal notice, Von Hilda snarled, "Is this information correct?"

"Almost," he squeaked. "But I have moved since I received my notice."

"WHAT? A wrong address? Get out you license-less moron! You don't deserve to drive. NEXT," she screamed.

One by one, Von Hilda systematically grazed her way through the menu of waiting room men. Each one was dismissed for one infraction or another and was told to vacate the premises immediately. And then there it was….my turn. I stood alone, but I was ready. I had checked and rechecked all of my papers. I had so many paper cuts I almost needed a blood transfusion. I took my seat in the diver license executioner's chair and waited for the switch to be pulled. The only thing missing was my death shroud.

As Von Hilda straightened up to unleash her attack, I was wondering just how bad and how bloody it was going to be. But just before Von Hilda demanded my papers, I kind of had one of those light bulb flickering moments. A thought was making a gallant effort to cross my mind. Thinking back, not one of the previous declared incompetent morons had spoken one kind word to her. Not one "Good morning." Not one "Those are really cool looking combat boots." Not one "Oh My Gosh! Did you have your stomach and your throat both banded to lose that much weight?" There had not been one compliment of any kind sent Von Hilda's direction. That was it. I was going to counter attack with a being nice strategy. What did I have to lose? There wasn't much left to chew on that she hadn't already chewed off in my previous attempts to obtain a legal license plate.

I know not from which it came, but in one single moment I ignored every common sense or good judgment I had ever had and offered Von Hilda this compliment. "I sure do like your new tooth. That is the prettiest shade of gold I have ever seen." Before my very eyes

I saw her melt. There was an instant bond between us. The sourest pickle in the barrel was turning into a spoonful of sweet relish. Her snarl was replaced with a smile. It was as if her cry for help had finally been answered. Our conversation took on a life of its own. We began to chit chat about the price of milk. We talked about the new channel 7 weather girl. She shared a brief antidote about one of her grandkids. And I naturally replied back with, "Oh that just can't be. You look way too young to have grandchildren." STAMP! STAMP! STAMP! STAMP! Her hand was like an automated stamping machine. All four of my documents got an immediate stamp of approval along with a brand new truck tag for Chuck.

As I walked out the door I heard a very soft, "Have a nice day sir" followed by a very very gruff "NEXT!!!!!!!" A compliment can sure go a long ways. I always did hear that you could catch more flies with honey than you could with a pitch fork.

The only thing worse than renewing a truck tag is to find out my driver's license has expired. Not just expired but has been for the past twelve months. Naturally it is usually a highway patrolman with a ticket book as thick as War & Peace that discovers my little lapse in memory. He wishes me a very belated happy birthday with a ticket to the tune of $65 plus any additional court costs. In addition to the hefty fine, I have to prove my repentance to the Governor of the State by attending a reformatory school for delinquent drivers to re-take and pass his required written and driving exams.

Could there be anything more fun than sitting in a waiting room with a bunch of sweaty, pimply faced, sixteen year old driving hopefuls waiting to take a test. It's been a long time since I have taken any kind of test, if you exclude blood work. The sitting and waiting and worrying of whether or not I could possibly flunk the test and end up having my fifteen year driving privileges permanently revoked was beginning to take its toll. But as I surveyed my sixteen year old competition, they didn't seem all that bright. I'm thinking if I yelled out the word Abracadabra most of them would think it was a country in Africa. Surely if they had a ghost of a chance of passing the test, it should be a breeze for me to sail through it.

There was a red headed freckled face boy that looked every bit of twelve. He was beyond nervous. He was so scared, his faced looked as if he had just licked an electrical outlet. There was a cute little blonde wearing a cheerleader outfit holding hands with her mother. She kept asking every thirty seconds, "Do you really think it's really going to be easier than the last four times?" Another young girl couldn't quit sobbing long enough to even give her name to the driving instructor. I definitely would want to keep an eye on her if she was driving and I was walking across a Wal-Mart parking lot. Of course there were a couple of good ole' farm boy studs that looked as if they had been driving trucks and tractors since birth. They were sitting together discussing the latest engines and transmissions they had rebuilt. In one corner, there was a young man with a thicker mustache than myself. I wasn't sure if he could read or write, but he looked very capable of being an excellent get-away driver. Then there was Tattoo Boy. He had more ink on him than a Sunday paper comic strip. And where there were no tattoos, there were piercings. His nose, ears, lips, eyebrows, and tongue looked like he had been hit with a hand grenade loaded with thumbtacks. His speech was so slurred, I'm not sure he could pass a sobriety test let alone a driving test. And finally in the far corner, there was back woods Bucky. Looking as if he had just walked in from Gap Tooth Junction, there was better than a 50/50 chance Bucky might need the test read to him. He also might need to be led to water if he got thirsty.

We were all ushered into the examination room. I got directed to a seat between Bucky and Tattoo Boy. I was almost embarrassed to have such an intellectual leg up on these two Simple Simons. We were all presented with an official two page multiple choice driving examination test. It was explained that we should take our time because there was no time limit. That had to be good news for Bucky. Since he was already about two puppies short of a pet shop, we might need to order him a pizza for supper and most likely a plate of biscuits and gravy for breakfast. We were told to "Begin."

As I started to read the first question, I couldn't help but notice pencils all around me flying through the pages marking answers. Even Bucky was half way through page one, while I was still trying to figure out the answer to Question #1. Is it okay to stop on an interstate highway and roll down a window and ask the driver next to you for directions to the closest McDonald's? Tattoo Boy was already on page two and leaving a blazing trail of hot molten number two-pencil lead in his wake of answers. What the heck is going on? The whole teen age bunch looked like they had just won the gold, silver and bronze medals in the Moron Olympics but they're passing me like I had the IQ of a lightening bug. How can this be? Are they even reading the questions? Here I am, clearly in last place and fighting my best just to hold that position.

I needed to get into the catch up mode fast. I can't get showed up by these sixteen-year-old twits. I was still trying to figure out Question #4. Whether I should donate my organs or sell my kidneys for cash, when I heard pencils begin hitting the table and seeing completed tests being handed in. This is stinkingly unbelievable. I struggled on answering questions about yellow lines and red lights and what to do when a school bus stops in front of you to unload a bunch of almost sixteen year old students. That one was easy. I chose answer number three…accelerate quickly and hope they jump out of the way

I was the last to finish the test. As I exited the exam room to turn in my test, my fellow dimwitted delinquents were already receiving their scores. "I got a 100."

"Me Too!"

"I got a perfect paper."

"I got a 99."

Even Bucky got a 98. He would have received a perfect score but he couldn't remember how to spell his legal first name, Theodosius. Good Grief! If all these dodos pass and I fail this test, I will need to enter a witness protection program. Before handing in my paper I asked the testing officer what was a passing score. "Seventy percent," was his answer. As my test was being graded, the red ink checks began to add up. For a minute I thought my test was actually bleeding. With one last question to grade, I had thirty-four right and fifteen wrong. If #50 was right, I passed. If it was wrong, I would be catchin' rides to everywhere from everyone. But Wait! Oh No! I had failed to answer question #50. Looking up at me and seeing my distress, the officer decided to give me a break. He was going to give me one last make or break shot at answering the last question orally. The question was, if a highway patrolman pulls you over and asks for a donation to the Highway Patrolman Retirement Fund, do you donate A.- $20, B.- $50, C.- $100? I chose D. – my entire life savings. YEE HAW!!!! I passed. I began getting pats on my back from my fellow delinquent doorknobs. Okay, one test down, one test to go. On we marched to the driving portion of the test.

We all filed outside and were assigned a driving test instructor. With my years of driving experience this test should be a snap. My instructor was a very quiet soft-spoken petite lady officer. Her name was Officer Patricia Waggin. She said to just call her Patti. Hummmm! Patti Waggin....what was the odds? After making sure that Chuck's safety mechanics were up to specs, we jumped in and got in line for our turn for the driving test. Remembering my experience with Von Hilda, I decided to compliment the officer on her shirt. She advised me to keep my eyes off of her shirt and on the road, to keep both my hands at 10 and 2 on the steering wheel, and my non-testing comments to myself. Humm! I suppose it must be against police regulations to accept compliments. As we waited our turn, we saw the red headed boy drive away at the break neck speed of a sleeping snail. Tattoo Boy on the other hand left rubber for two city blocks. One by one Bucky and the rest of his sixteen year old motley crew took off on their tests.

Getting the all clear sign, it was now my turn for departure. We leisurely headed down a seldom travelled side street. I followed Officer Patti's instructions explicitly and signaled for a left turn and then a right turn. As I approached a stop signed, she screamed as if I had slammed her fingers in the truck door, "Look Out!!!!"

I stomped on the brakes screeching to a halt. "What happened," I asked.

"You ran through a cross walk," she screamed.

"Where," I wanted to know?

"You're sitting in it," she said accusingly. It seems crosswalks do not necessarily have to be marked. All stop signs have an imaginary cross walks. There went five points. When I protested the point deduction, Officer Patti then marked off another three points.

"What was that for? I haven't even moved," I protested.

"That was for the three kids you ran over in the cross walk," she pointed out.

Leaving behind eight points and the bodies of three imaginary kids, we proceeded on with the test. Approaching the next four-way stop intersection, I was on the lookout for invisible kids, invisible grandmas in wheel chairs, and any stray invisible pets in the invisible crosswalk. Thanks to my good fortune, I didn't hit a single living invisible anything. But as bad luck would have it, there was now a vehicle stopped at each of the four stop signs. To the right was Tattoo Boy. To the left was the blonde little cheerleader smiling from ear to ear. And straight across from me was Bucky. It was as if we were all frozen in time. This was one of those curve ball moments. Unsure of exactly who arrived first, no one was sure who should be the first to go. Being older and the most experienced, I decided to break the dead lock and proceeded to cross the intersection. Seeing me move must have given the little blond cheerleader inspiration to proceed with her own test.

The only problem was she had been instructed to make a left turn.... right in front of me. I had to hit the brakes to avoid hitting her. Bucky on the other hand seeing both of us coming towards him, got nervous and jumped his truck up on the side-walk to avoid a head on collision. Tattoo Boy thinking he had the right of way after I cleared the intersection, had begun making his move. But when I hit the bakes in front of him, he had to make a hard right to avoid t-boning me. We all came to stop blocking traffic in every possible direction. I'm not sure about the other vehicles, but the red ink and points were flying off Officer Patti's score sheet in my truck.

Returning back to the testing facility, my only testing procedure left was to complete the parallel parking requirement. There were two upright poles marking the simulated parallel parking zone. No sweat. People make too much out of parallel parking. I pulled into the correct backing up position and prepared to stick the landing. I nailed it, almost. Just before I came to a stop, Officer Screams A Lot let loose with one of her Banshee War Whoops. "LOOK OUT!" What now, an imaginary fire hydrant? Crunch! Nope it was a real one. Officer Patti looked at me like she was trying to recall what poisons do not show up in an autopsy. There was no permanent damage to the hydrant, but Chuck now had a nice red dent in his bumper. Visibly shaken, Officer Patti climbed out of Chuck, ripped off my score sheet and tossed it at me. "A 71.You passed. Barely! Don't ever ever come back here again," she said as she staggered away.

Well it started out as a bad week, but Chuck now has a brand new two year license plate and I have a new three year driver's license. Since we both have a green light to be on the road again, it is now a good week. I think Chuck and I will go celebrate our new licenses. Maybe we will go look up Von Hilda with that good lookin' gold sweet tooth and see if she would like to go get an ice cream cone at the DQ. I'm pretty sure Officer Patti wouldn't take a ride with us, even if we offered her a free banana split with extra whipped cream and nuts on top.

CHAPTER 24

READY.....AIM.....DUCK.....

In the spring of 1944, my Dad graduated from high school one evening and boarded a train the next morning as a United States Army WWII draftee. Within three months he found himself in a fox hole in a faraway land with people shooting at him. This particular part of World War II was known as the Battle of the Bulge. Dad was able to make it home with few physical injuries and lived a reasonably good life down on the farm. Now here we are sixty years later in a rural community, laying dad to rest in a family cemetery plot.

As we prepared and planned for Dad's services, we were contacted by the local VFW (Veterans of Foreign Wars) Organization. They were requesting to be part of the graveside rites portion of Dad's funeral service. For his service to his country, they felt it was important to honor him with a seven man squad presenting a 21 gun salute followed by an official military flag folding ceremony. Many of the VFW members were good friends of Dad and had served with him in the same war. We were touched by their sincerity and genuine thoughtfulness in wanting to be a part of honoring Dad's memory.

While the actual funeral service took place at a local community church, there would be about a twenty mile drive to the last rites burial site. In fact, the cemetery was at one time part of the family farm where my dad had grown up. It was somewhat ironic that Dad had lived for nearly eighty years and we were now returning him to his boyhood stompin' grounds.

The funeral processional was made up of the hearse, the pall bearer limousine, the family limo, the VFW Honor guard van, and the customary caravan of family, friends and neighbor vehicles. Once we arrived at the cemetery, the pall bearers unloaded and prepared to carry Dad's coffin to the grave site. While waiting for family and friends to gather, I couldn't help but notice the VFW Troop unloading from the van. The average age had to be near 80 and getting older by the minute. If they didn't get a move on, the services would be over before they could all tumble out of the van. Also I couldn't help but notice that in addition to the squad leader there were only six old soldiers with rifles. Math had never been my strong suit, but I was beginning to wonder how the 21 gun salute was going to take place with only six rifles. In theory, seven rifles shoot three times a piece to have a grand total of 21 shots. Or there could be multiples of 21. There could be three rifles shooting seven times Or 21 rifles could shoot one time. Or if all else failed a single rifle could empty a full 21 round clip. However, if new math wasn't somehow involved, it sure looked like the six shot rifle team ceremony was going to be a few shots short.

Gingerly touching the old WWII Sergeant by the arm, I whispered, "Don't you need seven rifle guys shooting to make this 21 gun salute work?"

Being hard of hearing either from age or from being too close to a grenade going off during the big one, he yelled back, "Well, we kind of had an accident yesterday and we're a guy short today. But don't worry. We've got it all figured out. Randall and Keith are going to throw in a couple of extra quick shots and it should all even out." It seems the accident involved one of the eighty year old sharp shooters at another funeral service yesterday. One of the old timers got a cartridge jammed in his rifle. No matter how hard he pulled or pushed on the bolt action, the bullet was stubbornly stuck in the chamber. In an effort to gain better leverage, G.I. Old Joe finally resorted to placing the end of the rifle barrel on the toe of his boot so he could apply some serious downward pressure on the jammed bullet. It worked. Kerr Pow!! Although blanks are used instead of live bullets, they still contain enough gun powder to burn holes through leather, socks, and eighty year old toes. So Joe was now out of commission for today's service. Poor old Joe had made it through battles in Italy and North Africa. He had survived the Normandy Invasion and the Battle of the Bulge. He had seen non-stop combat for nearly three years and had come out with not so much as a razor burn. Sixty years later he becomes a military casualty at an honor guard ceremony. There is hope Joe will receive a purple heart for his act of bravery or for sure a purple toe.

As the graveside service commenced, it was kind of neat to see the frail old GIs all lined up in their uniforms awaiting their turn to perform. Some were tall and while others were short. Some had snow white hair while others were completely bald. A couple of characteristics they did have in common were they were all old and they all stood on unsteady legs. As the minister concluded his final remarks, a nod was given to the sergeant to begin the military honor. The old Sergeant yelled "Attention." Six arthritic backs cracked, but for the most part it would have taken a trained eye to spot any movement at all. "Ready arms." Slowly but surely the rifles began coming up to shoulders. "Ready."...... "Aim."..... And before another word could be said, Randall got in one of his quick shots. That first unexpected shot caused a chain reaction of many other shots to follow. Everyone was caught off guard. People jumped. People ducked. People began using each other for human shields. Gallantry and bravery was tossed aside and it was every man, woman and child for themselves. There would be no silver stars for heroics on this day.

Every once in a while we could hear the sergeant yell something, but for the most part the old troopers were firing at will. While some rifles were pointed skyward, others were aimed point blank level at scattering mourners. It was as if a happy trigger fingered firing squad had gone mad. Guns were going off. Spent brass was being ejected. Terror was in the air. It was as if we all had starring roles in an episode of COMBAT. The preacher screamed something about God and ducked for safety behind Dad's casket. The pall bearers looked like a bunch of circus clowns trying to see how many could crowd into the back seat of a limousine. The family scattered like scalded pups taking cover behind every available granite tombstone. It was as if the Dad's funeral service had become a reenactment of one of General Patton's fiercest battles.

After screaming his order to "cease fire" for nearly ten minutes, the sergeant finally regained control of the situation. In reality, I think the firing only stopped because the once upon a time storm troopers had finally run out of ammo. The sad part was the one half, once upon a time Dirty Dozen GIs thought they had performed in perfect gun shooting unison during the entire ceremony. This was probably due to all the hearing aids being turned to the silent mode. As they began marching back to their van, there was a lot of back slappin' going on with yet another military funeral job being completed well done. All in all, with the amount of brass casings picked up from the cemetery grounds, we estimated that Dad got somewhere in the neighborhood of a thirty-seven shot salute thanks to those premeditated extra quick shots. As the last shot echoed across the little country cemetery, a peculiar quietness fell over the hallowed grounds. Amazingly, only one lone elderly couple, too bone brittle to dive for cover, was still standing. With gun smoke still hanging in the air, the husband held his wife close and steadied her trembling hand. He consoled his frightened and feeble mate with these words of comfort. "It's all right Honey. They missed you again."

Isn't it odd how just a few words can break the tension of a moment? One minute people were cowering behind polished memory rocks fearing for their lives. A minute later, with no serious injuries acknowledged, grins started to break out. One by one members of Dad's departure farewell party began emerging from their hiding places with relieved smiles on their faces. One of my Dad's greatest attributes of life was he enjoyed humor. My Dad was one of the greatest practical jokers that ever lived. We all agreed we could have not scripted a better funeral service for him even if we had tried. If the gun fire hadn't been so loud, I'm sure we could have heard his laughter. I will be forever grateful to Dad's fellow comrades in arms for making his final day a pleasant, forever lasting, heart felt memory………..with just a touch of humor.

CHAPTER 25

THE GOOD...THE BAD...THE UGLY...

THE GOOD...ONE PARTICULARLY MISERABLY hot Saturday afternoon during our recent prolonged July drought, with absolutely not one hint of rain from the out of work pizza delivery boy moon lighting as our week end TV weather forecaster, I thought I heard thunder.

The Bad... Naturally the distant lone little rain cloud, looking much like the profile of Jimmy Durante's nose, didn't look big enough to snort out a sneeze let alone produce thunder. It was miles to the southeast, which meant it was in the wrong direction and the chances were slim to none that any rain would ever grace the presence of my farm from that direction. I never get rain from the east.

The Ugly... After mumbling to myself on what I actually thought about the raining on the just and the unjust alike scripture, I went back into my humble abode to finish watching the on the edge of your seat, exciting 2002 Texas Hold'em World Series of Poker Championship rerun. Being a farmer, I can relate to bluffing my banker into believing I won't lose thousands of dollars on a crop of soybeans. In fact, I have it in my will that when I die I want my banker to be one of the pall bearers. I figure since he carried me all these years, he might as well get first shot at finishing the job.

The Good.... Within a matter of just a few minutes, my TV screen went black with the words searching for satellite appearing at the bottom of the screen. Now that was odd, since the only previous times I ever recall losing contact with the satellite was during a heavy rain storm or failure to pay my monthly bill. A surprising close boom of thunder signaled maybe, just maybe, I might actually luck out in getting more than the usual three drops per square foot rain shower. But then again, the clap of thunder came from the east. I never get rain from the east.

The Bad… From my favorite fat man recliner, I glanced out the west window and noticed the wind starting to mess around with the tops of my favorite self pruning Chinese Elm trees. I can't thank the Chinese folks enough for sharing these debris scattering trees with America. Hearing something bangin' out east of the house, I grudgingly drug myself out of the comfort zone of my Lazy Boy to see if the lid of my gas grill might have blown up against the house.

The Ugly… In the words of my favorite American cartoon hero Popeye, "Well shiver me timbers and blow me down." Just as I pulled back the curtain of the back door window, I instinctively ducked as a sheet of tin from my neighbor's hay barn came slammin' into the side of the house. Before diving for cover, I got to see my gas grill go skating off the deck just before the tops of two trees came crashing down across my now not so hot hot tub. Whimpering like an orphan puppy, I belly crawled back to the west door just in time to see my guaranteed to stand up to an eighty mile per hour wind flag pole snap like a match stick. Trees were falling, sheet metal and boards were slicing through the air like missiles, and I was now in the center of the house running around like a cat chasing its tail. I was trying to figure out the best possible location for the county coroner to I.D. my body.

The Good… It was the mother of all storms. But this can't be because we never get rain from the east. From the roar on the roof, it was evident that the badly needed moisture I had been wishing for had arrived with a vengeance.

The Bad... However, it was too bad the long wished for moisture was descending in a frozen state. Screens began to puncture and windows began to crack and break, as the hail and nails from my neighbor's hay barn blasted against the house. Bam! Crash! Bam! It was if windows were being shot out by a Wells Fargo scatter gun.

The Ugly... Hail and wind was stripping leaves from the trees faster than Grandma used to pluck a chicken. A corn field across the road looked as if it was being pressed down by a steam roller. I saw three humming birds trying their best to pry their beaks loose from porch posts. They were no longer humming, but actually singing the words to Patsy Cline's rendition of "Please Release Me."

The Good... The violent storm only lasted a few minutes. In actual fear for your life time, that would be equivalent to about the same amount of time it took for me to change my underwear three times. It could have been four if I hadn't procrastinated in doing my Saturday morning laundry. Ultimately the house stood firm and the farm did receive about an inch of water in one form or another.

The Bad... The grandkids' recently completed Mt. High in the Sky tree house was now ground level after being crushed by an up rooted maple tree. It would have been nice if the grandkids could have played in once before it was reduced to a pile of kindling. Too bad tree houses aren't cover in a home owner's policy. Oh Well! What's another $800 lumber yard bill?

The Ugly... The storm aftermath left my farm in a close facsimile to Davy Crockett's Alamo. The local TV weather meteorologist/idiot classified the storm as a micro burst. According to Uncle Webster, the definition of micro is something very small or greatly reduced. Following that logic, my scaled down wind storm burst should have been something like a "puff." Well, I'm here to tell you my micro puff was more like Hurricane Katrina trying to fight its way out of the mouth of a Heinz Catsup bottle. Seventy-five year old trees were either broken off or uprooted. House shingles and barn roofs were ripped off and scattered all over the farm. Many of the out buildings were either turned over or blown completely away. A majority of my neighbor's hay barn had found its way into my yard, on top of my house, and had scattered my cow herd into three different time zones. My cows normally love a barn full of hay. But this was the first time they had ever had the opportunity to experience a barn full of hay room service.

The Good… The violent storm was confined to a very small area, mostly me and my neighbors' houses and barns. Yeah for us!!! With luck like this we should have headed straight for a Las Vegas slot machine. Neighbors only a couple miles away didn't even know a storm had occurred until they began finding my collection of paper feed sacks scattered in their yard. I had been wishin' for a break in the weather, but I just wasn't thinking on the lines of this much stuff getting broke by the weather.

The Bad… It was just the day before I had commented to co-workers that I needed a new project to work on, something fun just to keep me busy. I certainly wasn't planning on a project that would keep me busy all the way through my retirement years.

The Ugly… Picking up and piling tree limbs, dragging twisted sheet metal off the top of the house, patching up the roof and broken windows, and fixing downed fences are at best not fun time mid-July jobs. These jobs range from the not fun classification to the wretched miserable category rather quickly when the heat index clocks in at a sweltering 105 degrees. There is nothing uglier than a fat boy breaking out in a full sweat, unless it's a fat boy that has run out of sweat. Once that point has been reached, the face begins to contort, the body begins to bloat, and then the many years of bacon grease consumption begins oozing from the sweat pores. If you can picture a giant pork rind bubbling in an oversized fry daddy, that would have been me.

I think if there is a lesson to be learned here, I suppose it could be,

"Be careful what you wish for." Because, the next time you wish for something really really GOOD and you want it really really BAD, you just might get it in a really really UGLY way.

Like
Dude
Chill
Bummer
Loser
Awesome
Geek
Duh!
COOL

CHAPTER 26

I'M LEARNING TO TALK KA---OOOL

I SURE HOPE I am around when the aliens from outer space drop in to pay us a visit. I am particularly going to enjoy watching the little green men from Mars scratch their heads when trying to decipher our kid's communication code. Young people live in a different world than mine. It's impossible to understand their thought process. They seem to have different levels of intelligence. They can be masters of computer technology, but have difficulty in understanding the basic operational mechanics of a clothes hamper. They tend to have a different ranking of life essential priorities. While the early bird may get the worm, who wants a slimy worm if you can sleep til' noon and have a Ho Ho for lunch.

More importantly kids seem to have developed a continuously ever changing form of communications. Granted most of the words, but not all, can be found in Mr. Webster's dictionary. However it will be the context, inflection of the voice and pronunciation of words which could totally discombobulate our alien friends. If there is ever the hope and desire to communicate with our world, it will be important for our little green ET visitors to be able to recognize and understand our offspring's commentary. In a recent work related visit to school classrooms, I had a first hand exposure to the teenage Ebonics sweeping our country. Following is just a minute sample of teenage words and the definitions as I understood them.

Like – This word precedes 90% of all statements, questions and incoherent utterings. Example: Like I went to the mall and like hung out with the cool crew. Like it was so happening… "Like whatever the heck that means."

Scoping Out – To eyeball the hottest looking hunk (Neanderthal boy child) or babe (evil spend all your money on me girl child.)

Cool – Pronounced as a two syllable word (Ka-oool) for effect, when making eye contact with a hunk or babe.

Bummer– Something bad happened.

Bummed out – Something bad happened to them personally.

Dis'n Me – Abbreviation for disrespecting me. Correct interpretation, I'm mad because I'm not getting my way.

Hangin' Out – Doing anything or nothing with the cool crew to avoid any sense of productive activity.

Crash and Burn – After a long sleepless weekend with the cool crew, a thirty-six hour semi coma induced sleep.

Blow Off – Should have studied for a test instead of sleepin'. Just blew (past tense of blow) off a language arts exam.

The Buzz – The latest rumor about the school nurse and the Wrestling Coach.

Chill Out – Wrestling Coach's wife gets a new car, a 10 carat ring and a fist full of credit cards. She's chilled out for now.

Brainyack – A freakin' book worm nerd that sets the class test score curve.

Clueless – Opposite of brainyack. Even grading on the curve can't cure straight-line stupid.

Totally Rigid – Teacher refused to award extra points for Rowe vs. Wade decision essay answer. George Washington was not trying to decide whether to row or wade across the Delaware to attack the Redcoats.

Choked Totally – Failed the test.

I'm So Sure – Making up failed grade at summer school will be so much fun.

Duh – This sound designates a person who has the IQ of a cotton ball. His buddies call him Q-Tip.

A Baldwin – A term for good looking Bay Watch lifeguard type guy. My ego was somewhat bruised when I learned in adolescence lingo a Baldwin was one word and not two. I was hoping for "Bald One."

Boy Toy – Someone to pay for M&Ms (meals and movies) until a Baldwin becomes available.

A Barney – The something the cat coughed up guy loser bracket. A Barney does not have enough cash to compete with a Boy Toy. I'm familiar with this cash flow category.

Loser, Dweeb, Dork, Wuss, Nimrod, Dipstick, Dufus Ray, Geek Tragedy, Moron, or Sleeze Bucket – All a step or two below the Barney bracket. A member of this element will most likely be homeless. Usually sells blood for a Big Mac with fries. Their only hope for economic survival would be an unexpected inheritance from a never before heard of long lost Boy Toy uncle.

A Babe – Has blonde hair, a face full of makeup, wears tight sweaters, is at least two years older and has a valid driver's license.

Eye Candy – Has blonde hair, a face full of makeup, wears tight sweaters, at least two years older and has failed the driver's license exam three consecutive times. Other synonyms may include hot stuff, fox, pure cane sugar, or love goddess.

Park It – Sit your butt down on the couch.

Couch Commando – A 24 hour non-stop, flat on your back, with an idiot box remote in one hand and a Ding Dong in the other.

Calorie Fest – A 24-hour junk food raid.

Awesome – The best ever (Taylor Swift concert)

Totally Awesome – Concert tickets were freebies

Gross – Description of nourishing food (broccoli, spinach, pickled beets, etc.)

Sweet – Description of anything good. Such as an unexpected passing grade on a test, finding a $5 dollar bill on the ground, a free pizza, or getting a pet monkey for your birthday.

My Bad – A major screwed up. Spilled a can of Coke on mom's new plush $$$$ Sierra Mist colored carpet.

Gone Ballistic – Mom (Lizzy Borden) having an axe swingin' mental break down about the stained carpet.

Toasted – Getting burned by a five-year-old little mole brother spilling his guts about who spilled the Coke on the carpet. Caught-Burned…….Thus toasted

Skunk Eye – A look…..A mother's "I should have eaten you at birth," look.

Dude – Any guy old enough to have a driver's license. Male adults with families and 40 hour work week jobs are considered old dudes.

Dip Stick / Wing Nut –These are mostly adults that they consider to be crazier than a road lizard. Not recommended as terms of endearment.

Go Ahead!! Knock Yourself Out – Permission given by kids to adults. Example: Question: Would it be okay to move this desk? Reply: Go Ahead!! Knock yourself out…..Dipstick.

In Your Dreams – To ever believe that I will ever be able to comprehend the teenage short cuts of speech.

So there you have it, the language that could possibly save our planet from an alien invasion. How could our kid's linguistic jargon possibly save us from an episode of the Twilight Zone? Well think about it. Can't you imagine the little green Martians frantically thumbing through Mr. Webster trying their best to break this teenage code? It's not possible. Our kids have a communication that changes daily. Talk about.... "Go Ahead and Knock Yourself Out!" Our little green buddies will be knockin' themselves out alright, just trying to beat it back to their own Swiss cheese planet.

Personally I like being around kids and trying to keep up with their latest variations of the English language. Every time I say bummer it makes me feel Ka-oool. In fact, I use their teenage lingo a lot. I think it is important to talk their talk if we want them to walk our walk. So if all of you old dudes out there are getting bummed out trying to get through to your couch commando, you might want to just chill a bit. Like the latest buzz is our kids are all right, they just like hangin'out with their friends at the mall like we hung out with our friends at the pool hall. So I'm so sure, that if we don't go ballistic and cut them just a little slack, our next generation will be just as totally ka-oool and totally awesome as we thought we were. Go ahead! Knock yourself out. It's fun to talk Ka-ool.

I'M LEARNING TO TALK KA---OOOL

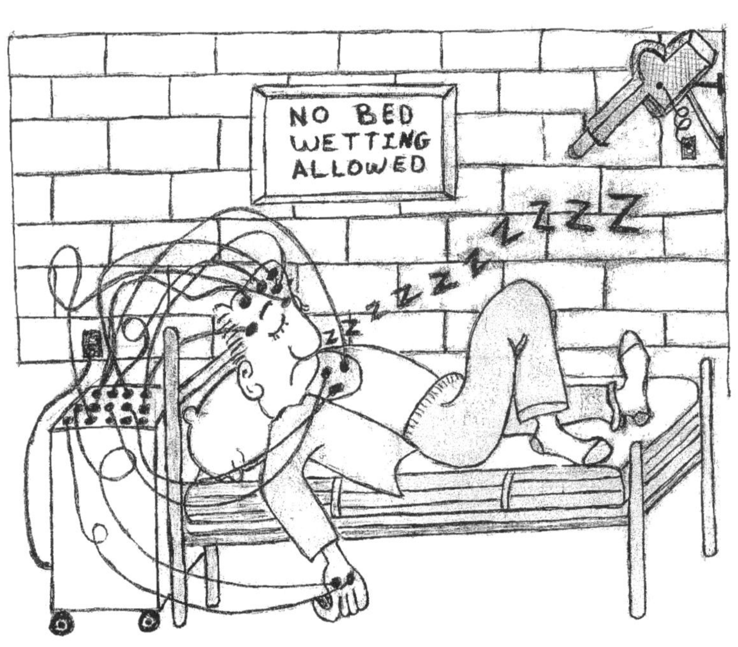
NO BED
WETTING
ALLOWED
ZZZZZZZZZZZ

CHAPTER 27

THE HOUSE OF FORTY WINKS

I DON'T UNDERSTAND IT. Regardless of how many hours I stay under the covers, I drag out of the sack each morning like I have just been run over by a herd of hungry hogs. It wasn't always this way. In my more robust years, I could really work. I mean good old heavy liftin' sweat rollin', back breakin' farm type work. I could stay with it all day and half of the night. I would then come home, wolf down a supper that could have met the dietary needs of a third world country, watch most of Johnny Carson's Tonight Show and then take a nice long trip with Mr. Sand Man. But now that I have one of those cushy feet up on the desk town jobs, I don't seem to have any spin left in my spin cycle. I may spend eight hours under the sheets, but I am lucky if I get at best a couple of actual hours of quality shut eye during the night.

One evening while I was trying to switch TV channels by beating my low battery remote on the end table, I heard the words of a commercial, "Are you tired, wore out and feel like the last time you had a good night's sleep was during the Carter administration? Do you snore so loud hotels have placed you on a do not reserve list? Have neighbors placed For Sale signs in your yard? Well, Sleep Apnea may be your problem."

Well, hold Aunt Gertie's big white horses. That snake oil salesman just described my no sleep symptoms to a T. "Do neighbors in a four mile radius complain about your snoring? Do you wake up choking and gagging like you have just been hung on an episode of Gunsmoke? Have you ever rested your eyes at a stop light on your way to work, only to open them and find the five o'clock rush hour traffic whizzing by? If so, you need to make an appointment with Dr. No Doze immediately and ask about Sleep Apnea." I was on the phone faster than a hound dog could grab a hambone making my sleep problem appointment.

In less than eight hours I was sitting in Dr. No Doze's office. "Un Huh. Un Huh. I see," said the doctor as he listened to my lack of sleep symptoms.

"So what do you think Doc? Do I have it? Am I going to make it?" I asked through drooping eye lids. The doctor first wanted to give me the proper medical definition to explain the dreaded sleep deprivation disease.

In a straight forward doctor to terminally ill patient voice, he told me, "Sleep Apnea is when a person actually stops breathing during their sleep." Oh! My Gosh! I knew it. I knew it. I was a goner for sure. I was just hoping there would be enough time to get my affairs in order. All except for that $5 Super Bowl bet I made and lost to my buddy. The Steelers should have never won that game. Recognizing my anxiety, he immediately tried to put my fears at rest by reporting there actually had never been a confirmed case of Sleep Apnea resulting in a death. Whew! That was a close one. However the good doctor went on to say, it was the lack of sleep, the weariness, the sluggishness, the wanting to fall face first into your morning bowl of Post Toasties which are the culprits that causes people to become accident prone. "And it's most likely going to be an accident that's going to take you out," he said grimly.

"Yikes!!!!!!!"

In order to have a conclusive Sleep Apnea diagnosis, I was referred to the clinic of a top notch nod off specialist. After meeting with Dr. Van Winkle, he booked me for an all night sleep over to run a series of sleep disorder tests. Scheduled to be at the house of forty winks by 9:00 p.m., I arrived 30 minutes early in my NASCAR Tony Stewart PJs with my tooth brush and favorite drooling pillow in hand. To my surprise, I found seven other puffy eyed guys already sitting in the waiting room ahead of me. Well, only actually five were sitting, two were passed out on the couch already snoring their bull frog rendition of "Old Man River."

As I checked in, I noticed the building was constructed somewhat in the shape of a pizza. There were eight rooms in the outside circle with a nurses' monitoring station directly in the middle. One by one, Nurse Ratchett led us off to our testing hammocks for the night. My room had the appearance of a cell at Sing Sing. The concrete walls were bare. There was not a single throw rug on the frosty 30 degree tile floor. And more importantly, there wasn't a television in sight. How was someone supposed to fall asleep in a cold, quiet as a church mouse, dark lifeless joint like this?

Before nappy nap time, my nurse hooked me up to a sleep testing machine. No less than 16 electrical wires were glued to my head to monitor my brain activity during the night. Brain activity? Boy, were they ever going to be in for a surprise. By the time she finished smearing my head with model airplane glue, I had almost passed out from the fumes. Oh! So that was how they planned on getting us to sleep. Of course the head was just the beginning. More wires were attached to my chest, each arm and leg and for a finishing touch a little red glow in the dark thingy-ma-jig was clamped on to my favorite nose pickin' finger. Looking at all of the electrical wires plugged into my body, I was sure glad I had finally kicked the bed wetting habit.

Just before tucking me in for the evening, Nurse Ratchett pointed to a peep show hole in the ceiling and remarked that my night's sleep would be captured by a hidden video camera. It was a relaxing thought that I may one day be able to spot myself on a starring role on America's Funniest Videos. Click....the lights were out. Thunk... the door was closed. Except for my red glowing ET finger, I was now alone in the darkness of doom.

For thirty minutes I laid there in my solitary confinement wondering if sleep might ever show up. I was just on the verge of drifting over into never never land when it happened. My next door buddy in room # 3 started cranking it up. I swear the snore was like a garden tiller without a muffler. It wasn't long before the ex-marine in room #8 joined in with his snort and whistle routine. Shortly after, the FBI wanted poster look-alike in room #2 started talking in his sleep. It was something about he really didn't mean to cut up his mommy and daddy with a meat cleaver. The physco in room #5 moaned and groaned and then would break out into a fit of giggles. The want to be lumber jack in room #7 could have single handedly clear cut the entire redwood forest by the sound of his chain saw snore. The poor fellow in room #1 was gagging and slurping like he was at an all you can eat hog trough buffet. For a while, I thought a stray dog had found its way into the sleepy hollow facility, before realizing it was only the guy with the basset hound face in room #6 barking out messages in Morris Snore Code. And that just left room # 4 ....wide awake me! Great! Of all days to leave home without my cyanide capsule.

With windows rattling and a Grand Canyon snore echo ringing in my ears, I settled in for yet another long sleepless night. However, surprising as it might be, my bunk house buddies kind of got a soothing La-La-Bye rhythm going. I'm not sure of how or when, but eventually my own lights went out. I wouldn't find out until the next day of my own contributions to the snoring concerto.

The next morning (5:00 a.m. sharp) Nurse Ratchett appeared like the Grim Reaper to unglue me. Slowly and methodically she applied a solvent to dissolve the glue from each of the 16 electrodes attached to my head. I quickly learned that the solvent not only worked great on glue, but dissolving head hair as well. My patch work head of hair looked as if my two year old granddaughter had given me a hair-cut with a nose hair trimmer. Nurse Ratchett suggested that it might be good if I would purchase some of that (soot in a can) hair spray for camouflage just until the bare spots had grown back in. The rest of my body wasn't quite so fortunate. With late for breakfast hunger pains setting in, Von Ratchett abandoned the use of the solvent and just began yanking off the remaining body censors as if she was skinning out a 'possum. Yeeeeeeeeow!!!!!!!!!

Unglued, unwired and still mostly undressed except for my Tony Stewart PJ bottoms, I was led down a corridor to the snore clinic control central. Waiting for me was the doctor of snore, a couple of nurses, and a half of dozen groggy looking interns. Together they were going to evaluate my night time video along with the corresponding snore graph monitor. Watching my video with company was quite the humbling experience. Sitting there with nine strangers, I got to watch myself dig and scratch at every conceivable body crevice. Better yet, the movie came with sound. I moaned and groaned and made gurgling noises like I was gargling with peanut butter. During the night, I tossed, I turned, and at one point looked as if I was doing the stop drop and roll put out the fire routine. Later in the show, I really got on a rhythmic snore beat and did a reasonably good job of snoring out the theme of Bonanza. If I thought my sleep over buddies were loud the evening before, they were nothing but a bunch of lightweights compared to my off the chart decibel level snores. I found out later that my sleep buddies #2 and #7 had actually quit the study during the middle of the night and went home because they couldn't take my snores any longer.

It was during one of my rollin' around fits that my red glowing ET finger tip must have fallen off. Of course when the oxygen sensor contact was broken, a flat line signal immediately appeared at the ever present Ratchett observation control station. Always alert at her post, Nurse Ratchett came charging into my room preparing to make a code blue call if necessary. However, after sizing up the situation, she was much relieved to find that it was only the disconnected sensor.

For the next several minutes, we all watched the video as Nurse Ratchett proceeded to track down the runaway finger clamp while I slept on. She searched over, around and under (and I mean under) every portion of my body. All the while throughout the entire search, I didn't miss a snoring beat. Using the lead wire as a locator, she tried to pry me up to make a grab for the sensor. No good. I was too big. So she pushed and shoved in an effort to get me to roll over. Nope. I was stiffer than a corpse. As the video rolled on, we watched in amazement as Rachett Woman actually climbed in bed with me. In a series of Hulk Hogan wrestling maneuvers, she finally braced her back against the bed rail and used her knees to tilt me over just enough to jerk free the little plastic finger gizmo. Throughout the entire episode, I was out like a light. It was if I had been put down with a horse tranquilizer. Here I was in a clinic because my last good night sleep was somewhere back in the mid '70s. But yet, I didn't crack so much as an eyelid during my wrestling match with Nurse Ratchett. Even the doctored chuckled, "I thought you had a staying asleep problem?"

The Richter Snore Scale confirmed that I indeed had contracted the dreaded sleeping sickness. During the night I had gone 12 minutes and 23 seconds without actually breathing. Coincidentally, that was about the same length of time of my wrestling bout with Nurse Ratchett. The doctor's antidote for my Sleep Apnea was a night time beside air compressor. A compressor, capable of inflating farm tractor tires, would blow 300 PSI (pounds per square inch) air up my nose and somehow that in turn would force my mouth shut and prevent snoring. And if I wasn't snoring, that meant I was actually sleeping. So I guess the bottom line is, I am always going to have the incurable Sleep Apnea disease, but the service station compressor should make my nighty night life much better. But if by some strange phenomenon

I would happen to mysteriously pass from this world in my sleep, at least I know that I went out in a quiet, non-snoring manner.

CHAPTER 28

THE LOOK

THERE IT WAS "THE Look." This wasn't just one of those run of the mill looks. This was "The Look." "The Look," which can turn mortal men into cosmic dust. "The Look" that says, "You best like your Pork and Beans straight from the can mister, because that's exactly how you're going to get'em." "The Look" that reminds all men that the "Death do us part" of the wedding nuptials was put in there for a reason. In fact, it has been said that it was "The Look" that created the tradition of the wedding veil. According to ancient Roman Law, the bride's veil was a requisite in warding off evil spirits…better known as "The Look." If not for the veil, all grooms may have sustained instantaneous blindness before the ceremony could even be concluded. I don't know of any man that has been able to stand up to "The Look." In some specific instances "The Look" has actually been fatal.

"The Look" is a woman vs. man stare down competition. Women stare….men fall down. No matter how hard they try, men will lose every time. It is like staring straight up into a July sun at high noon without blinking. At first the eyes begin to water. Then they begin to dry out followed by the cracking phase. After enduring "The Look" for an extended period of time, one or both eyes begin to twitch like a frog in an eighth grade science experiment. Shortly thereafter, the entire central nervous system begins to deteriorate. From this point "The Look" will most likely become fatal. I know of no man that has successfully stood up to "The Look." I had a friend that tried it once. He was bound and determined to not be a spineless twit to something as non-physical as a look. He went as far as to go into dress shops and practice staring at female mannequins. Hours upon hours he practiced. But when it came down to the actual one on one confrontation.....well, when it was all said and done he was found wondering aimlessly along a country road, taken to a hospital and declared legally blind. He now has to have "The Look" drive him down to the coffee shop for our Friday morning bull sessions.

While males have been armed with extreme levels of knuckle dragging testosterone, females have been more favorably armed with "The Look." In reality, there is no amount of manly chest beating that can ever match up to a female look. It's as if women have the Tomahawk cruise missile and men are still chucking dirt clods. If a woman wants to buy something really bad, it can be the "pretty please" look. Man melts. If a man does something kind of squirrelly, it can be the "you are embarrassing the heck out of me" look. Man wilts. If she wants to go out to a movie and he doesn't, it's the "I'm going to go home to mother" look. Man pauses and weighs the pluses and minuses of that look. Regardless, a woman versus man contest is no match. "The Look" of a woman will always win out.

If they are of the female gender, they come anatomically equipped with "The Look" at birth. "The Look" can come in all shapes, sizes and ages. If you are a man, think about it. Think about all the looks you have received from the opposite sex during your lifetime. It is as if a cerebral blue print is being followed by pink newborn baby girls all the way through grandmotherhood. How many of these looks have been cast upon you? There is the:

Mother – The I am the judge, jury, and executioner look.

Sister – The mom and dad will always believe me over you every time look.

Girl Friend – The I am totally in love with you until somebody with a cooler car comes along look.

Daughter – The you even look at me wrong and I will cry look.

Sunday School Teacher – The forgive him for he knows not what he says, does or thinks look.

Wal-Mart Greeter – The just grab a cart and get away from me look.

Teacher – The I wonder if his parents were on crack look.

The Red Cross Blood Mobile Nurse – The I don't think you have a pint of blood to spare look.

Daughter-In-Law – I am so so so glad your son didn't take after you look.

Granddaughter – The I can wrap you around my finger and tie a knot in you without you even knowing it look.

Girl Scout – The only one box of cookies cheapskate look.

Avon Lady – The if you don't buy something, I will be back every day for the next two weeks look.

Return Clerk at Clothing Store– The you must have been dreamin' if you thought you could fit your fat butt into these two sizes to small Wranglers look.

Female Pharmacist – The I don't think this prescription is going to cure the cat fight going on in your head look.

Baskin Robbins Lady – The it is obvious that you are going to want to sample all 31 flavors look.

Lady Jehovah Witness – The I'll be seeing you again bright and early next Saturday morning, please have your pants on look.

Driver's License Bureau Lady – The you're not bright enough to be behind the wheel look.

Bank Teller – The Wow! Your pay check is way below the poverty level look.

Female Co-Worker – The wish you were an ant and I had a magnifying glass look.

Waitress – The I hope that quarter tip doesn't bankrupt you look.

Lady Barber – The trim what look.

Lady Tax Accountant - The Ha Ha Ha snort snort Ha Ha Ha why aren't you on welfare look.

Woman City Cop – The I'm not sure he could pass a sobriety test drunk or sober look.

Nurse Deep Needle – The bend over and take it like a man you big sissy look.

Life Insurance Lady – The we don't cover humans with life expectancy of a Mayfly look.

Lady Boss – The you are living proof that every village does have an idiot look.

3rd Grade Neighbor Girl – The he's a sucker for every fund raiser look.

Supermarket Checker – The I'm so sure these chips and dip are on your fatso diet look.

Grandmother – The I know I am crazier than a loon, but you have to be nice to me if you want to stay in my will look.

Mother-In-Law – The you will also be trimming my toenails once a month when I move in with you look.

Wife – The I don't want anything for Valentine's Day, but your life won't be worth bee spit if flowers don't show up at my work look.

From girl scouts to grandmothers, all females come equipped with come-hither smiles, seductive charms, and a weapon of mass destruction "The Look." Women may have gotten their start from one of man's ribs, but they have learned how to non-surgically remove his backbone with very little effort. One prolonged lethal glare can turn a man into a spineless ameba. According to national statistics, women will out live men on average seven to ten years. Why do men die at an earlier age, because they choose to? While on earth, the only available choices to man is to love, honor and obey, and hope lightning strikes before "The Look" of a woman does.

But when it's all said and done, look or no look life wouldn't be all that much fun without them.

RIP

CHAPTER 29

SOMETIMES IT'S BETTER TO LAUGH... THAN IT IS TO CRY

SOMETIMES HUMOR CAN HAPPEN in the most unlikely places. Who would ever dream that a funny bone could get tickled during the last rites of a graveside ceremony? I realize a traditional funeral is a serious and solemn occasion and I probably shouldn't have laughed out loud, but people can express grief in many different ways. Sometimes it's better to laugh than it is to cry. Anyway, that's my story and I'm stickin' to it.

It was a chilly, blustery day and the grayish, overcast sky was spitting out a sprinkling of rain the day of the funeral. As I drove along the muddy gravel road in the funeral procession to the cemetery, I couldn't help but think what a dismal, perfectly tailor made day for a funeral. But this wasn't just any funeral; this was the day we were laying my Great Aunt Mary to rest.

Aunt Mary was one of the kindest, sweetest women who ever lived. She never had kids of her own, but loved children immensely. Needless to say, that worked out great for me and my brother. Since she lived on a farm not far from us, we got to see her often, which translated into us kids getting spoiled absolutely rotten. What can I say? It was a tough job, but somebody had to do it. In addition to all the good fortunes, which came our way in the form of Cracker Jacks, soda pop or Hostess Twinkies, Aunt Mary taught us some wonderful lessons of life. She taught us to be optimistic, be positive, to always look for that silver lining, and most of all, in tough times "Sometimes it's better to laugh than it is to cry." As kids, those were really good times. And now years later, here I was preparing to say my final farewell to Aunt Mary.

The cemetery was on an almost treeless little knoll located in the middle of a rural farming community. Besides being the community cemetery, this was the family cemetery of many of my pioneering ancestors. As I followed the funeral procession into the cemetery driveway, I noticed several friends and family members already gathered at the burial site ready to pay their final respects. This was a true testament of respect for a life well lived.

When the funeral procession came to a stop, we all exited our vehicles and respectfully made our way towards the grave site. Side by side, my brother and I solemnly stood just outside the tent, which had been erected to protect family members from the disagreeable weather elements. Braving the chilling wind, we all crowded in to listen to the preacher's parting spiritual thoughts.......And that's when it happened.

Before I relate what "it" was, it is important to understand the differences between me and my brother. My brother is well educated with a college degree. I was always told I had a sweet smile, but was always considered to be the simple one. My brother is spit and polish. I'm still learning how to spit. He has lived in big cities and has traveled the world. I ended up staying on the farm but have left the county a couple of times to go after tractor parts. He's a suit and tie person, while I am more at home in a pair of "Relax Fit" Wranglers. But more importantly, unlike myself, my brother always thinks ahead. Just like today, he thought to bring an umbrella along just in case of rain.

But his was not just an ordinary umbrella. This was a sophisticated NASA prototype of the latest advanced rain repellant technological design. Even though it was a compact model, about the size of an Oscar Meyer weenie-dog, with one push of a button, it would mechanically flip and flop and unfold like an 82nd Airborne paratrooper's chute. When completely extended it would cover an area about the size of Rhode Island.

Once again, another notable difference between me and my brother is how we go about getting something done. Being simple minded I'm all for taking short cuts as long as it serves the purpose. Take his umbrella for example. If I was going to use this umbrella contraption, I would have held it straight up like a lightning rod, pushed the button and WALLA…jobs done. My brother, on the other hand, being more aware of upper crust society etiquette, takes time to think things through and considers all options and/or any potential safety hazards. To insure he would be in compliance with all OSHA safety regulations, he would methodically point the umbrella down and away from him like it was a loaded assault weapon before engaging the umbrella opening process. He would then gently squeeze the hair trigger button to release the computerized snap-into-place weather protection unit. Once unfolded, he would then proceed to systematically raise the umbrella behind him until reaching the desired height and elevation. I think I have sufficiently given the "always do it absolutely perfect" picture of how number one perfect son does stuff. Now back to "it." The tickle your funny bone "it."

It was somewhere about "Thou anointest my head with oil" part of the 23rd Psalm when the wind began to blow and the rain came peppering down. Seeming like the appropriate time to unveil his high and dry head cover, my brother pulled his umbrella out from one of his side coat pockets. Giving me one of those sibling rivalry "I bet you wish you were smart enough to think about bringing one of these" smiles, he began his step by step umbrella raising procedure. Pointed down and away, the umbrella did its spectacular 'flippin-floppin' and snapped open as if computer activated. The only hitch unbeknownst to my brother, one of the little aluminum support rods had unfolded directly underneath the dress of a chunky lady slightly behind and to one side of him. I couldn't help but notice it was in a perfect dress snagging location. Right at that moment, I had a revelation. There was a choice to be made. It was as if I was being faced with a test on morality and ethics. I could choose to do the honorable thing and warn my brother to save him from a potentially embarrassing situation. Or …..maybe…..I could …..just….stall ….around…. a little bit….and see…how Mr. Macho Brother….might handle…..the situation. What to do? OOOPS!!! Too late. There she blows.

Sure enough, as brother dearest began elevating the umbrella into position, the dress was snagged like a perch on a hook. The kindest physical description of the about to be exposed lady was she was a tad on the portly side, the port side of the Titanic that is. This could explain the multi-pleated, free flowing funeral mourning dress attire she was wearing. With the wind blowing at a pretty good clip and the funeral service tent making lots of flapping noise, the lady was intently listening to the preacher and was completely oblivious to the fact her dress was now about half mast. To her credit however, she did have on several layers of some kind of elastic body control under garments. In fact, I had never seen that much "stretched-to-the-max" spandex in one place in my life. I almost wavered and came to my brother's rescue. But then again, I was a little apprehensive about accidentally startling the lady. If either one of us made one wrong move, that spandex might snap and she could easily wipe out the preacher, four pall bearers and up to as many as a half a dozen other family members. So I just stayed put and kept my mouth shut.

I think it was the next gust of wind, which must have reached areas unaccustomed to having a wind chill factor that sent a warning signal to the lady that all was not right in her underneath world. She immediately began trying to control her high flying skirt. About this same time, with the umbrella coming to an abrupt halt about shoulder high, my brother thinking the wind had caught his umbrella began putting some real muscle into his umbrella raising effort. With one good upward yank, he shot the black dress up around the lady's neck like black smoke billowing from the Pope pickin' Vatican. Of course with her skirt now eyeball high, the lady was completely blinded from the real reason of why her dress was unfurling like Old Glory. Even though it seemed to be a losing battle, the lady was making a valiant effort to contain her high in the sky flying dress. Not to be bested by a little breeze, my brother began pulling for all he was worth on his uncooperative umbrella. Still blaming the wind, both were still absolutely clueless of the jerk and yank contributions being made by each other.

Okay! There was still time for me to be my brother's keeper. But you know what? I may be a little on the slow side, but I still have a memory.....a very long memory. And, every little childhood indiscretion I had suffered at the hands of my big brother came rushing back in a flash. And besides, it was the funniest darn thing I'd ever seen. So I just decided to let this cemetery-striptease-tug-of-war just run its natural course. Being an adult male, my brother at first seemed to have a slight strength advantage on this tug and pull competition. However, a friend of the lady joined in on the fracas in an attempt to help gather in the yards of flapping dress material. Well now, that was a little more like it. One guy against two women, for the most part, is considered to be a fairly even match. And who am I to interfere in a fair contest. Game on.

The harder the two women tugged, the harder my brother pulled. Back and forth they went a tuggin' down and a pullin' up.... all the while all three of them thinking the wind was the culprit. The preacher was just starting to explain how it was all right for friends to grieve.....and, how it was all right for close family members to cry for a loss.......and I suppose, how it was all right for me to do what

I did next. I couldn't help it. I laughed. Not a little muffled snicker, but a laugh you might hear when a joke is told down at the pool hall. Immediately all eyes turned in my direction. But as luck would have it, all those looks somehow by-passed me and settled directly on my brother and his dress hiking victim. When he turned around and recognized his part in the outdoor peep show, my brother suffered a colossal "blood rushing to the face" melt down. Well …Well…Well!!! So Mr. Smooth as Silk is human after all. Well, welcome to my rough cut world brother. It was about time he got reminded of his country roots upbringing and what it feels like to be one of us just plain and ordinary common folk again.

While I kept right on laughing, several mourners jumped in and tried to straddle the high flying dress situation. The lady was mortified. My brother was an apologizing emotionally wounded wreck. And as for myself, I was still having a pretty good laugh over his predicament. In fact, I couldn't stop laughing. Extremely upset, my brother whirled and gave me a look that could have melted scrap iron. With his embarrassment fast migrating into anger, he wanted to know just exactly what I thought was so darn funny. Just in a nick of time, I remembered something that really saved my bacon. With the straightest face I could muster, I said, "Don't you remember, Brother, what Aunt Mary always told us? "No matter how dark the skies or how bad the times may seem, sometimes it's better to laugh than it is to cry?" I guess he had forgotten Aunt Mary's advice, because he still didn't laugh.

SOMETIMES IT'S BETTER TO LAUGH...
THAN IT IS TO CRY

DOCTOR
BACKSIDE
SNAP!

CHAPTER 30

ALL'S WELL AND MY END IS WELL

A FEW WEEKS AGO I developed an annoying rash on the back of my neck. Nothing serious, but it was persistent and would never quite go away with my home brewed remedies. Since our current family doctor was in the graduating class of Methuselah, my wife encouraged me to go to one of the new young doctors in town that might actually know something about curing ailments. An appointment was made. I didn't know him and he didn't know me, but before the appointment was concluded we were both going to have formed an opinion of each other.

Once I was weighed and criticized for my excess baggage, I was placed into a holding cell to await my new Dr. Kildare. After a 45 minute wait, a doctor opened the door seemingly to be studying my medical chart. Good grief! Doogie Houser looked every bit of fifteen. "What seems to be the problem today," he asked? I explained about my rash. He asked if I had ever had it before. I told him yes about 30 years ago during my puberty years in grade school. I added puberty years specifically for his youthful benefit. I proceeded to explain what the rash was called and what medication had been prescribed to cure it.

With a worried look on his brow, he said, "Hummm....a reoccurring illness. That can be a sign of diabetes." Catching me somewhat off guard, I tried to explain my theory of 30 years between flare-ups not seeming to fit the definition of a reoccurring illness. However, my uneducated medical opinion seemed to fall on deaf ears. Like it or not my diabetes test was already in motion. Faster than Jesse James, Dr. Quick Draw whipped out a sharpened instrument from his pocket, which closely resembled an old fashion ice pick. In one swift motion the sharpened point was jabbed into my only good typing finger to induce blood flow. Yeow! Just my luck, he only winged me. Yeow! #$#@% He sure hit pay dirt on the second try. After collecting a microscopic sample, he gave me a roll of gauze to control the fountain of blood spurting from my finger. In a matter of seconds his computerized machine confirmed that I had luckily not contracted the dreaded diabetes disease. That was the good news. The not so good news was my finger would be out of typing action for the next week.

Still smarting from my wounded finger, the pint sized doctor seated on a four-wheel stool came scooting up to get a close look at my watering eyes. Eyeball to eyeball, he asked me somewhat of a peculiar question. "How many times do you get up at night to relieve yourself?" Not particularly sure what that had to do with my back of the neck rash, I told him I really didn't know and didn't see why it mattered. He showed little appreciation for my comment. In fact, it was as if I hadn't even spoken at all. Still staring at my eyes, he suggested that I must drink a lot of alcohol.

I said, "No I don't."

"Then you must drink a lot of coffee?" He questioned.

Again "Hun uh."

"Well how about soda pop?" He began sweating me out with his Gestapo interrogation tactics.

Another "Hardly at all" was my answer. Totally mystified, he quizzed me on what was my drink preference. The only drink that came to mind was iced tea. That got an immediate "AH! HAAA!!! With pink or blue," he grilled? Clueless as to my choice of colors, I asked him what he meant by pink or blue? He explained pink was

Sweet and Low and blue was Equal. I cautiously admitted to having an Equal addiction. "AH! HAAA!!! That's it."

"That's what?" I asked.

"That's what's making it longer and harder. Surely you have noticed it getting longer and harder?" He asked. Now thoroughly confused and somewhat alarmed, I slowly backed away to create some distance.

In my deepest big boy voice, I asked, "Making exactly what longer and harder?"

"Your nose," he answered. "Haven't you noticed it getting bigger?" It seems the caffeine of the ice tea combined with the chemical sweetener can in rare cases cause the nose to contract some kind of rhino somethin' somethin' somethin' nose disease. The symptoms include an enlarged and hardening of the nose. However, not to worry. I had been diagnosed in the early stages of my Pinocchio Honker growth spurt and there was medication available that should easily whittle it down by at least a third. Gosh! I hope there's enough nose left to hang my glasses on. With a still bleeding finger and now developing an inferiority complex about my gigantic nose, I was fast losing confidence in my fresh out of kindergarten doctor. My old doctor was starting to seem smarter by the minute, even if he was getting a little short on minutes.

By this time, my new doctor had walked around behind me and pulled out my shirt tail. He began thumping on my back like he was picking out a ripe watermelon. Gradually in a bear hug fashion, his squeezing fingers had made it all the way around to my chest. Oh!! Oh!! Dr. Romeo's wondering hands began roaming around a little too freely in my not so comfort zone. As he began fondling my breasts, I was trying to figure out what my breast might have to do with the back of my neck. With a handful of breast in each hand, he asked me if I knew what a mammogram test was? I thought about asking him if he was planning on asking me to go steady. Instead I replied that I had heard of that woman's test and emphatically placed extra emphasis on the word woman. That tripped his trigger and he fired back that it was not just a test for women....it was for men too. With the booby exam still in progress, I was beginning to feel like I was being criminally violated. A couple of more quick squeezes and the doctor announced that my left nipple was a little harder than my right one. He was 99% sure there was nothing wrong, but to be 100% absolutely sure he was going to schedule a boob smashin' test for me the following morning at the local hospital.

I began protesting about the upcoming tit torture, and I was immediately reprimanded. I was told that when I reached my wonder years of 40, there would be an entire regiment of health prevention tests that I would need to have performed on a regular basis. By now I was growing beyond upset, so I thought it would be important for him to know what I was thinkin'. For starters I told him I was pretty sure I was already past 40 and no one could make me take a test if I didn't want to. All Dr. Pain and Suffering heard was that I was past 40. "Just how old are you," he asked?

"Forty two," I indignantly replied.

"Well, you know what past 40 means don't you? Please stand up and drop your pants," he ordered.

No, I didn't know what past 40 meant, but like a trained monkey I stood up and dropped my drawers. With no warning or explanation, Dr. Strange Love took me down with a tactical Hulk Hogan arm bar move and pinned me face first cross ways on an examination table. What the heck was this about? I was about to find out.

Yeow!!!! In mere seconds I got to experience one of my first ever good health prevention tests.....the one finger plunge exam. Blood rushed to my bald head like an over ripe tomato. My eyes slightly crossed just before they began bugging out of their sockets. My grinding teeth were begging for a bullet to bite down on. Then this Dr. Kevorkian madman asked the weirdest question. He asked me if I would please strain. I was already groaning like a Mamma Grizzly bear trying to deliver a breached two headed cub with non-retractable claws. Puffin' like the little engine that couldn't, I don't know what else I could have done to prove that I was straining with all my might. This dude was a bigger quack than the AFLAC duck. He wasn't a doctor. He was an executioner. My Gosh! Did I have a lisp when I asked him to "Please check my rash"? I'm certain I pronounced rash correctly. All I know is that he sure as heck missed the back of my neck by a good three feet.

Trying to recover from my lube and go experience, I gingerly bent down to pull up my Fruit of Looms. While I was bent over, the doctor made a comment about my follicle deprived Q-Ball head. "What do you think about your hair?" he asked.

"Which one," I shot back?

"Would more hair improve the quality of your life?" He quizzed. Dumbfounded as to the way he segwayed from one body area to another, I said I hadn't thought too much about it, but maybe. But that maybe would sure as heck include being brought up to speed on just how the procedure would take place. I sure didn't want another surprise attack from south of the border like I had just experienced. He proceeded to enlighten me about some experimentation being done with applying some kind of heart medicine rubbed on the head. Supposedly by smearing the gel to the scalp...walla ....hair would magically appear.

"Kind of like one of those Chia plants," I said.

"Pretty much," he agreed.

Noticing buckets of sweat still running off me, he wanted to know if I always sweated that profusely. "Not always," I said. "Just when somebody tries to shove a Louisville Slugger up my hind end." It was meant as a joke.....kind of. He didn't see the humor. With all the bed side manner of a bed pan, Dr. Straight Face stated that sweat could cause ill side effects for any hair restoration project. It seems sweat can carry the magic hair growing potion to other parts of the body. This could cause hair to show up in unwanted places. Now that is something I could really look forward to........tuffs of hair growing off the end of my ever growing Woody Woodpecker nose.

So...after being stabbed, fondled, probed, and hair humiliated I was really beginning to miss the misdiagnosis of my previous pre-historic physician. Good grief! I go to a new up to date clinic to get a cure for my rash and come away with a complex about my hoe handle nose stuck on a hairless head. I was somewhat surprised as the doctor was leaving the room when he said, "By the way, you were right about that rash. I'll write you out a prescription and it should clear up in a few days." To this day I still don't know when Dr. Jeckell examined my neck. Of course there were a few minutes that I was border line un-conscious, so it could have been then. I suppose if there was a moral to this story it could be, "All's well and my end is well" at least until next year's health preventive test. By the way, I did skip the mammogram. Also, when I got home I simply raved to my wife about how fabu-lous her recommended new young doctor was and that she should make an appointment just as soon as possible to go get her own stuff checked out. I can't wait to hear the results from that checkup.

ALL'S WELL AND MY END IS WELL

FURY

CHAPTER 31

IT'S THE LITTLE UNEXPECTED STUFF

One of my greatest fears is fast becoming a reality. I am slowly but surely turning into a grizzly, gripey, grumpy old man. Getting old isn't what it's cracked up to be. I didn't plan to be this way. I think it's just part of the fermenting process of time which can sour an outlook on life. In most cases, it's not my normal belly aching of a new world order conspiring to raise my taxes, health insurance rates, or gas prices which irritates me the most. It's the little everyday unexpected stuff that seems to really tie a knot in my shorts.

It's little stuff, like a train blocking the highway when I am already 15 minutes late for work. Or, my last light bulb burning out in the upstairs bathroom, while I'm trying to shave, which made me late for work in the first place. Or worse yet because of the darkness, mistakenly picking up a tube of hemorrhoid shrinking cream and giving the old bicuspids a good brushing. After that little mouth watering experience, I couldn't even form words to call my office to let them know why I was going to be late for work. I tried, but all I could do was whistle. It's this little unexpected stuff which is gradually pushing me over the edge of sanity cliff.

Sometimes it can be something as pure and innocent as a child's swing that can change your entire outlook on life. When my grandson Benton was born, I knew that boy needed a swing. Grandpas are programmed to think that way. So I did the grandpa thing and went to Wal-Mart and bought one of those impossible to fall out of little blue plastic swings. I surveyed the yard and found the perfect swing hangin' tree limb. With only a few close calls of standing on a wobbly ladder, I was able to install the swing without doing any real permanent bodily injury. Benton loved the swing and for the past several years got many hours of enjoyment from it. But as time went along, a sugar fortified diet assisted Benton in out growing his Blue Angel aircraft. The first clue was when his legs turned as purple as concord grapes because of the blood circulation being cut off by the now, way too small leg openings.

The best way of solving the problem was to let little sister Olivia inherit the small blue safety swing and build Benton a new and improved big boy version. One day I spotted just the perfect grandson swing. It was a 16" truck tire hung parallel to the ground by a geometric assemblage of metal chains. WOW! It was exactly what I had been looking for. And more importantly, it looked simplistic enough that even I couldn't goof up the installation. So once again, I raided the grandkids' college fund, bought all the necessary parts and "Walla" the new space shuttle size swing was in place. Benton loved it and Grandpa almost broke his arm trying to pat himself on the back for doing such a good swing building job. One would think that should be a very happy little ending to a simple little swing story. But no!!!!! Nothing is simple because of all the little unexpected stuff that will come back to bite you in that all time favorite biting place.

The other day I was out mowing the yard. Normally yard mowing is a fairly insignificant Saturday afternoon chore. That is only if there is no little unexpected stuff to go wrong. As my magnificent riding Murray mower approached the new swing, I decided to reach ahead to prevent the tire and chains from rubbing against the mower. It seemed like a logical thing to do. Either for fun or stupidity I held on to the tire swing as I mowed through the swing area. Just as I let go of the swing, I approached my favorite exposed tree root grinding area. Once again logic betrayed me as I stopped to do the responsible thing of raising the mower blades to avoid the roots. While I stopped to adjust the blade height, I forgot an important basic rule of physics, "what swings one way will eventually swing back" KERR SMACK!!! The off road mountain climbing lugs of the swing nailed me right between my shoulder blades. I couldn't decide whether to pass out or throw up. All I remember is I couldn't breathe and I kept tasting cranberries. And, I hadn't had cranberries since last Thanksgiving.

As I wondered why no one warned me this was the day that the sky was going to actually fall, my foot slipped off the clutch and my mower made a diagonal lurch right into little sister's blue swing. Somehow one of her swing ropes got hooked on the mower deck lever, while the other looped around my neck like a common horse thief's hangman's noose. But that didn't stop my mighty mower from powering onward. As the swing ropes tightened, the front wheels began pointing skyward and the blades turned into propellers for a lawnmower take off. At the same time, coughing and gagging, I began imagining tomorrow's headlines, "Local Man Lynched For Doing a Crappy Job of Mowing His Yard." It must have been survival instinct alone which made me reach to turn off the key. Of course, being semi-air borne just placed me at the perfect elevation for a one last back of the head shot from Mr. Snow Tread. Evidently Mr. Goodyear not only has a steel belt but a black belt in karate as well. This second womp on the back of the head sent me directly into the 5th dimension of the Twilight Zone. At that particular moment, being hung from a cottonwood tree didn't seem to be such a bad idea after all. I think it was late Sunday evening before my eyes finally uncrossed.

So what is the best answer on how to deal with the little unexpected stuff that can drive us crazy? Well, group therapy and sometimes doubling up on the PROZAC seems to take the edge off. I'm not for sure what is worse, the little unexpected stuff that seems to be driving me crazy or that I am rapidly turning into a grizzly, gripey, grumpy old man. When I watch my grandkids, they run, they laugh, they play and yes, they fall down and get boo boos. But invariably, they always seem to get right back up and continue on their merry way. They just let the chips fall where they may and whatever happens...happens. I think I'm green at the gills with envy that I don't have a grandkid's philosophy on life.. I can't run. My laugh is a sneer. I forgot how to play because of work. And when I fall down, my freakin' boo boos usually land me in the emergency room.

Since no one has actually found the fountain of youth for the inevitable old age ripening process, I think I have come up with a new home remedy to deal with my rusting out years. The next time life sends one of those little waves of unexpected stuff crashing into my little chunk of paradise, I think I will go swingin' with the grandkids. I might be too old to be a swinger, but it can't hurt to hang out with those who still can.

IT'S THE LITTLE UNEXPECTED STUFF

CHAPTER 32

MY NEW YEAR'S RESOLUTION......AGAIN

As I SETTLED BACK into my warm soft LAZY BOY recliner on New Year's Eve, I began watching my all time favorite Jimmy Stewart rerun of Its A Wonderful Life with my grandson, Benton. During the first commercial, I began to think about my 51st annual New Year's resolution......lose some weight. I have some fairly obvious telltale signs, which proves to the world that "You can have your cake and eat it too." I have places I could no longer reach to scratch. Sometimes I break out into a sweat when trimming my toe nails. I can live in denial as well as the next person, but when looser clothes, like sweatshirts, parkas and tarps can no longer hide the love handles, it's time to take action.

Yes Siree! This time I'm going to do it. No more make'em and then turning right around and breakin' them. This New Year's resolution I'm going to keep. Once and for all, I would like to put on a pair of my blue jeans that didn't already have stretch marks. It would be nice to wear my John Deere belt buckle and have people actually see the tractor. I'm tired of having to lift up those four extra chins just so I can shave. I've made up my mind. Once and for all, I'm going to go all out and fight the fat. "Good bye Fat Ben..... Hello Mr. Thin Ben."

In some sense, the holiday season can be compared to one enormous ongoing meal-a-thon. Halloween is the appetizers. Thanksgiving is the main course. And Christmas is the dessert. Ever since last Halloween, I have been on an eating frenzy. Well, maybe I should say since the week before Halloween, because it was pretty slim pickens by the time the real trick or treaters got there. I can't help it. I love Snickers candy bars. When I spot a Snicker, my tongue starts slappin' me on the forehead. Whether it's a bite size, miniature, regular, or giant size Snickers...I love them all. I have about as much will power as a drunk turning down a free drink at happy hour when it comes to passing up a Snickers candy bar.

By the time the Halloween candy is finished off, it's time to partake of the meal of all meals, Thanksgiving. On one weight conscious Thanksgiving, I tried to count my calorie consumption and wore out three sets of batteries in my food intake calculator. Thanksgiving is a time to reflect on what we are thankful for. Most of all, I'm thankful for gravy. I love gravy. There is turkey with gravy and mashed potatoes with gravy and dressing with gravy and anything with gravy. Gravy could almost be a liquid Snickers.

Every great meal needs to be topped off with a dessert....just a little something for the sweet tooth. That is why Christmas was chosen to follow Thanksgiving. There are sugar cookies, and fruit cakes, and divinity, and peanut brittle, and peanut clusters, and..........*fudge.* Oh man! Fudge is soooo good. Especially, fudge with nuts. Stir in a cup full of pecans with that sweet creamy chocolaty fudge recipe and...WALLA....a little chunk of chocolate heaven. Fudge with nuts comes in a close second, right behind a Snickers and maybe tied with gravy.

So now here I am at New Year's Eve, with a summer sausage in one hand and a cheese ball in the other, and keeping my eyes open for any stray Snickers. As I sink a little deeper into the cushions of my chair, I make a pledge to myself. "Ben Boy, you better enjoy this moment, because tomorrow it's all going to be different. Tomorrow is going to be a new day. A fat free day."

Kicking up the recliner foot rest, I lean back and mentally begin preparing my plan of thinness. I suppose the first step towards achieving my Governor Swartzenager body would be to introduce myself to better eating habits. In the past, my idea of a low fat diet was just to lie down on the couch while I ate my chips and dip. I also had a theory that if I drank a Diet Coke while I ate my three Little Debbie ding dongs, the calories would become diluted, and actually become some of that good cholesterol. Well, chips and dip, you are history. Adios, ding dongs. From now on it's nothing but health foods for this soon to be body beautiful.

The logical first stop for healthy food happiness should be the Supermarket. Hmmmmmm! Let's see. I've never looked for health foods before. I wonder what aisle they're in. Of course! Now I remember. It's called the produce section. I remember going there a couple of times to get just enough veggies to fill the rotter, somctimes better known as the crisper. I do this on special occasions just to impress my health conscious company that may be by for a visit. But not this time. It's going to be an all fiber diet for this boy. I need lots of carrots, lettuce, green beans, cabbage, and broccoli. (Well, maybe not the broccoli.) Broccoli is too much like a weed. Anyway, if I follow my rabbit diet strategy, I should consume enough fiber to produce a complete set of wicker patio furniture by mid-summer.

Just eating right won't be the total cure. If I really want to drop the pounds, I need to exercise more….at least more than walking back and forth from my recliner to the refrigerator. In the past, I have made some half hearted attempts of getting up at the crack of dawn to exercise with some of those early morning TV fitness freaks. But there is always some Miss Lucy Long Legs who invites all of us beginners to sit down on the floor, lift our left leg high up in the air, bend it backwards behind our head and then try to tickle our right ear lobe with the big toe. And, that was just the warm up.

The best four star exercise joint I ever went to was a place called the Looking Good Fitness Center. The minute I walked through the doors of this house of health, I could almost feel the cellulite begin to drip off me. I could smell the sweat. I could hear the moans and groans. I could see a variety of machines with bars and weights and pulleys and cables all designed to inflict bodily pain. Bald men were panting. Sweat was running. Women were straining. Big Mama Leotards were stretching. The last time I had seen this much beef was when I hauled a load of steers to the stockyards. This was an absolutely GREAT place to lose some weight.

Immediately I was greeted by an energetic young woman just beaming with fitness. She was about the size of a stick. I've seen more meat on antlers. "May I help you," she asked, looking at me as if I was lost and looking for directions to the closest McDonald's.

Doing the normal guy thing of sucking my gut half way up into my chest, I replied, "Yeah. I was thinking about buffin' up a little."

"And just what do you hope to achieve?" She asked.

"Well, what would it take to get me looking like one of those Bay Watch life guards on TV," I asked?

I believe "An Act of God," was the mumbled reply.

The first step was to choose an exercise plan and to select a weekly, monthly, yearly schedule of payment. My request for an hourly rate was denied. Next was the all important weigh in. As the flashing numbers on the scale began to soar, I felt relieved when the final flash showed me 10 pounds lighter than I thought I actually weighed. My enthusiasm was quickly doused when I was informed the flickering number was actually my percent of body fat not my weight. Ouch!

Stick girl then invited me to a free trial workout on their very latest fat burner machine, better known as "The Cremator." With a few limited instructions and one push of a button, motors began to whine. Pulleys began to whirl. Rubber belts began to scorch. I was hanging on to the kill rope like a chad in a Florida election ballot. After completing a regiment of fat removing exercises, which lasted for eternity (almost 23 seconds) I fell off and inquired if she had 911 on speed dial. With sweat rolling off me like I was employed at one of Cathy Lee Gifford's shirt factories, I politely excused myself and crawled out of JocksMart in a state of dizziness.

I don't care what anyone says, I'm going to whip myself into shape this New Year. If Richard Simmons and I have to sweat to the oldies every night of the week, I'm going to remove myself from the ranks of the swollen society. Starting tonight, right after that wrinkle free Dick Clark counts down that falling silver ball in Time Square, I'm going to start taking care of myself. I'm going to eat right. I'm going to exercise more. I'm going to ....Grandpa....Grandpa..... Wake up Grandpa." Huh? What? Oh my gosh! I must have dozed off. What the heck time is it anyway? Well Good Grief! It's almost New Years. "Grandpa, can I have a candy bar," my five year old grandson wanted to know? With dreams of thinness quickly fading from my mind, I groggily replied, "Well sure Benton. And Hey! I've got a good idea. Why don't we both celebrate New Years? Maybe Grandpa will have one of them Snickers too."

M+M
M+M
IVORY
SHAMPOO

CHAPTER 33

GOD BLESS GEORGIA AND GOD BLESS BEN GAY

GEORGIA? WHY ON EARTH Georgia? Almost a year ago, my youngest son accepted a really good job in Atlanta, Georgia. Although I was happy for him since it was a job he would really enjoy, my heart almost went into a code blue because of my grandkids being moved thirteen hours away. When you are around a grandson for seven years and a granddaughter for three and had the joy of watching all of their T-Ball games, pre-school programs, Halloween costumes and Easter egg hunts, words cannot explain the heart wrenching loss of when it is taken away. Georgia. Of all places Georgia. The poor kids won't have a chance. I give them a year before they contract that deadly "You All" accent disease. It will only be a matter of time before Hee Haw becomes their number #1 favorite TV show.

However, it has now been ten months and with Georgia schools on Spring Break the grandkid express is on its way back to Missouri. Yee Haw! If I had a tail, it would most definitely be waggin'. This is a special occasion and Grandpa is definitely excited. I immediately got out the yard rake and leaf blower and started cleaning up the family room. I even got out the dust bath towel and scraped off a few of the most visible dust bunny areas. I have to get crackin' because the GK-(grandkid) Day invasion begins tomorrow.

The van hadn't even come to a stop before Benton and Olivia were bailing out for a fun filled day and night at Grandpa Ben's farm. With batteries fully charged and sugar highs off the chart, they hit the door on a dead run. I got a brief hug and a slurripy wet kiss on their way in as I went out to haul in their overnight back packs. A quick good bye to the other grandparent chauffeurs and I thought I had mistakenly stumbled into a nudist camp when I re-entered the house. Yikes! Shoes, socks, jeans, shirts and underwear were tossed in every direction and two naked grandkids were hollering for their swimsuits so they could go swimming in Grandpa's out door bath tub (hot tub). Splashin' and dunkin', it took less than an hour before we were all pruned up and the color of vine ripen tomatoes. Before we passed out from the 102 degree heat, I suggested we get out and cool down and rest a while.

What better way to rest than a good ole' game of hide and seek. There is nothing worse than one of those stick in the mud, snorin' life away, rockin' chair grandpas. So when it came my time to hide, I didn't pick a tree or lilac bush for a hiding place, I stuffed my not so petite size body on the concrete slab between the air conditioner and house. My knees were the first to go numb. Knee caps and concrete is not a good match. Then the hearing disappeared when the jet propulsion AC fan kicked on about three inches from my ear drum. The longer I stayed wedged in my hiding place tomb, the faster my arthritis permanently cemented my joints together. Where is a full body epidural when you need one? Trying to hold out as long as I could, I figured I was about 15 minutes away from becoming a permanent concrete yard ornament if they didn't find me pretty quick. There might have been a chance of saving my back if I had only known my two little red headed wonders of joy had given up seeking after the first two and a half minutes of looking. They had a sudden urge to go check out the $46 worth of junk food in the kitchen cabinet. Now I understand why grandpas look all bent over and need a walker just to get around. Old men shouldn't be hidin' when young people really don't give a whing ding where they're at anyway.

While I was on trash detail picking up M&M and Ding Dong wrappers, Benton and Olivia headed out for one last quick dip in the hot tub before supper time. Grandkids think an outdoor hot tub is the coolest place ever to take a bath. I take full responsibility for not explaining why bars of soap and shampoo should never be put in a hot tub. I will admit the three foot high suds and bubbles were kind of neat. It brought back fond memories of Lawrence Welk and his champagne bubbles. The tub has since been drained and refilled and so far so good on the $800 circulation pump.

Before starting supper, I tossed a load of wet swim suits and towels into the dryer. Our evening meal, upon special request, consisted of pepperoni pizza, peanut butter and jelly sandwiches, chips and dip and frosty cans of Mountain Dew. The kids wanted to know if I was baking brownies for dessert. I told them no, but maybe through their power of suggestion, a chocolate aroma did seem to be permeating through the house. I finally tracked down the chocolaty smell to some M&Ms in one of the swim suit pockets in the clothes dryer. The chocolate pretty well came out in the rewash, but I am now the proud owner of some every color of the rainbow bath towels. The second load of laundry held Olivia's new glittery pink jeans. It never occurred to me that the glitter wasn't attached permanently. Naturally the next load was grandpa's BVDs. Although it does add a certain stylish flair, I'm hoping the hot pink glitter fades out of Grandpa's skivvies before my next doctor's appointment. I wouldn't want Doctor Wilson to think I prettied up just for him.

After four grueling hours of after dinner "Sponge Bob" cartoon network, I for one was certainly in the mood to be horizontal. All three of us climbed into bed and within minutes the grandkid lights were out. Those kids may have been asleep in spirit, but their bodies transformed into a nonstop spastic robotic machines. It's hard to understand how a body can receive rest when it is in perpetual motion. Their sleep pattern was similar to that of a slice of bacon as it wiggles and jumps around in a frying pan? I got kicked and kneed and elbowed and punched until I thought I had been through a 15 round prize fight. My nighty night time was about as much fun as a series of rabies shots. Finally, I drug myself to the couch, if not for rest, for my own safety. Sometime during the night I woke up with severe chest pains. I first thought I was having the big one, but soon discovered Olivia had tracked me down and was lying with her bony little elbows embedded into my chest. With her face only inches from my own she whispered the sweetest words, "I love you, Grandpa Ben." I'm glad her words were sweet, because her breath could have pealed the paint off a barn floor.

After a breakfast of frozen waffles, fried bacon and spilled on the floor Sunny D, we packed a lunch, loaded up the fishing poles and headed to a favorite fishin' spot. I tried to give lessons on the correct way to cast a rod and reel, but somewhere along the line the grandkids have inherited an "I can do it by myself" stubborn streak. I'm not sure where that trait came from, but I know for a fact it is not my side of the family. Through a constant vigil, I kept both kids a safe distant apart hoping to avoid an errant fish hook in the eye. It's too bad I didn't take the same precautions for myself. Yeow!!!! With one hook in the back and one in the ear, needless to say my nerves were on constant edge each time I heard the zing of a fishing hook missile sailing through the air. Every time I heard a cork pop the water, I ducked as if I was on a Dick Chaney quail hunting trip.

Only 20 minutes of cork bobbin' had passed when Olivia thought it was time for a snack. Opening a package of Lunchables, she soon found out crumbling up the crackers and tossing them into the pond made great floating fish food. So did the ham and cheese. Of course when lunch time finally came around, everyone had a Lunchable meal except for grandpa. Come to find out, it was his meal that served a greater good of saving the lives of fish that were too lazy to bite a juicy worm on a hook. Oh well! Missing one meal won't kill a grandpa. Fish hooks might, but not a missing a meal.

Grandpa did have the forethought to take along a fish basket just in case a trophy fish was landed. I soon learned anything retrieved on a hook was considered to be a trophy, including moss. I tried to show the proper way of putting a fish in the basket and then tossing the basket back into the water. I should have been clearer about the importance of maintaining a good firm grip on the nylon cord when making the toss. Burr!!! Grandpa had almost forgotten how (shiver me timbers cold) waste deep April pond water can be.

Sunburned and back home, we spent the rest of the afternoon having wet sponge fights in the yard, climbing in the tree house, swingin' on the tire swing and making yet another trip to the hot tub. There was just enough of the fun day left to hurry to town for a McDonald's Happy Meal and a quick trip to the city park playground. At the Golden Arches drive through, Benton told me what he wanted to eat and I placed his order over the intercom. I kept trying to ask Olivia what kind of Happy Meal she would like, but I couldn't even get an eye contact from her let alone a verbal response. Naturally, the order lady in the drive through squawk box quickly became impatient, then irritated and finally down right insulting. After about a half a dozen tries, I finally gave up and asked Benton what the heck was the matter with his sister. It seems Olivia has quite a pretend imagination and at any given moment may give herself a complete new identity by changing her name to someone else. Finally Benton figured out that Tuesdays was her day to be called David and when asked, David said a Chicken McNugget Happy Meal would be fine with him or her or whoever the heck she was. Whew!!!! I knew Georgia might have an ill effect on these kids.

All in all I had a great time with the grandkids and I know they had a good time back on the farm. We crowded in six weeks' worth of fun in less than 24 hours. The laughter has since died down and the farm is certainly a bit quieter. But there are plenty of reminders of good times. The 150 flies now buzzing around inside the house reminds me of how many times Benton and Olivia opened (not closed) the doors to go have fun. Getting ready for work, I noticed I was sporting yet another stylish pair of boxers decorated with hot pink glitter. I am also sun burned, have swollen joints, and am making baby 'possum whimpering sounds when I do strenuous activities such as tying my shoes. There are aches and pains in places only site specific to grandpas. But, it's nothing that a bucket full of Ben Gay won't fix up. "Maybe the old grey mare ain't what she used to be"… but this old work horse of a Grandpa did put forth a valiant effort to have grandkid fun.

I will have to admit that I now fully appreciate and have a total and complete understanding of God's Plan of giving young people the primary responsibility of having and raising kids. And maybe the Divine Plan also includes a reason for creating a 13 hour distance between grandpas and grandkids. Grandpas sometimes forget how much energy it takes to keep up with young legs and young minds. Maybe long distances are designed to allow grandpas time to remunerate, rejuvenate, and recuperate between visits. As for this Grandpa, I love my grandkids and I always want to be ready with open arms, plenty of get up go and have the fish hook removin' pliers handy for their next visit.

I have rethought my previous worry. Maybe my fears were unfounded in what affect Georgia may have on my grandkids. I probably should have been equally concerned for the well being of Georgia. The paths of two rambunctious Missouri grandkids might make Billy Sherman's March to the Sea seem like a cake walk. Until my next grandkid adventure, all I can say is, "God Bless Georgia" and "God Bless Ben Gay."

GOD BLESS GEORGIA AND
GOD BLESS BEN GAY

ANNUAL
CHILI COOKOFF

CHAPTER 34

THE GREAT CHILI COOK-OFF

POLITICS IS POLITICS. DURING every political campaign season we see hopeful candidates more than willing to step up to the plate and do nontypical things to attract votes. They shake hands with complete strangers and make them "better days ahead" promises with no intentions of keeping them. Some kiss some of the ugliest, snotty nosed babies that a mamma possum would have abandoned at birth. Others hug the elderly like they are a long lost family member that had just been named in their will. And almost all candidates will take part in any community event whenever and wherever there is a crowd of potential voters. And yes, there was a time that I was one of those promise makin', ugly baby kissin', old person huggin' electioneering hopefuls.

One problematic concern with primary elections is the prime campaign season for electioneering takes place in the heat stroke month of July. July gives the heat of the campaign a completely different meaning. In my bid for a county race, I showed up at an annual small town festival to meet and greet my fellow citizenry on one of those heat scorching July Saturdays. On this particular day of the festival was scheduled the event that was expected to draw the largest crowd, the annual Chili Cook Off. In retrospect, the person in charge of scheduling events must have had the I Q of a cotton ball to plan a Chili Cook Off in 105 degree, cook an egg on the sidewalk, July temperatures. However, being billed as a sanctioned stepping stone to compete in the national indigestion cook off title, 35 chili bean competitors showed up to contend for the colon crippling crown.

As bad luck would have it, judges for the event were still recovering from a jalapeno hang over and turned out to be no shows. Event planners quickly scrambled and thought it would be fun for the local political candidates to be substitute chili taste testers. We were assured it would be lots of fun. My opponent, Big Mike was a big strappin' fellow who immediately jumped at the chance for free political exposure and better yet…free food. Not wanting to look the part of a spoil sport, my finicky stomach and I put on our best game face and accepted the chili connoisseur judging position. How bad could it be? Who doesn't like chili? With cup, plastic spoon, and tally sheet in hand, we made our way into the chili bean pot arena to begin scoring the pots of liquid fire.

First up was…. Carl's Coyote Killin'Chili.

My fears eased somewhat as I watched Big Mike lap it up like he was a starving third world orphan. However, my fears returned in a flash as soon as the infernal fluid passed through my lips. Yikes! Holy Mother of Mona Lisa.! What kind of sick twisted mind could concoct such a lethal Molotov cocktail recipe? The crowd burst into applause as I began coyote yipping at an imaginary moon. Surely this was the worst one.

Entry number two was….. Herbie's Heart Stoppin' Chili.

Have mercy on my poor cellulite laden soul. I no longer have a pulse. I felt like I had molten lead in my mouth. I did. It was from the fillings in my teeth. In mere seconds, I forgot how to breathe. It would be 100 to 1 Las Vegas odds on whether or not shock paddles could even revive me. I lost all peripheral vision. My entire body broke out into a river of sweat causing the red stripes on my new campaign patriotic flag shirt to dissolve into one solid pink color. I was now promoting Breast Cancer Awareness. Naturally, Big Mike was cool as a cucumber.

Lisa's Lip Remover Chili.... smelled funny. One quick sniff and my nose hairs mysteriously vaporized. I developed an I Dream of Genie nose twitch and began snorting out involuntary snot bubbles. Tingling sensations ran down my quivering spine as I lost feeling in all extremities. I began having hallucinations and fantasies about Desert Gila Monster nibbling on a Polar Bear ice cream sandwich. Lisa seemed offended when I told her that her chili had most likely caused me permanent brain damage.

Thanks to.... Clyde's Colon Cleansing Chili......my intestine was now a straight pipe. I was passing gas faster than a NASCAR pit crew. Va-Rippppp!!!!! Paramedics were summoned to assist four people behind me that were overcome by my toxic Mexican spiced fumes. Great! I'm not only burning at both ends, but I am now taking casualties. It's too bad Big Mike hadn't been down wind.

Angie's Afterburner Chili.... will no doubt guarantee me a place in the halitosis hall of shame. Geeze Louise !!!! I am now belching pure fire. The little flipper ma-jigger in the back of my throat is all shriveled up with third degree burns. My mouth feels like I have been bobbing for tater tots in a Fry Daddy. My breath could peel the paint off a camp for bad boys out house floor. I now can hear a slosh when I walk. It must be the internal bleeding. I would have thought the chili heat alone would have seared shut any severed arteries.

Harold's Hair Lip Chili.... was an unexpected treat. Yee-ow-ee!!! A hand grenade could have been put under my tongue, the pin pulled, and I wouldn't have felt a fang. Oh no! I know wonger have the ability to pronounce words with (th) sounds. My froat is frobbing and I wonder if my new wisp is temporary or will be a permanent forax condition. Big Mike seems to be frilled with the chili eating fun.

Living up to its title was.... Nellie's Nuclear Waste Chili. Holy

Smokes! Someone needs to call 911 and report this Chernobyl uranium spill to the EPA. My nose feels like it has been snorting Roach Repellant. My vision blurred for a few seconds just before the right retina detached and skedaddled to the back of my eye socket. The normal pigment color of the skin on my throat has now turned a bright struttin' turkey gobbler red. My one good eye now has an iridescent greenish glow. Meanwhile, Big Mike is in his food sampling comfort zone. He has already done away with the spoon and is drinking the chili samples straight from the cup. It is evident that my opponent intends on making this election a real horse race.

I will have to admit, Big Mike is a candidate that will reach out to voters. He certainly lent me a hand in guiding me to Babb's Battery Acid Chili cookin' booth. In an effort to demonstrate political courtesy, I decided to give Big Mike the first go ahead taste on Babb's chili. Observing no noticeable flinches, I proceeded with my own tentative taste. Holy Smoke Stacks!!! If this is supposed to be a joke, it is beyond cruel. This chili should be kept away from small children and postal employees with suicidal tendencies. My tongue felt like it had been snagged by a hundred fish hooks dipped in poison dart juice. I swallowed a can of Coke to extinguish the combustible heat source only to spread death and destruction to my entire esophagus. The chili heat is drying up my tears before they can run down my cheeks.

I am so thirsty. A sun baked leather saddle bag is less dehydrated. Big Mike thinks we may be able to get a drink at Mamma's Mount St. Helen's Chili booth. After having a sip of water, I proceeded to have a sip of her ......Sweet Mary's Mamma!!! A corpse has a better chance of recovering from this witch's brew. My mouth began having a melt down. All I could taste was pain. My throat felt like it had been sand blasted with fragments from a broken rubbing alcohol bottle. My lungs finally gave up on trying to breathe. Inhaling and exhaling was just too painful. Without warning my body began convulsing in dry heaves. I waved off two people wanting to perform the Heimlich

Maneuver so I could run over and dunk my head in the Methodist women's galvanized pop cooler tub.

Fred's Fire in the Hole Chili immediately cured my dry heaves. I am now in my full body up chuck mode. In fact, I am heavin' up fish sticks that I had eaten in my freshman year of high school. Big Mike asked me to please quit screamin' and I didn't even know I was. My ears are ringing and my merry–go–round world is now spinning. I can no longer distinguish between still and moving objects. Please.... someone...anyone....slam my head in car door to help ease the pain.

With a permanent limp, I stagger on towards the last and hopefully the least Connie's Instant Coma Chili cooking station. As I hesitantly try to sample the entry, the chili slid out of my code blue mouth and began raising blood blisters on exposed skin. My tongue felt like it had been stretched and seared on a George Foreman grill. I stumbled and fell dragging most of the pot of molten lava chili on top of me. This chili DNA evidence may be a good thing. At least the county coroner's autopsy may be able to prove what killed me.

And, what about my political opponent? I think Big Mike could swallow live charcoal briquettes, devour raw meat with an Idaho potato and cook a Full Meal Deal internally without feeling a thing. He wore his multi-chili stained t-shirt with pride. I've seen road kills with less visible damage. Each reddish splotch served as a courageous chili campaign insignia for each of the individual chili entries he had tasted. Evidently spices and peppers and beans and lethal south of the border heat sauces have little to no effect on his cast iron colon. Looking down at my near lifeless body, Big Mike offered me a hand up and wanted to know what I thought about going through the molten maze of chili pots one more time just in case we needed a tie breaker. That settles it. I'm done. Big Mike gets my vote.

CHAPTER 35

...AND WHEN THE BOUGH BREAKS

I HAVE LEARNED THAT artificial intelligence is no match for natural stupidity. As bad as I hate to admit it, adult males are a little strange. You put a guy on a horse and he automatically thinks he's a cowboy. You put a muscle shirt on him and he thinks he is Mr. Universe. Or in my case, you put a chain saw in my hands and I immediately become the Tree Terminator. Recently I was sprucing up the place with my trusty chain saw and tried to do a smart thing. Now the key word here is smart. According to Mr. Webster, smart in the context of a verb can be defined as.... "Having quick intelligence, shrewd, sharp, or witty judgment." Since my IQ has matured to the level of somewhere in the neighborhood of my weight divided by my age, quick intelligence doesn't seem to be a relevant factor anymore. On the other hand, smart in the form of an adjective can mean to have a "stinging sensation" or "quick inflicted pain." With both of these definitions in mind, this is how not to trim a tree.

I am probably the only person in Barton County who has a yard full of self-pruning Chinese Elm trees for shade. In my defense, I inherited these trees from the previous owner, Wong Chow Drop Bough. However, I have no defense, except for suffering from brief episodes of insanity, for planting my beloved sweet gum tree. Why people choose to plant species of self-destruction is a mystery to me. The slightest of breezes can cause Chinese Elms to litter the yard with a countless number of limbs. And just as soon as you get the yard picked up, a sparrow can cough and another six-foot limb will come tumbling down. Even more exciting is a really good ice storm. Ice on these trees could make General Sherman's March to the Sea look like a stroll in the park. This summer I decided to beat the weather to the annual tree trimming punch. With a ladder in one hand and a chain saw in the other I headed out to wage tree trimming war.

After doing my lumberjack imitation of hacking and sawing and hauling several loads of underbrush, I was down to my last lone limb. It wasn't a huge limb, but it was an extremely long limb. This parallel to the ground limb extended well past 30 feet and reached right over the top of one of my out buildings. The limb was just begging to come down, and I was more than willing to oblige. This is where smart...the verb...entered the picture. Now I could have just sawed the limb off at the trunk, but that would have meant the entire weight of the limb would have come crashing down on the building. So in my infinite wisdom, I made some C minus high school geometry calculations to prevent this possible damage. Making my first tree incision out about 12 foot from the trunk would allow the leafy part of the limb to drop and I then could come back and finish Mr. Thick Limb off at the trunk with a second cut. After pattin' myself on the back for being so tree cutting savvy, I leaned my ladder up against the outstretched limb, climbed up and went to work.

Regardless of how smart we think we are, we seldom are able to recognize an eminent disaster, even when it is staring us in the face. Not one time in my previous smart discussion with myself did self ever tell me what could or would take place if I proceeded with this limb cutting plan. In one brief instant, I learned lots about tree trimming. I learned there is a significant difference between just leaning a ladder against a limb and extending a ladder an appropriate distance above a limb. I learned once the heavy end portion of the limb heads for the ground, the remainder of the weight lessened limb will snap up with jet propulsion speed. With ladder collapsing in one direction and the chain saw being thrown in another, I was instantaneously transformed from a tree cuttin' Paul Bunyan to a tree swingin' Tarzan. I learned quickly how Tarzan got his yell. So there I was, sixteen feet up in the air, hangin' like grandma's knickers on the wash line.

As my panic began to subside, I tried to evaluate my situation, which was bad......extremely bad. I made an attempt to use my failed high school trigonometry skills to figure out the length of my ever shortening life expectancy. I kept telling myself, "I know that I am six foot. I know that my completely stretched out arms adds a minimum of another two foot. Therefore if ground is sixteen feet from my hands, that makes it only eight feet from the bottoms of my feet. How bad can that be? That's not so far." Baloney! A Green Beret Storm Trooper would have second thoughts before making this jump without a chute. There was little doubt that hurt was soon going to be involved in my latest drop from the tree mathematical equation. Not just a little hurt, but a bucket full of hurt. Looking below, I tried to select the best possible location for my pinpoint landing. My first problem was I had body parts a lot bigger than a pin point. As I kept a firm grip on my life line limb, I tried once again to be smart and weigh any other possible life preserving options. Unfortunately, a heavy body and a weak grip were fast making my mind up for me. With all of the grace of an upside down barn yard cat clawing at nothing but air, and of course screaming all the way, I finally had to let go.

Now eight-foot may not seem like such a distance, but I think in that eight feet I fell like a screeching opera star for at least 30 minutes. It is amazing how much momentum a potato chip and dip enriched body can pick up when gravity is involved. Thanks to a recent Discovery Channel program about sky diving, I kept remembering, "Do not lock your knees." I was soon to realize locked knees were going to be the least of my worries. KERR WOMP!! I don't really remember the touchdown of my feet. But, I will never forget the eye crossing pain of the foot bone connected to the leg bone and the leg bone connected to the knee bone and the knee bone scored a direct hit to the chin bone. To add further insult to already significant injury, I was in a mid tongue Nancy girl scream when my chin hit that all important unlocked knee. I immediately lost the ability to speak English, Chinese and Russian. Not that I could speak Chinese or Russian, but it would have been nice to have had the option just in case I would have ever wanted to pursue a career with the C.I.A. My fall was definitely in keeping with Mr. Webster's adjective definition of smart (stinging sensation or quick inflicted pain). Ouch!! Oh double ouch!! That really smarted! I whimpered like an orphaned cocker spaniel puppy. There was definitely going to be some marks left from this little fiasco.

Floating in and out of a semi-conscious state, I kept seeing this beautiful star constellation that looked just like Woody Woodpecker sitting on a Chinese Elm tree limb. Usually when I do something stupid, every neighbor I have within a five mile radius just happens to be driving by to witness my performance of foolishness. So, I immediately tried to jump up and found out I already was up. My normal 6'2" body had been crunched into that of a rodeo midget. I did a quick body check and wondered if it was possible to bleed internally and externally at the same time. I did find out I could throw up a really long time after I thought I was finished. More importantly I learned that when a bough breaks, a lot more can be rocked than just a cradle. I still drool my oatmeal at breakfast and make slobbering sounds when I smell fresh cut tree bark. With my new out stretched arms I now have no problems with scratching an itch in the middle of my back. And my Wrangler inseam went from a 32 to a 16. The good news is I can now share britches with my six year old grandson.

Getting old is not easy to accept. Finding out that you're brain cells are diminishing at the speed of light is even harder. Maybe Mr. Webster should revise his definition of smart to include –"the mid way point between genius and insanity." Which could be translated as, "50 year old men are idiots if they climb ladders to trim tree limbs."

CHAPTER 36

YOU CAN'T HIDE FROM MOTHER NATURE

HUNTING IS SUCH A great hobby. It offers so much more than just the hunt. It's good exercise (sweat like a pig). It teaches patience (naps in the woods). It teaches outdoor skills (pullin' ticks and scratchin' rashes). More importantly, hunting gives people an opportunity to experience nature at its best (cold rains, waste deep creek crossings, mosquito attacks, and skunk sprayings.) And that is where this story takes place on just one of those memorable hunting occasions.

There they were...Three huge struttin' turkey gobblers. They were bigger than huge. They reminded me of the Cartwright boys, Adam, Hoss, and Little Joe minus Pa riding out to check on the cattle in the south meadow. All this time I thought I had been calling to just one lonely love sick old bird. But no, there were three bearded Casanovas and they were headed directly towards my very best seductive come check my feathers out call. They were still more than a hundred yards away, but my blood was already starting to boil like a can of Campbell's soup. My neighbor sure gave me an early birthday present when he gave me permission to hunt on his magical turkey paradise. He's definitely made my Christmas card list this year. Better yet, it seems that I was the only hunter in his woods today. Maybe I better make that a box of Christmas candy instead of just a card. I did have to hike nearly a mile to get here, but who cares when you have three giant leaf shakers baring down on you. This was a turkey hunter's dream come true and all that I could think of was, "Don't screw this up. Don't move a muscle. Don't bat an eye. Don't even breathe. Turn blue as a Smurf if you have to, but don't spook these birds." I sat scrunched up at the base of a dead oak tree frozen like one of my parent's concrete lawn ornaments.

When hunters get together, they often try to out lie each other about who had the most perfect hunt. This was about to be one of those coffee shop tale swappin' perfect hunts that I would be getting to tell for years to come. The weather was absolutely picture perfect. My decoys looked great. My camouflage looked better than a real multi-flora rose bush. And my, "Why Don't You Come Down And See Me Sometime Big Boy"calls could have won a professional turkey calling championship. I sank just a little bit lower as the three turkey amigos slowly and methodically made their way towards my perfect turkey hunting story ending.

Just out of old Betsy's range, through cat like slitted eyes, I was trying to decide which one of the Gobblezilla turkey fans would look best over my fire place mantle. All of a sudden the three turkey bad boys stopped dead in their tracks. Three heads popped up as if they had received a direct call from the Butterball psychic hot line. In the next instant, they turned on a dime and ran like someone was ringing a Thanksgiving Day dinner bell.

What in the name of Southern Succotash just happened? I know I didn't move because the Blue Jay was still sitting on my shoulder pecking away at the camouflaged buck brush berries imprinted on my turkey hunting coveralls. Not only had I stopped breathing, my heart hadn't pumped blood in the last five minutes. What in the world could have made those three Tom Terrifics turn tail and head for a different time zone? It was then I heard the unwanted music dreaded by all turkey hunting ears. “Having any luck?” The only luck I was having was all bad. My bad luck was that at this most inopportune time some Wonderin’ Willie had chosen to come bouncing through the woods behind me and had spooked my birds.

Every community has one, the guy that thinks he has a permanent hunting easement on all land, the guy that regards no hunting and no trespassing signs as open personal invitations, the guy that thinks he is the original Rambo of the Woods. There he was….our guy….known in our neighborhood as Rambo Red. Again I heard him holler out, “You havin’ any luck?”

To myself I thought, “Well not now you freakin’ turkey terrifying idiot.” But regardless of what we may be thinking, it can sometimes benefit self-preservation to keep your thoughts to yourself when facing a wildlife felon with a loaded shotgun. Since my run for your life turkeys had probably reached Zimbabwe by now, I crawled out of my almost perfect turkey hunting hiding place to face my almost perfect turkey hunt spoiler.

Trying to remain calm and prison free, I reluctantly put Old Betsy back on safety. I sure would hate to read in the local obituaries of Rambo Red’s untimely demise because of an accidental slippery trigger finger. In less than a hospitable way, I explained how I had permission to hunt and was assured by the landowner that no one else would be on his property today. Rambo Red dismissed my words with a shrug and said he never had and probably never would ask permission to hunt from anybody. He went on to brag about how his military training (most likely a cook stationed in Oklahoma) had made him an expert in jungle warfare. His camouflage expertise was so good that he could slip on and off of any farm without anyone knowing he had even been there. He went on to say that his camouflage clothes and face paint was so good that he could blend in with nature to the point of becoming invisible to an untrained eye. In fact, people had come within three feet of him and never had a clue that he was within spittin' distance. Well, I don't know about people, but my three turkey friends sure spotted him and quickly did the "Now you see me, now you don't" disappearing act.

I began packing up my decoys as Rambo Red sauntered off across the open field muttering how he was invisible to the world. There was really no reason to continue the hunt with him roaming loose in the woods. I decided to call it a day and made plans for a new turkey hunting strategy for tomorrow. Hopefully with any luck at all, Rambo Red would choose some other farm to practice his invisible trespassing skills.

The next pre-dawn morning I decided to set up my shooting quarters closer to where the turkeys had first appeared the morning before. If I could cut down the distance, I might have a better chance of tagging one of the three gi-gantcha-normous leaf rakers. Everything was just about as carbon copy perfect as the previous day.... good weather, good location, and best of all no signs of Rambo Red. There was one slight difference. At the gobble hour, it became evident that the turkeys had chosen a roost exactly where I had sat down the day before. In essence, we had just traded places for this day's hunt. Go figure. For three hours I listened to their lovesick gobbles echoing across the field. I gave them my very best come hither calls to no avail. On this day, they were in no mood to show themselves. I really couldn't blame them after yesterday's Rambo Red scare.

I have learned a long time ago, that it is nearly impossible for my 250 pounds to sneak up on a turkey. Their Superman eyesight gives them a distinct advantage of being the spotter instead of the spot tee. So in general, I usually just wait. I can almost wait forever. Not particularly because I have the patience of Job, but more because of an inherited family trait of pure laying on the porch hound dog laziness. Why chase after something that will more likely than not end up coming to you anyway? But somehow today was different. Listening to those feather shaking gobbles was beginning to get under my skin. My patience was quickly being reduced to that of Judge Judy getting ready to pronounce sentence on a dead beat dad for back child support. The temptation to sneak up on those bearded beauties became too great. I prepared to make my movement. Little did I realize the impact that movement would have on my hunt.

There isn't a Las Vegas book maker alive that would have given odds on me making it across an open field unspotted. General Custer would have had a better chance at his last stand. So that option was out. Unlike Rambo Red, I didn't consider myself invisible. What I needed was a tactical Normandy Invasion plan that would hopefully get me within gunshot range unnoticed. Checking out the surrounding terrain, I began formulating my sneak attack movement. My best bet was to crawl on my hands and knees through the woods to a creek about fifty yards away. From there I would drop off into the shallow water and wade my way west using the creek bank for cover. Once I got to a fallen maple tree, I could hoist myself up to dry land where I could hide in a patch of small sprouts and bushes. From this point if I hadn't been spotted, I would try to make a determination of how close I might be to a potential Thanksgiving feast.

I followed my movement plan like a road map. I crawled. I waded. I climbed up into my hideaway patch of bushes. I hunkered down and listened for gobbles. Yep!!!! They were still there, somewhere just over the next rise. I could sure give that Rambo Red a lesson or two on how to sneak up on a death wish tom turkey. Since the bush area provided little hiding cover, I picked out a big oak tree about twenty-five yards up ahead for my ambush site. So far my planned movement had worked to perfection. However, in just two short steps my movement plan took a turn for the worse.

Something unexpected happened. No, I didn't spook the turkeys. No, I wasn't struck by lightning. And no, I wasn't abducted by aliens. But what did happen made me freeze in my tracks. Sometimes nature can be incredibly cruel, especially when it decides to come calling unannounced. The best advice that I can offer to all wanna-be turkey hunters is this. Do not eat Mexican the night before a hunt. Of all times, why now? I could feel a churning sensation deep inside the inner chambers of my soul. A growling noise from unknown depths signaled an eruption was close at hand. Maybe I could weather this brewing storm by thinking happy thoughts. Nope!! I was having an internal melt down and I was wishing for flame retardant underwear. I looked in the direction of my truck and decided there was no way I could do a mile long scissors walk. Shear panic was upon me. I definitely had not counted on this movement in my earlier pre-movement planning.

By the increasing and magnifying snarling sounds of my intestine, I was seconds away from having a major accident not covered by my homeowner's policy. I didn't have to be a fortune teller to foresee this was not going to be a pleasant colon blow experience. In fact, the knife piercing ache somewhere south of my belly suggested this could reach Hiroshima bomb dropping proportions. In these untimely calls of nature, when a facility is impossible to reach, I usually look for a place of privacy of a fallen log or a big tree to back up against. There's no need to traumatize furry little animals or song birds if you don't have to. But nothing was close and there was precious little time to look elsewhere with so little warning. I needed something to lean on or in this case hang on to and I needed it now. My intestinal fortitude was screaming that speed was of the essence. The only thing close enough to help support me in my upcoming EPA violation was a squatty little elm tree surrounded by a few scattered bushes. My options were few and my choice was clear. With gritted teeth and clinched fists, I shortened my normal big boy stride and took a dozen little Peter Cotton Tail hops to the unfortunate little elm.

If the turkeys weren't gone by now, they were sure to be headed to a friendlier climate in short order. At this point, shooting a turkey was the least of my worries. I immediately felt my bean burrito drop at least two levels in my lower regions. I tossed old Betsy aside out of any potential harm's way. I grimaced in pain as I threw off my back pack. I dropped my camouflage coveralls, long johns and my plaid boxers down to my ankles. As fast as I could, I bent over and hung on to the tree bark like a hangin' chad in a Florida election. With a mighty painful groan, I let nature do its thing. Lightning struck. Thunder rolled. My body shuddered as nature erupted with the force equal to that of Mt. St. Helens. This was one time I was thankful to be viewing nature from the opposite direction.

Awe-Chee-Wawa. I felt like a bucket full of Mexican hot peppers had just clawed their way through my digestive tract. Sweat was pouring off of me in rivers. One final high pitched scream as relief passed over me and through me. But wait just one colon cleansing moment! That scream wasn't mine. With a choking chicken grip on my tree of life and death, I could only get a partial glance of movement in the bushes directly behind me. In fact the bushes were so close I could have spit or done something that (rhymes with spit) on them. And I just may have. Well I'll be darned. I guess Rambo Red was right. He really can blend in with natural surroundings pretty well. Gagging and coughing and screaming words dipped in a high pitch sissy sauce, Rambo Red, or should I say the now Rambo Brown, became a world class sprinter. He crossed the open field in a dead run. He never slowed down. He never stopped. And, he never looked back. Poor fella, I don't blame him for not wanting to look back. He probably will never be able to get rid of his last visual image of my assault on nature as it is. In my tree huggin' position that I was still in, I was kind of glad he didn't stop to ask if I was having any luck like he did yesterday,

No, I didn't get a turkey that day, but my walk back to the truck was a lot more pleasant than it might have been. I was able to score on a Mr. T towards the end of the week without any further nature call complications. As for Rambo Red, he has been nowhere to be seen. I haven't seen him under any bushes. I haven't seen him roaming the woods. I haven't even seen him driving on the road. Rumor has it that he may have moved to Arkansas. I hope his movement went as well as mine. To this day I think Rambo Red thought I had spotted him underneath that gooseberry bush and was trying to teach him a trespassing lesson. But that simply was not the case and I categorically deny that accusation. However, if there is any lesson to be learned by Rambo Red, it is probably this. He might be able to paint up and dress up like a walking blackberry bush to sneak around to fool all of us neighbors, but then again sometimes no matter how hard you try to hide, you just can't fool Mother Nature.

YOU CAN'T HIDE FROM
MOTHER NATURE

VOTE
VOTE
VOTE
VOTE
VOTE
VOTE
VOTE
VOTE
VOTE

CHAPTER 37

TOSSIN' MY HAT IN THE RING

I'M NOT SURE WHY folks choose to enter small town politics. I suppose it goes back to the school yard days of getting picked last for the dodge ball game. There comes a point in life when we all feel the need to be picked first for something, if for no other reason than to help re-inflate our sagging egos. In one of my more unbalanced years, I chose to throw my hat in the ring for a county-wide position. The way it turned out, I probably should have thrown my body under a rolling tractor tire. It would have been quicker and less punishing.

Running for an office in a local election requires tons of self commitment. In a rural community, voters are usually scattered out far and few between. So in order to have a realistic chance of getting elected, the bushes have to literally be beat to death in a search of every possible vote. For the most part, only one out of ten houses may contain an actual registered voter. But since voter houses are not identified with a big red X, the only solution is to stop at every house, trailer, or homeless shelter teepee you come to and knock on the door. To make the primary campaign even more enjoyable, it takes place during heat of July and August. I lost 22 lbs. the first week alone, just from sweat. I hit the campaign trail on a dead run, but ended it on a delirious dehydrated crawl.

Anyone that may be having an incoherent moment and possibly contemplating a future in politics, I would like to share with you just a part of my house to house campaign experience. When it comes to potential voters, there is one of every kind and one of all kinds. And.... I'm pretty sure I met them all.

At one farm stop I think I met the oldest, quite possibly the very first pioneer farmer of our county. While he may have been small in stature, he looked incredibly tough and unbelievably leathery. In fact a well aged saddle bag with eyes would be a pretty fair description. I immediately learned that he was upset. He wasn't upset about something, he was upset about everything. Someone had forgotten to tell him the war was over and I'm not referring to the Gulf War. I'm thinking he was just waiting for supplies and ammunition, and the South and his General Lee were going to rise again.

On another stop, I happened to notice an older gentleman sitting on his front porch. I stopped, walked up to his porch, introduced myself, and we had very nice exceptionally long visit. We pretty much solved the world's problems right then and there on his front porch. Amazingly enough, only after about two hours he announced that he liked me and wanted to know what he could do to help me. My reply was fairly simple, "If you would vote for me I certainly would appreciate it."

His reply was even simpler. "You know, I've never ever got around to signing up to vote." The last time he thought he voted was for a Roosevelt. I didn't hear him say whether it was FDR or Teddy because I was already in my truck making dust.

Sometimes you can judge a voter by the kind of pets they keep. At one country stop, I spotted a guy and his wife working in their garden. Yee Haw! Not one but two possible votes. As I began my walk across the gravel driveway, from around a lilac bush I spotted this mountain of hair rushing at me. Unsure of whether it was a dog or a horse with teeth, I froze in my tracks. The mouth slobbering Cujo came to a gravel sliding stop with his nose buried into my crotch clear to his eyeballs. As I looked down and made eye to eye contact, I interpreted his low guttural growls to say "Go ahead punk! Make my canine chewing day."

My life expectancy continued to deteriorate with the farmer's less than reassuring words, "You might want to hold still, I don't think he will bite." I was really hoping for more comforting words. I was so scared I was afraid to breathe. In one snap my entire gender could be changed. It was only the snarling vibration in my crotch that kept me from returning to my bedwetting days.

Speaking of wetting, it's not only the size of the dog in the fight, but the fight in the dog that can have an unnerving impact on an election campaign. Answering my knock on the door, a young lady showed up with a screamin' baby in one arm and a rabid Shih Tzu in the other. She had no more than opened the door when her phone rang. Needing a free hand to answer the call, she gave me the option of holding one or the other. The Shih Tzu looked like a dirty dish rag with bugging eyeballs and snarling vampire teeth. The snarling baby, on the other hand, I don't believe had teeth. I chose the snarling little varmint. I should clarify. I chose the Shih Tzu. Between both out stretched hands, I held the growling bug eyed little beast at arm's length. When the potential voter turned her back to me, I whispered words of wisdom to my struggling little captive. "Keep it up you little yipping Shih Tzu and I'll put the farmer squeeze on you." He kept it up, so I fulfilled my campaign promise and clamped down with a squeeze. As I gave him my squeeze, he returned fire with his pee. The little fire hose peed up and down my shirt like he was putting out the great Chicago fire. Nothing like campaigning on a hot day drenched in doggie dew.

The people themselves can sometimes liven up a demanding day of campaigning. At one house in town a guy answered the door with painted toenails, eye shadow, and the softest, coldest, clammiest hands I have ever touched in my life. He was living proof of why some animals should eat their young. Yuck!!! I rubbed the side of my wranglers for three city blocks just trying to get rid of the creepy feeling off my "please vote for me" shaking hand.

Sometimes folks can surprise you. One evening when I was hoofing it around town begging for votes, I had a Hell's Angel veer off the street to block my path with his Chopper. He had a dew rag on his head, a beard half way down his no shirt belly, and tattoos visible on every exposed part of his body. I didn't know whether to make a break for it or just wait for the beer bottle to crack me over the skull. I was somewhat taken back when he asked if I thought Senate Bill 108 dealing with potential cuts in higher education had a chance of passing the House Budget Appropriation Committee. Wow! Who would have guessed Road Rash would even have had a coherent thought, let alone be a student of state politics?

At one door, I had no more than said hello when a lady grabbed my arm, pulled me in the house and said, "Get on in here. My husband's got something he wants you to eat."

Pushed into a kitchen chair, a plate of something was slid in front of me. "Try one of those," said the grinning husband.

"What is it," I asked.

"It's good," he said.

"Good for what," I asked again.

"To eat," he snickered. "Haven't you ever had a deer popper," he wanted to know? "Try it. You'll like it. You want my vote don't cha?" Well, he had me there. I really did want his vote. So I popped in the deer popper. Or, maybe a better description would be the blasted deer popper started popping me. Holy Chernobyl Uranium Spill !!!!! My tongue immediately went limp and my mouth quickly followed suit. I eventually learned that a deer popper consists of a smidgeon of deer meat, wrapped in some kind of nuclear enhanced cheese, soaked thoroughly with some type of cruelty to animals hot sauce, then stuffed into the hottest Mexican fire eater's jalapeno pepper known to mankind. After creating a sweat pool on the floor, my head actually started to bleed through the sweat pores. My right eye swelled shut and the left one began an uncontrollable twitch. I lost my ability to speak words. I could make whooo whooo sounds, just not words. If elected, I promise to make deer poppers illegal.

Voters want to know if elected will you work hard for them. Walking up a sidewalk, I met a potential voter coming down his porch steps. I introduced myself, shook his hand and gave him one of my self flattering brochures. Right there in front of me he read it and kept making approval sounds like he was enjoying what he was reading. "Well, you certainly seemed well qualified for the office," he said. "We need more people like you in office today," he added. SWEET!!!!! I was becoming so light headed I could hardly keep my feet on the ground. He wished me good luck and I headed on my way trying hard not to pat myself on the back. "Hey," I heard my well wisher's voice behind me. "You wouldn't have a minute to help me carry a table would you?"

"You bet," I volunteered. It's the least I could do for a vote. As we walked around the back side of the house there was a U-HAUL trailer backed up to some sliding doors. I helped carry the table. Then I helped carry the dining room chairs. And then I helped carry the refirgerator, kitchen stove, washer, dryer and deep freeze. Then we started on the hide-a-bed couch, two recliners, a love seat, two sets of bedroom furniture and a back breakin' hope chest filled with all of grandma's prized possessions… and maybe even grandma by the weight of it. My light headedness of voter exultation was quickly being replaced by too much bending over and lifting dizziness. Puffing like a freight train, I mentioned something about my pace maker starting to act up. I really didn't have a pace maker, but he didn't need to know that. Good politicians are known for shading the truth. I almost went to one knee when he said, "That's all right. I'll just leave the rest of the furniture for the moving crew. They'll be here in a little while." As I staggered off, I got a pat on the back and heard something about being an angel in disguise. But just before crossing the street, I turned and asked if he had bought a house on the other side of town. "Oh no," he said. "I took a job out of state and I have to be there the day after tomorrow." Great!!!!!! Mr. Butter Me Up wasn't even going to be in the county for the primary election. That no good lying snake in the grass. He should have been a politician himself.

There can be awkward moments when campaigning. One knock on the door was answered by the cutest Shirley Temple looking little girl I had ever seen. I asked if her mommy or daddy was at home. She nodded yes and motioned for me to come in. I did. She walked over to the TV and sat down in front of it to watch cartoons. She also had a bowl of grapes for a snack. Looking back and seeing me standing by the door, she patted the floor next to her and invited me to watch an episode of Sponge Bob Square Pants. I was enjoying my grapes and deeply engrossed in Sponge Bob looking for a buried treasure when Mommy and Daddy walked in. I'm reasonably certain I lost those two votes, but the grapes were good.

Sometimes a mistaken identity can lead to an awkward moment. One evening when I was out door knocking, I remember it was close to supper time because I could smell something cooking from the house I was approaching. Picking my way through a yard resembling the debris field of an EF5 tornado, I walked up some rickety steps and approached a one hinged screen door. Before my knuckles could even get close for a knock, the door flew open and this wild eyed, red faced, shirtless, long haired, full bodied tattooed maniac screamed, "What the hell do you want?" This guy was wound tighter than a Timex. I was so scared I forgot what I wanted. I could barely remember who the heck I was. Having just enough composure to control the alligator tears swelling in my eyes, I squeaked out that I was running for a county office. I guess it was my brochure in hand that was possibly mistaken for a search warrant. Seeing that I wasn't the law, the Son of

Satan relaxed a bit and said over his soldier, "Its okay. It's just some dude running for an election." I immediately started looking for a red dot on my heart. Thinking back, I'm almost positive that wasn't a hamburger I smelled being cooked over a Bunsen burner.

"We were hoping you would come by," said a lady as she met me on the front porch. "We were just talking about you today and Fred said that he hoped that you would be stopping by. Look, I'm on my way to my daughter's to pick up the grandkids, but he is in there watching TV, so go on in and visit with him. He's sure going to be glad to see you," she added as she jumped in her car. Off she went. This stop would have been much more enjoyable if I had an earthly clue as to who in the name of Grandma Moses Fred and his wife were. But what the heck! If this guy was excited to see me, I was going to be just as excited to see him. I opened the door, wandered down a hallway, and following the sound of Vanna White turning over her Wheel of Fortune alphabet. I entered the living room to find my "couldn't wait to see me fella" stretched out on a couch doing his Rip Van Winkle imitation. I was at a loss as to what to do next. Was he just resting his eyes? Was he taking a short nap? Or was he down and out for an all night count? Wishfully thinking that he might wake up at any moment, I decided not to disappoint him by leaving without a visit. I sat down in a recliner to wait him out. I had won three rounds of Wheel of Fortune and not one eyelid had even cracked.

Just when I thought he was about to come out of his snoring coma for a visit, he only gave a couple of snorts and stirred around instead. Not opening an eye, he reached down and unsnapped his Levis and then began to scratch a really bad itch in his big boy region. My retinas were beginning to burn as I watched the digging, the pulling, the rearranging and the unmerciful scratching. I was wishing that my own eyes would close…permanently. Excited to see me or not, every fiber within me was saying that I needed to make a break for it. If he woke up and I was sitting there staring at him, I'm not sure what

I could have said to him…except for, "I didn't know you were left handed." I quietly tippy toed over to Mr.Scratchmo, gently placed my campaign flyer on his chest and then made a get-a-way faster than a get a way car at a 7-11 heist.

Sometimes a campaigning can cause eye strain. As I bounced up the steps of a trailer, I put on my best vote for me campaign face and gave the door bell button a push. I waited an appropriate amount of time and pushed the button once again. With no answer, I was just about to stick one of my campaign brochures in the door when I felt a vibration. I can only associate the vibration of being similar to the foot steps of Big Foot walking across a ping pong table. When the door opened, there stood the biggest wet woman I had ever seen in my life. Not that I have seen that many wet women. Orca had heard the doorbell and had come straight from the shower. She was as slick and shiny as a seal. The hand towel she held in front of her covered absolutely none of her private areas. I'm sure Eve's fig leaves would have covered more. I tried my level best to maintain eye to eye contact with the dripping damsel. But, I could tell I was beginning to develop a lazy right eye, so I bore down and focused with all my might. I handed her one of my vote for me refrigerator magnets that was considerably bigger than her cover up towel. I'm not sure that an entire refrigerator could have provided enough cover for that much exposed flesh. I apologized for interrupting her Nestea plunge and then fell off the porch backwards.

On a hard day of campaigning there is always the need for pit stops. Of course knocking on a stranger's door and asking to use their restroom will probably not gather too many votes. So what a campaigner does in a rural election is to look for a lonely country road absent of residences. On one of these fateful occasions when Mother Nature began calling, I needed to find a watering ground fast. As luck would have it, I happened to be in a rather sparse neighborhood of the county. I wheeled on to a tree lined gravel road and drove to a rise where I would be able to look in both directions. Being proud of myself for finding such a secluded location, I went about doing my water reducing business. Have you ever just seemed to sense something isn't quite right? There was no dust from either direction. I was standing in the cover of shade trees just off of the road. I was reasonably certain I was safely hidden from any peering eyes, but there was this impending sense that my privacy was about to be interrupted. Oh! Oh! Hearing hoof beats, I quickly turned to see if I was about to be trampled by a stampeding horse. What I hadn't counted on was being in Amish country. Ma and Pa Bonnet and Suspenders, riding in a horse drawn buggy had slipped up behind me from a nearby hay field. I only had one hand to wave at them as they trotted by. A big sign in the back of my truck with my name plastered on it, left no doubt as to whom I was. If there was any consolation at all from this embarrassing situation, I learned that our local Amish do not participate in elections.

On the last day before the election, I decided to make one last attempt to find any of those elusive votes. I went to a small town and began walking streets and knocking on doors. It was a pleasant evening and I found several folks sitting on their front porches. I had made it to the last house of a dead end street just as the sun was setting. A middle aged guy was sitting on a porch swing and greeted me with a very friendly wave. I reached out and shook his hand and everything went down hill from there. It turned out that my last potential voter had a speech impediment. He could not pronounce the letter L. In fact he substituted the letter R for words that had Ls. I was immediately taken back when he asked, "Are you rooking forward to your erection?"

My what? His unexpected question hit me in the face like a bucket full of ice water. "Excuse me," I asked?

"Your erection, are you rooking forward to it," he yelled louder. Not only was the guy speech impaired, but his hearing was shot to. To compensate for the hearing loss, he screamed almost every word.

Everyone in the neighborhood was now on the edge of their porch swings anxiously waiting for my reply. I could already hear a few scattered chuckles coming from nearby porches. I tried to dodge the question by diverting his attention to one of my informational pamphlets. As he was scanning the material, I tried faking a heart attack and said I needed to run back to my truck for my nitroglycerin pill.

As I trotted down his sidewalk, I heard his screaming parting words, "Good Ruck on Your Erection Tomorrow." There was no use to run now. His announcement had been heard for at least three city blocks. Where was a real heart attack when you needed one? Walking down the street somewhat dumb struck, I got a chuckle and a "thumbs up" from every front porch I passed. I wasn't sure if the "thumbs up" was for the upcoming election or erection. I'm sorry to report that on Election Day, I lost out on both accounts.

TOSSIN' MY HAT IN THE RING

YOU RANG AMIGO

CHAPTER 38

ADIOS AMIGO AND REMEMBER THE ALAMO!

DOESN'T IT TICK YOU off when someone always gets the best of you? That's the way it is with my brother. Our lack of maturity and good natured sibling rivalry has gone on for years. But no matter how well I plan a practical joke, he usually finds a way to top me.........sometimes without even trying. One such occasion occurred recently on his 55th birthday.

All through our lives, our Dad would find ways to drive me and my brother nuts with his warped sense of humor. His all-time favorite demented joke was to call us, at the butt crack of dawn, on his own birthday and sing the Happy Birthday song to himself. I know. I know. It sounds stupid, but in his own morbid way he thought it was funny. I always tried to give him the benefit of the doubt and just marked it off to the double dipping of his Prozac. Not only did he get a buzz out of getting to wake us up, but he got the added thrill of trying to make us feel somewhat guilty for not remembering his birthday. Well good grief! No reasonably sane person is thinking about birthdays (anybody's birthday) especially at 5:00 o'clock in the morning. And, he wouldn't just sing in a normal manner. He made sure each and every note was not just a little off, but an eye crossing teeth gritting off key. His vocal rendition could be compared maybe to a heart broken hound dog baying at the moon or a garden tiller running wide open without a muffler. Like I said, he thought it was funny and that is all that mattered to him.

Well anyway, we lost Dad last year. So in his memory, I suppose my dim witted brother thought it would be fun to keep up dad's family tradition of singing the before the rooster crows Happy Birthday song. On his July Birthday the traditional call was made to me. Of course to keep the tradition in tact, the tune had to be heard in the wee hours of the morning. When that phone jingle jangled in the pitch black of night, I flew out of the bed as if I had been bit by a cobra. In the dark, my house is pretty much a mine field of household booby traps. Stubbing my toe on the bed post and tripping over the vacuum sweeper, I finally crawled through an assortment of grandkid LEGOS to make a grab for the phone. Immediately expecting the worst kind of news, because what other kind of news is there before the chickens wake up, I uttered a weak and gravelly hello. What I heard back was the saddest.....the most pathetic.....the most mournful Happy Birthday song I have ever heard in my life. Dad would have definitely been proud. Naturally my brother thought it was absolutely hilarious. It's funny how some kids will grow up to have the same sick twisted traits as their parents. My brother is definitely turning into our dad. That means a daily handful of little orange pills and a therapist's couch is just around the corner.

Although I am four years younger than my brother, I feel I am definitely much more mature than he is. Rarely do I stoop to his adolescent antics of playing practical jokes. Wink! Wink! However, this past Tuesday was my birthday and it was only out of respect for my elders that I thought I should repay his earlier thoughtfulness of our dad's Happy Birthday song. To make sure my singing debut would happen at the proper hour, I set my alarm for......3:00 AM…….the absolute perfect witching hour for a family wake me up telephone call.

My brother lives in Texas......way down in Texas. In fact he is so far down in Texas, on a windy day he can spit across into Mexico. I could hardly wait to get my birthday started off on the right note, especially if that note was going to be really off key. Wiping the sleep gunk from my eyes, I still had the alarm clock ringing in my ears as I dialed his number. When the receiver picked up on the other end, I heard exactly what I wanted to hear. There was this really husky drowsy barely audible "Hello." It was great. He's such a deep sleeper I could just picture him trying to figure out where he was and how he got there. Perfect. It's show time. I immediately began belting out one of the most painful eye crossing Happy Birthday songs that could have only been sung by a harpooned walrus. I was moaning. I was groaning. I had real passion when I went diving down to do justice to the really low notes. There is little doubt that I could have won the grand champion prize in a bull frog croaking competition.

I had just gotten to the second "Happy Birthday to Me" part, when I heard a railing of words I couldn't quite make out. It sounded like his wife was now awake and she was giving him fits for ruining her beauty sleep. This was even better than I could have imagined. I was getting two practical jokes for the price of one. As I got to the final happy birthday stanza, I cut loose and let it all hang out. I threw in just a couple of high pitch screech owl notes just to add a little extra pizzazz to my operatic happy birthday sing along. Wow! Pay backs are beautiful. My ultimate practical joke was being carried out to perfection. If Daddy was looking down, I know it would have brought a tear of pride to his eye.

Trying to suppress my giggles, over the phone I could still hear a heated discussion between my brother and his wife. I couldn't make out much, but there was one generic expression I immediately recognized. "Who the @# +% is it?" Oh! Oh! Hold the phone. Something's not right. My brother had been a minister for quite a few years and I really couldn't imagine one little cock-a-doodle-doo phone call would cause him to back slide all the way back to using sailor talk. The agitated voice was becoming shriller and more intense by the minute. To make matters worse, this voice had a very distinctive Spanish flavor to it. Oh! Oh! This might not be good.

My most favorite word immediately came to mind when I realized what had happened. CRAP! Somehow I had accidentally dialed a wrong number and had just woken up some poor Mexican and his senorita from their night time siesta. I tried to explain who I was trying to call, but my rudely awakened Poncho Villa was cutting me no slack. Most of his ranting and raving was in a Spanish English mixture of four letter words. Words that I don't remember ever hearing before or even spelled out in the hundreds of Dora the Explorer movies that I have watched with my grandkids. Although my Spanish is pretty well limited to a Taco Bell menu, I was pretty well getting the drift of his message. Which was, "Leesten here you scum sucking blankety-blank-blank Gringo-- I've got caller ID and I weell find you. And when I do, I'm going to reep this.....And then I'm going to teer that.... And then I'm going to slice you and dice you and feed your body parts to wild peegs....." And those were just the words I could make out. Of course there was a barrage of other more colorful Spanish phrases, which I presumed to have something to do with an autopsy of a cadaver. As the verbal onslaught continued, there were a couple of times I thought I actually could feel his spit coming through the phone line. It's funny how the inflection and voice tones of a completely different language can still be so universally understood. Even though I couldn't translate all of his meaning, it was obvious that inflicting pain was foremost on his mind. It didn't take much imagination on my part to visualize what particular body cavity of mine he was planning on reeping and teering.

Poncho Villa was fast making a believer out of me. Any second, I was about half expecting a butcher knife to reach through the phone and slice off one my ears. Trying to offer an apology is next to impossible to someone who is spittin' words out faster than a chain on a wide open chain saw. As hard as I tried, I couldn't get a word in edge wise. Poncho's one tract mind was on a mission. And that solitary mission was trying to figure some way to knock the goodies out of my piñata from 950 miles away.

As his threats grew more menacing, I broke my number one rule of being a coward at all costs. I did the bravest thing I could think of doing at 3:00 AM in the morning. When he paused to take a breath I said, "HEY! Listen up you little Speedy Gonzalez want to be. I called you by mistake. I've tried my best to apologize. Now why don't you just pull down your sombrero and give it a rest. But if you are bound and determined to not let it go, here is my name and address and why don't you jump on your Barney the Burro and trot right on over here. It will only take me a minute or two to give you a good lesson in basic manners 101. Adios my little Amigo friend and above all else.....Remember the Alamo," and then I hung up.

Whew! Finally my little Santa Anna session was over. Still, I probably shouldn't have given Poncho my brother's name and home address. Maybe I should warn my brother that he might be having an early morning visitor. But since I had already lost confidence in my phone dialing ability, I sure didn't want to take a chance on accidentally getting another wrong number. Oh well. What the heck. My brother really likes a good practical joke. If Poncho would happen to show up at his front door in the next few minutes, I'm sure they would see the humor and sit down and have a good laugh over it...or not. Who cares? It's my birthday and I'm going back to bed and have a sweet dream about being serenaded by a donkey cart load of singing senoritas.

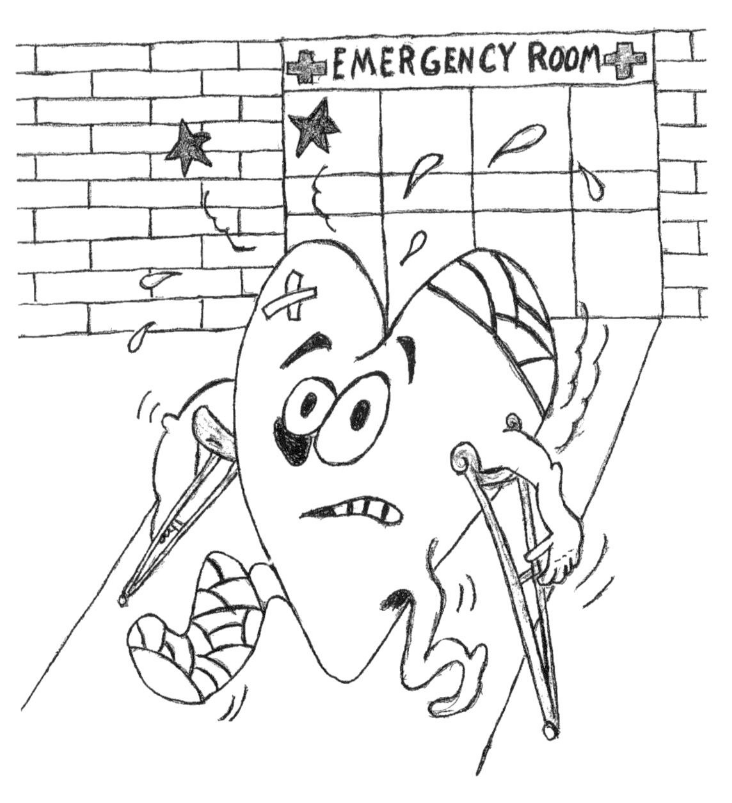
EMERGENCY ROOM

CHAPTER 39

AND THE BEAT GOES ON

YIPPITY DOO DAH! I made it. Made what, you might ask? Well, I finally made the BIG FIVE 0. A half of a century. A bicentennial occasion. A Roman Numeral "L." Wow! This is the first time I have ever had an "L" associated with me, which wasn't preceded by at least two or three X's on the shirt tag. Anyway, I have proven my old high school principal wrong and did beat his life expectancy odds of me and that's what counts.

The entire year leading up to this mid-century milestone, folks have been helping me to prepare for this special event. The AARP has now included me on their monthly "Wrinkles Are Us" mailing lists. I certainly enjoy reading about the many upcoming silver haired, camera on a stick, proctology procedures heading my way. I should try to include those KODAK moments in the next annual family Christmas letter just for fun.

Today's kids seem to show very little sympathy for the plight of us old folks. A pimply faced 15 year old waitress recently singled me out at the local Chinese "CHU MI FAT" Restaurant and asked if I wanted the five percent sixty-five and older senior citizen discount. No tip for that little chick-a-dee wannabe. On my home phone, I had a message inviting me to a meeting on how to pre-plan and more importantly pre-pay my own funeral service. Although it sounded like it could be a real hoot picking out my own wooden box and naming some really uppity ups that I never associated with to be my pall bearers, I don't think so. Why would I want to deprive my kids of that little get even chore?

There have been more and more signals that my body is in the hurry up aging process. My hair is disappearing from some areas of the body and showing up in the most unwelcome regions. I now have a forehead which reaches from my eyebrows to the beginning of my Wranglers and enough hair growing in my ears to attract a pair of nesting cockatoos. Fearing driver rejection, I now take my deer hunting range finder with me to those pesky license bureau eye exams. I would at least like to see if the big E is standing up or lying down before they permanently jerk my license. As for my good eating habits, my four major food groups consist of Ruffles potato chips as my vegetable, a Milky Way counts towards the dairy, Meat Lover's Pizza provides adequate protein, and a platter of rice crispy treats covers any cereal grain requirements. My doctor is always criticizing my eating habits. He tells me that every slice of bacon I eat will take eight minutes off my life. I love pessimistic doctors. If that bacon diagnosis was really true, by my bacon consumption calculations I should have kicked the bucket when Pilgrims first hit Plymouth Rock.

Of course all of the little minor league feel bad signals take a definite back seat to the "Oh no! It's the big one Elizabeth heart attack." Having two parents that made rib splitting a recreational past time, I have had plenty of experience in learning the early warning signs of a heart attack. There was the tightening of the chest, nausea, and tingling in the neck and arms. Other symptoms could include shortness of breath, cold sweats, and the desire to stretch out on the couch and watch Dr. Kildare reruns. Feeling a little woozy one day, I began mentally checking off the ticker quitter signs and realized I had just made a perfect code blue score. By all accounts I was one shovel full of dirt away from pushing up daisies.

Still, not wanting to jump to conclusions I drove to my doctor's office to see if he wanted to second my opinion. Good Grief! Chest Pains? Sweating? Tingling Arms? Shortness of Breath? The craving for watching an episode of Marcus Welby M.D.? Who was I kiddin'? The verdict was unanimous. The doctor, two nurses, a rubber glove salesman, and three waiting room patients all jumped right on board with my unprofessional heart attack assessment. I was a walking dead man. A nitroglycerin pill was shoved under my tongue, an ambulance was called, and my next of kin was immediately notified. The ambulance ride to the Intensive Care Heart Unit ranked right up there with a runaway lumber wagon. The only shock absorber in the entire vehicle turned out to be me. Since the ambulance/hearse was not equipped with the bring 'em back to life shock and awe electrocution paddles, the NASCAR car/ambulance driver made certain he hit every pot hole as a precautionary method to keep me resuscitated.

If the ambulance ride didn't kill me, the ER nurse "Attila the Hun" sure gave it her best shot. She jerked my stretcher out of the ambulance and wheeled me down the hallway in a dead run. I thought I was in a demolition race for life derby as we crashed into every gurney, wheel chair and bed pan in sight. As we came to a turn left or right dead end, Attila made a quick left towards Intensive Care. That was good because a quick right would have landed me right square in the middle of the John Doe morgue.

Once in my room, two janitors hurriedly wheeled in a mega watt heart monitoring machine next to my bed. The colossal heart cart had gauges and wires hangin' from every direction. Attila immediately ripped off my shirt and began super gluing little round patches to my chest. Electrodes from the machine were attached and the power switch flipped to the on position. Nothing happened. No lights flashed. No gauges moved. No nothing. Attila went into an immediate life-saving action by removing the super glued patches. Rip!! Rip!!! Rip!!!! Yell!! Scream!!! Cuss!!!! I felt as if I was auditioning for an Australian NADS hair removal commercial. Attila was ripping patches of hair off my body the size of coon skin caps. Have mercy on my hairless chest soul!!!! Water board torture would have been a breeze compared to this type of inhumane treatment.

Another nurse suggested shaving might help to form a better electronic connection. Attila whipped out her own personal mustache shaving BIC and began raking off my chest hairs and at least two layers of skin. YEOW!!! Another set of patches were glued in place and wires reattached. Flipped the switch! Nothing. Five hundred bells and whistles on this heart checkin' contraption and there wasn't one little hint of a mechanical hum. Without hesitation, Attila resumed evaluating my pain tolerance. Rip!! Rip!!! Rip!!! No time for screamin' or yellin'. I headed straight for the cussin'. Cuss!! Cuss!!! Cuss!!! Mopping up my bloody chest with a bed sheet, Attila gave me a quick "sorry about that" as she tried to reattach the pointy part of my left nipple.

My chest was bleeding like it had been blasted by a double barrel Winchester. Finding new places to inflict pain was not going to be easy. But Attila was a professional life giver or taker and she sought out new undisturbed territory. This time, she pulled out a new trick play from her Brave Heart play book of torture. After raking off what few remaining chest follicles there were, Attila pulled out a wood rasp to thoroughly rough up the presumptive glue down area. Attila had learned this rasping technique from a retired horse barn carpenter. No time for yellin' screamin' or cussin'. I just started bawlin'. Once again there was the now or never flip of the switch. It was never. Not one light. Not one bell. Not one whistle. Writhing in pain and now completely free of any body hair, I screamed, "For the love of Lassie, do not touch me one more time. Just pull the plug and let me die." And just by accident, I had provided them with the operating procedure needed. Someone had actually forgotten to plug the million dollar monitoring machine into the 110 wall outlet. I had lost all of my chest hair and the sticky out part of my left nipple all because someone wasn't bright enough to bend over and push in the plug. I was now more confident than ever that I was in the perfect place to actually fix my ailing heart.

It's amazing how a million-dollar machine can spit out data once it has juice. Since the machine data was showing that I wasn't in any immediate danger of buying the farm, Attila suggested we go for a walk. Anywhere away from the full body barber shop torture chamber was fine with me. But as it turned out, Attila, bless her sadistic little heart, was only planning on watchin' while I on the other hand, did all the actual heart kerr thumpin' walkin'.

As we rounded a corner, there was a tiny frail gray haired wisp of a woman pluggin' away on a treadmill. I kind of felt sorry for the old gal. Although she was plodding along at a steady pace, she looked as if she would have been much more comfortable behind a nursing home walker. Never the less, in a minute or so they shut it down and had granny hop off and she was led behind a screen. I am sure she was being removed as an act of kindness so that she wouldn't have to watch a real man treadmill work out.

Attila told me the treadmill exercise would be a mere six-minute stroll in the park. As soon as my heart rate got up to 175, the walk would be over. The first 30 seconds went smooth. I was moving like a fat tick on the back of a lazy hound dog. However, the next five and a half minutes were pure hell. Attila cranked the speed up to a pace that would have qualified me for the Olympics. She then changed the elevation to simulate a climb of Mt. Everest. I was huffin'. I was puffin'. I was thinkin'. Just how big is this darned park that I was strollin' in? Although my light headed dizziness was close to becoming a full fledge black out, I continued to focus my tunnel vision on the quick climbing heart rate monitor. …5….10…15…150… My lungs were screaming. My legs were burning. My spine was cracking like a plumber's butt. This excruciating test of pain was just wrong on so many levels. How bad can a heart attack be anyway?

Finally....finally.... the magic number of 175 popped up on my heart rate radar. I pitched off the rubber moving mat like a jumper off the Golden Gate Bridge. Half carrying and half dragging me, Attila pulled me behind the corpse viewing screen. I was breathing so hard Attila and her fellow inmate nurses must have thought I was going into labor. They smeared a Vaseline jelly all over my belly to give me a sonogram. I assume it was to see if it would be a head first or breached delivery. While I was sucking for air like a drowning victim, Attila said the silliest thing, "Okay! Hold still and don't breathe." Are you freakin' kidding me? Was she insane? No problem on the holding still part. I was so exhausted I could barely move. But don't breathe. What kind of maniac would make you run full tilt up a Pike's Peak mountain side and then ask you not to breathe? In her previous life, Attila had to have been a Nazi SS Storm Trooper.

After barely surviving my six minute eternity treadmill trot and finding out that I was not pregnant, my greasy belly and all was then put through another batch of heart checking tests. When it was all said and done, my kerr thumper pumper was given a clean bill of health. What the test did show was that I had gas. Great! So much for eating Mexican food after nine o'clock. The good news is that Rolaids are going to be my new best friend. The not so good news is that it has been two months since my Attila the Ripper incident and I'm still yellin', screamin', and cussin' every time I hear Velcro being ripped apart.

Honestly, with all things being considered, fifty is not all that bad. I may be a little fatter, somewhat slower, and a whole lot balder..... all those dreaded senior citizen "er" words which afflict the elderly. But as far as a 50 year old heart goes, it's still a pumpin' and I'm still a jumpin' and the beat goes on.

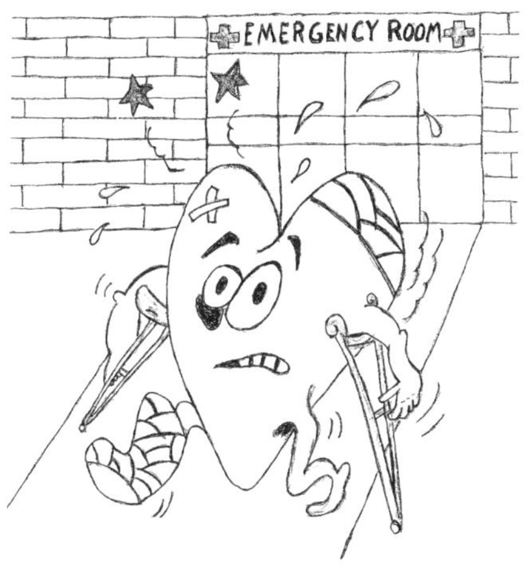

AND THE BEAT GOES ON

CHAPTER 40

DAD'S TOP TEN LESSONS OF LIFE

ALMOST EVERY KID NEEDS a role model. Someone to look up to. Someone that can teach those valuable lessons of life. Lessons like how to keep your mouth shut so flies can't lay eggs in your brain or how to pee your name in the snow or the magical sounds made when getting to pull a finger. In many cases this role model responsibility usually falls on the shoulders of the Dad. My Dad taught me these valuable life-long lessons and so many more.

Lesson 1...To Be One with Nature

My Dad might be best described as what you might say a little bit on the jittery side. Being a WWII vet, loud noises seemed to spook him. When I was growing up, our family lived on a farm. Like most seven year old boys, I enjoyed running around the countryside pretending to be a cowboy or sometimes even an Indian. When I was in my Geronimo mood, I would try to walk as quietly as possible and sneak up behind our collie dog or old yellow tom cat and then cut loose with a "stick 'em up white man" yell. The collie dog would fall all over himself trying to make a clean get away. The tom cat on the other hand would go straight for the stars like he had been launched from an Apollo launch pad.

It was so much fun watching the dog and cat do their terrified yoga moves, I had the bright idea that it might be fun to sneak up behind Dad and let go with one of my very best white man scalping war hoops. I was bare footed and I didn't make a sound as I snuck around a lilac bush to get right behind Dad. I was one with nature. I was the best invisible Indian ever. He didn't have a clue there was an Indian within 50 miles of him. Dad just happened to be getting ready to cross a barbed wire fence when I let loose with the shrillest high pitched Comanche Indian "stick 'em up white man" screech ever. Dad let out a scream of his own and kind of did a collie/tom cat combo jump. He was all over himself, but still could have qualified for the Olympic high jump. He almost cleared the barbed wire fence from a standing position. It would have been better for me if he had been able to jump the fence cleanly. Instead, on his downward descent he ended up straddling the skin puncturing barbs of the fence. As the barbs found their mark in his south of the border regions, he again let out another scream that included some army talk words. It was at this point I was pretty sure our white man/Indian treaty was probably broken. So I jumped on my imaginary painted pony and made tracks for happier hunting grounds.

Lesson 2...Getting Priorities Right

Dad always had his priorities right. One morning while Dad was outside doing morning farm chores, mom had us boys at the kitchen table eating breakfast. The morning quiet was broken by the loud honking of a truck horn, an engine roaring and lots of yelling outside. Suddenly the back porch door was flung open and Dad rushed through the kitchen and made a bee line to his bedroom closet. We sat there staring as he ran back out of the house carrying his brand new Remington 12 gauge shotgun. About two minutes later while we were still munching our Post Toasties, Dad ran back into the house yelling for all of us to get out. The house was on fire. It wasn't much of a fire and Dad and our milk hauler got the fire under control with a couple of well-aimed feed buckets full of water. But still, it was good information to know where the family ranked on Dad's in case of fire priority list.

Lesson 3...Community Involvement

Living in a rural community, we also attended a small rural country church. One particular year, in an effort to increase church attendance, Dad and Mom's Sunday School Class thought it would be good to host a community party and invite some potential church member prospects. It was the fall of the year, so the class chose a harvest/Thanksgiving type theme that would be held at one of the class member's barn. The barn had been decorated with corn shocks and pumpkins. A hay tunnel had also been constructed for an entrance to the social event.

On a crisp November evening, several of the usual church goers and potential class members arrived at the party location and began visiting outside the barn entrance. All the young farmer couples began swapping their grain harvesting stories. At the appropriate time, it was announced that it was time to begin the church party festivities inside the barn. In order to start the fun, everyone had to enter the barn by way of the hay tunnel. The tunnel entrance was pitch dark. The tunnel itself was long with a very low profile. It was just high enough that an adult could barely squeeze through while crawling on their hands and knees. Everyone began crowding towards the tunnel entrance, dropping down and beginning the hay tunnel crawl to the party.

Once Dad began his crawl, he soon learned the tunnel was built in the form of a maze. There were some side passageways that would lead only to dead ends. With folks wondering in and out of the side tunnels, the tunnel traffic would literally slow to a terrapin turtle crawl. Navigating through the dark tunnel was not easy since the visibility was an absolute zero. But Dad wasn't concerned about finding the way out because he knew Mom was just ahead of him leading the way.

Every once in a while, there would be so much congestion in the tunnel the crawlers would actually have to come to a complete stop to let others figure the way out. Being young and somewhat frisky, Dad thought it would be down right funny to have some fun with Mom. Whenever the crawlers stopped he would reach up and give Mom a pinch on the rear end. With each pinch Mom would whisper back, "Quit that!" Of course every "Quit that," was just like saying "Sick 'em" to a farm dog. For the next ten minutes there was a continuous pinch followed by an instant "Quit that." Dad was having the time of his life. He was laughing all the way through the tunnel. He was still laughing when he finally made it through the tunnel and jumped up to face the upset neighbor lady whose rear end he had actually been pinching. It didn't take long for Dad to stop laughing. In fact, I had never seen a smile actually dry up, crack and then fall off of a face before. The happiness seemed to be gone. Dad was no longer happy. The neighbor lady never was happy. And by the time Mom found out what had happened, she for sure wasn't happy. Dad turned into an apologetic wreck and I'm pretty sure the neighbor lady and her husband decided against ever becoming Methodists.

Lesson 4...Religious Values

From time to time Dad would haul me to what might be referred to as spiritual meetings. I'm not sure if it was to keep me on the straight and narrow or just to scare the crap out of me. One cold winter night, he dragged me to a way back in the sticks one room country church for and old fashion Pentecostal Revival. The church was so far back in the boonies, the hoot owls were even afraid to hoot. As we walked into the church, I started studying the congregation. I wasn't for sure if this was really a revival or a Deliverance type Gap Tooth festival.

Preacher Pete was a fire and brimstone type of an evangelist. He wasn't five minutes into his sermon when all heck broke loose. Revival???? It was more like we had just entered the fifth dimension of the Twilight Zone. One corn fed beauty jumped up and started acting crazier than a spider monkey hopped up on Mt. Dew. She was chanting some kind of jibberish that made absolutely no sense. It wasn't long before four or five other fat girls jumped out of their seats and began pretending to stomp crickets. Bouncing up and down the aisle, they too joined in with the same mumbo jumbo chant. Before long the religious heavy weights began dragging the church going men folk out of their church pews. They were huggin' and bouncin' and pantin' and jibberisin', all over the place. If any four walls ever needed to be surrounded by a SWAT Team, it was this old fashion Pentecostal Revival.

One hefty soul sister made a grab for me, but I ducked and slid to safety to the other side of Dad. One bald headed old dude started giddy upping around the room like he was breaking a wild mustang. He was hollering about his wife going to visit her two old maid sisters, Sodom and Gomorrah at the Great Salt Lick…..or something like that. Almost everybody was on their feet by now. I will have to say the chunky girl reunion really did have the old church a rockin'. The gals were chantin'. The guys were whoopin'. The windows were rattlin'. And I thought for sure the old church floor could give way at any minute.

Pretty soon everybody seemed to get tired of the frog hopping, because most of them hit the floor and started floppin' around like a carp on a creek bank. Preacher Pete even went down like he had been hit with a beer bottle in a back alley. This is when the serious moaning and groaning got underway. Some were on their backs, some were on their bellies and almost every one of them had their eyes rolled back in their heads. They were wiggling around on the old wood church floor like pieces of bacon frying in a cast iron skillet. The squawkin' and screamin' carried on for at least twenty minutes. They sounded like a bunch of guineas being chased by a coyote.

My eyes were big as saucers. Dad on the other hand was grinning from ear to ear. I think he was reliving his childhood church memories. Except for two hard hearing old timers asleep in the corner, Dad and I were the only two still sittin' upright in the church pews. All of a sudden Preacher Pete jumped to his feet and began singing "Shall We Gather at the River." Holy Moly! Surely Preacher Pete wasn't thinking about taking us all out for a late night polar bear dip in Cottonmouth Creek. If so, Dad or no Dad I was going to make a break for it. I would rather take my chances on a 15 mile late night hike home than going for a Decem..burr skinny dip. But gradually all the sweaty guys and chunky girls rolled up to their feet and joined in with the singing. Then like a light switch being flipped, the service was over. No one really spoke. Everybody just kind of had a creepy smile on their face as they walked out of the church. They walked and I ran. I made a bee line straight for our '57 Chevy pickup, jumped in and locked both doors. Dad had to give me his mother's maiden name, name what team won the '62 World Series and count from 87 to 41 backwards before I would even unlock the truck door for him. I never did figure out whether Dad had my salvation or traumatization in mind that night.

Lesson 5...Giving Life Direction

Sometimes Dad attempted to give my life direction. As a kid, I lived for the Fourth of July fireworks. Fire crackers and bottle rockets were my favorites. I would use my Black Cats to blow up crawdad mounds and my bottle rockets to teach baby birds how to fly before they even had all of their feathers. After the fire crackers had exploded there would always be plenty of shredded Chinese newspaper scattered around the farm. Once in a while I would tear apart a dud fire crackers just see if I could make out the tic tac toe headlines of a Chinese newspaper. One day my curiosity was killing my cat because I didn't even know where China was. So I went and found Dad working on his almost always broke down tractor and asked him, "Hey Dad, where's China?"

"Right underneath your feet son," he replied. Wow!!! There have been Chinese people making fireworks right under my feet this whole time. Who knew?

"So we just kind of walk on top of Chinese people," I quizzed.

"Yep," nodded Dad as he continued to work on the tractor carburetor.

"Wow! How deep are they," I asked?

"Don't know for sure. Why don't you go find a tater fork and see if you can't dig down and find one," he said. Gee! Whiz! What a great idea. Dad was always giving me good ideas.

I found a secluded location behind the milk barn and started diggin' for one of them firecracker makin' Chinaman. Digging a hole in the July heat is not easy work. The dirt was hard as a rock. But I was an energetic ten year old and I was determined to find China. But after five days of back breakin' hole diggin', my enthusiasm rapidly began to decline when I hit the Great Sandstone Wall of China. I only had a five foot deep hole and there was not one sign of a Chinese firecracker factory anywhere. My Dad thought my search for China was kind of funny. My China excavation had kept me busy for five days and out of his hair for the same time. But....it wasn't quite so funny when he unexpectedly backed his rear tractor tire into my five foot deep China hole a couple of months later. I'm not for sure, but I think Dad might have been speaking some form of Chinese when he crawled off the tractor.

Lesson 6...Sense of Humor

In Dad's later years, he acquired a sick and tormented since of humor. Every March 27th, "his birthday" at six freakin' o'clock in the morning, he would call me at my home and sing Happy Birthday to himself.... like I had forgotten his birthday. Naturally the entire song would be off key and it would be a compliment to say his vocals resembled the croak of a love sick bull frog. Six o'clock in the Morning??? The neighbor's rooster doesn't even wake up that early. Who remembers birthdays at six in the morning? Geeez!!!! Louise!!!! I don't even remember my own birthday at six in the morning.

Lesson 7...Good Intentions

Although he had good intentions, Dad didn't always think things through. At Christmas time Dad would always have in mind some elderly person that had lost their spouse and he would always try to deliver them a box of candy or some little gift to brighten their holidays. If he knew of someone in the hospital, he would make a special effort to stop by for a visit and usually take along some kind of gift. One Christmas, Dad found out that one of his WWII Army buddies was hospitalized, so he made plans for a cheer him up visit. He took along a box of chocolate cherries and a pair of house slippers for gifts. The gifts were accepted with maybe an arched eyebrow thank you from his Army pal. It seems Dad's buddy was a severe diabetic and the disease had progressed to the point that it had been necessary to amputate one of his feet. Dad probably should have forgotten the sugar enhanced chocolate cherries and for sure skipped the slippers.

Lesson 8...Obey Laws if Possible

Dad didn't have a lot of respect for rules or regulations or even most state laws. He thought most laws were merely suggestions and usually meant for other people…not him. Dad's number one hobby was fishing. He especially enjoyed going trout fishing at a state park. One of his favorite fishing holes was designated for artificial bait only. But many times those pesky trout just couldn't be enticed to bite a feather or a piece of plastic or rubber. However, Dad discovered through trial and error the benefits of digging up some grub worms the day before the fishing trip. He could chop them up into little pieces and put a little piece of worm on the point of the artificial lure hook. The trout seemed to be a heck of a lot more interested once they got the scent of honest to gosh real live worm juice. In no time Dad would have his five fish limit much to the dismay of all the fellow fishermen. Even when no other anglers were having any luck at all, it was a rare occasion that Dad didn't come home with a full stringer.

After one particular successful fishing trip, my brother and his grown son happened to stop by for a visit. As Dad was showing off his prize catch, it wasn't hard for the two of them to catch the fishing fever. Although my brother and nephew were from out of town, it didn't take long for them to talk Dad into letting them use his fishing gear for a bright and early next morning fishing trip. Dad showed them exactly what bait to use and how to use it….including the worm bits. He assured them that if they followed his instructions to the letter, their stringers would also be full.

It was an hour drive to the trout park, so they left Dad's home at 5:00 AM sharp. What was even more amazing is that they were back home by 8:00 AM fishless. Not only were their stringers not full, they no longer even had stringers. It seems under cover state trout wardens seriously frown upon using illegal (chopped up grub worm bits) in an artificial bait only section of the river. The penalty included being kicked out of the park, confiscation of all fishing equipment, and a $65 fine a piece. It is remarkable how fast a couple of $65 fines can cure a bad case of fishing fever.

Lesson 9...Helping Others

Dad finally retired from the farm and he and Mom moved to town. Although Dad no longer farmed, he did keep some of his smaller farm equipment. He kept one small tractor and a brush cutter. He enjoyed driving out to the farm and chopping up any unwanted weeds or sprouts. Dad never did understand that there was a difference between country and city etiquette. In the country, if you saw something you could do to help out a neighbor, you just went ahead and did it. No permission was asked. No thanks were needed. However in town, folks pretty well wanted you to stay on your own side of the property line. Dad somehow missed the stay in your own yard memo.

One afternoon on a return trip from the farm, Dad spotted a neighbor that must have had lawn mower problems. The grass in the back yard was about three foot tall and for sure was in need of a mow job. Thinking of nothing else except lending a helping hand to someone in need, Dad threw his tractor in gear, jumped the ditch and began slicking the place up with his brush hog. The chopped up grass really began to fly. Due to the height of the grass, it was hard to see what might be in front of him. He did spot a crabapple tree and decided to go mow a few circles around it. As Dad approached the tree, he was feeling pretty darn proud of himself for doing something to help out one of his new town neighbors. He wasn't quite so proud when he started hearing a Clang!!! Clang!!! Clang!!! Dad somehow had mowed over a steel chain and it was being drug into the mower and was wrapping around the mower's turning blades at a remarkable pace. To make matters worse, there was a once ferocious German shepherd attached to the end of the chain. Before this mowing incident, this dog was known as "Fritz the Fang." He was the canine terror of the neighborhood. Kids were not allowed to go within 50 yards of this man killer for fear of losing an arm or a leg. However, there was something about being nearly neutered by a 2700 RPM weed chopper that pretty well took the bite out of Von Barks-A-Lot. To his credit, Dad was able to shut down the mower, just before the German SS Hound was turned into a Berlin Bratwurst. After the attempted good deed experience and from the urging of the local city police department, Dad decided it was probably best to not help neighbors out unless they specifically requested his assistance. And as for Fritz, he became the most docile neighborhood pet on Hagny Street.

Lesson 10...Don't Bother Sick People

Dad was a 78 year old WWII vet when he was diagnosed with terminal lung cancer. Even though his energy level was slipping daily, he tried to go for short walks every evening for exercise. Returning from one of his walks completely tuckered out, he collapsed into his living room recliner. Mom was sitting on the couch reading the late afternoon mail when I stopped by to check in on them. As I sat down, Mom told dad that he had received a letter. Already half a sleep, Dad asked from whom. Mom replied that she didn't know. Well who signed it was the next logical question. Mom said she didn't know because she hadn't opened it. Becoming more agitated by the minute, Dad wanted to know why in the world she hadn't opened it. The answer was because the letter was addressed to him and not her. Well that was the last straw. Good Grief!!!! After 56 years of marriage, why all of a sudden she now decides to not want to read his mail? "Open the letter," he complained. Mom opened the letter and began to read to herself.

After a couple of moments Dad said, "Well, what does it say?"

Mom slowly and carefully began to read aloud. "Dear James Reed, if you were in Germany during the years of 1946 or 1947, there is a good chance you might be my father." Tired eyes flew open. Dad immediately snapped out of his exercising coma and became an Olympic sprinter. Jumping out of his Lazy Boy, he crossed the room in about three hops.

"Might be what? Give me that," as he grabbed the letter out of Mom's hand. Mumbling as he read, he must have also been doing basic math in his head. "Well this couldn't have been me," he said. "Cause I left Germany in '45."

"So your only defense that you are not a father is that it's only the wrong year that makes it impossible," quizzed Mom.

Either from the shock of the letter or maybe left over shell shock from a too close exploding German Panzer shell, Dad stood there in a wobbly daze. Then finally he spoke, "Leave me the heck alone. I'm a sick man."

The lessons of a father, they served me well.

DAD'S TOP TEN LESSONS OF LIFE

CHAPTER 41

I'M NOBODY'S NUT DINNER

IT SEEMS LIKE IT is getting more and more difficult to have a simple plain ole' run of the mill ordinary day. I'm not sure if it is an old age thing or maybe I have just set my bright chipper day bar way too high. Every day it seems as if there is yet another new disruptive obstacle that has been placed in my path just to remind me that my good time days are long since behind me.

Every morning, I am barely able to roll out of bed and point my compass north. But when I do, I can easily identify each and every one of my different body parts by the various pains I feel. Knees hurt. Shoulders hurt. Upper, middle, lower back hurts. Head is spinning. So much for a good night's rest. With moans and groans, I stumble into my kitchen and set my Breakfast of Champions toaster arrow for my favorite light brown toast. And sure enough, just like clockwork, ... Kerr Boing... up pops the usual smokin' black tar asphalt shingle. On my way to work, I usually can coast in on fumes to the local Gas-N-Git, providing I have a Hurricane Katrina tail wind pushing me along. And naturally, just as I'm stickin' in the hose to fill up my gas guzzling Chuck (Chuck is my truck) the goofy grinnin' snack bar attendant runs out to raise the gas price from $2.69 to $3.49. Yep! Definite signs that it's going to be another great day.

The work day doesn't get much better. An irate individual calls and chews me up one side and down the other and then spits out any leftover pieces back at me through the phone. Once he stops to finally take a breath, I reassure him that I work for the soil conservation service and not a local lawn mower oil changing service. I didn't charge him $100 for anything. Another somewhat deranged customer stops by the office to request some specific topography maps. Thinking he was interested in constructing a lake, I spend a considerable amount of time pointing out specific county drainage areas. My eyes might have slightly crossed when he said he had no interest in building a lake, but had been detailed from the California Sasquatch Society to locate some upper elevation Bigfoot nesting sites in Southern Missouri. A day just can't get any better than this.

So just how should one of my unordinary run of the mill days come to an end? Maybe like this. I live in rural America, sometimes referred to as "out in the sticks." Directly in front of my house is my metal rural mailbox. Every evening when I come home from work, I pull Chuck up beside my mailbox to see who was first out of the gate in sending out their 60 day past due late notices. However, on this particular wintery evening with the sun already set, retrieving my mail would be somewhat different. As I reached inside the box, I felt the hard hairy skull of some unknown creature. YIKES!!!! I thought I had actually found that California Dude's Sasquatch nesting site. I lost part of my thumb nail and the skin off all four knuckles as I jerked my hand out of the metal box. Holy Moly!!! There is definitely something about unexpectedly touching something hard and hairy in the dark that can really cause the kerr thumper pumper to skip a few beats. Where are the shock paddles when you really need them?

Either I or the creature let out a high pitched Girl Scout scream. If I was betting man, I'm pretty sure I would place Las Vegas odds on myself. Throwing Chuck into reverse, my off road tires began digging trenches in the gravel road. Braking to a stop 30 yards away, I switched on my high beams and aimed Chuck's lights straight at the mailbox lair.

After my arrhythmia was once again stabilized, with windows shut tight and doors locked, I put Chuck into drive and carefully made a wide circle to shine his lights directly inside the open mailbox. I could barely make out the head of the creature. He lay motionless. I presumed he was playin' 'possum just waiting for the right moment to unleash his attack. Grabbing a tire tool, I got out of my truck and approached the mailbox monster ready to do bodily harm if necessary. Giving a couple of quick jabs with the pointy part of my tire tool weapon, I decided the animal was either dead or in a hibernating coma. On a more careful inspection, I found that it was not a mail monster at all. It seems that my two Honolulu granddaughters thought it would be fun to send Grandpa a paradise island surprise. So to surprise Grandpa, they had actually placed a stamp and address on an actual Hawaiian coconut and mailed it all the way to Missouri. I will have to admit, Grandpa was most definitely surprised.

For days I was extra cautious when opening my mail box lid. But as time went by and as my scraped knuckles began to heal, I had almost forgotten about going postal over the Hawaiian coconut incident. For sure, on any given day I usually have plenty of other asinine occurrences that could ruin any chance of me having just an above average decent day.

But believe it or not, this one particular Friday had not been so bad. I made it to work without having a flat tire. It had been a moron free day at work. And my new medication was keeping my suicidal tendencies in check. What more could a guy ask for? All I had to do was make it home and it would be one of the best plain Jane, run of the mill ordinary days I had had in a long time. Another hundred feet or so, Chuck and I would grab the mail and we would be home free.

Even in the fading light I couldn't help but notice that my mailbox fold down lid was about one third the ways open. Once again my mailman had been carless in securing the mailbox lid latch. So what! If the wind blows a 60 day late bill out of the box, it can just be my 90 day past due late notice next month.

After rolling down my truck window, I finish lowering the mailbox lid and reach for my daily bills and the usual fist full of junk mail. What happened next nearly returned me back to my formative bed wetting years. From inside the box came a ferocious growl. It was a growl a hungry King of the Jungle lion makes when he first spots his daily Happy Meal. I jerked my hand back losing the other part of my thumbnail and reskinning all four of the almost healed knuckles. In a single bound, a saber tooth monster sank claws into my arm and then joined me in Chuck's cab. Even in the fading light, I could see that his eyes were blood shot and the hair on his back was standing on end. His back was arched and it was obvious that a lunge at one of my vital organs or private parts was close at hand.

Like the bravest three year old little girl that ever lived, I screamed at the top of my lungs. Four times I tried to throw open my truck door only to receive a new dent each and every time from my six inch away steel plated mailbox. I made a fear motivated attempt to climb out of Chuck's driver side window. I am now reasonably certain that due to my plump Poppin' Fresh physique, it would be virtually impossible for me to be thrown out of Chuck's side window even if T-boned by an eighteen wheeler. Sometimes it just isn't possible to squeeze a big fat camel through the eye of a Ford Ranger needle window.

Hearing a snarl and a guttural hiss, I whirled to face my attacker. While it was obvious the hideous hairy beast would have no trouble what so ever in carving me up like a Thanksgiving turkey, it was apparent he was confused in the unfamiliar surroundings of the truck cab. In the dimly lit cab, the front window, the passenger side window, the back glass, all looked like means of escape to him. He became an evil rubber injected super villain as he bounced and ricocheted from window to window to window like a fur covered medicine ball on steroids.

It wasn't until after three more truck door opening dents that my light bulb of a brain gradually clicked to the on position. It finally occurred to me the only way I might escape a mutilating death, would be to back Chuck up and bail out. The gravel chewed away at my Mr. Good Years as I slammed Chuck's transmission into reverse. The engine roared. Sparks flew. Gravel sand blasted three of my neighbor's cows. Chuck went from zero to 70 in six feet. As we raced backwards, we went into one ditch, bounced back on to the road, only to find ourselves back in the opposite ditch before coming to a stop. But the good news was Chuck's driver side door was now free. I pulled my ejection seat door lever and bailed out like a crop duster clipping a power line.

Using the don't lock your knees and/or don't bite your tongue off method of hitting the ground, I rolled up against a barbed wire fence and then jumped up and sprinted for my life. I was sure the son of Satan was right on my heels. I gave a quick glance over my shoulder before collapsing into a heap in the roadside ditch. Twenty yard dashes can sometimes be killers for those folks who have neglected their own physical fitness. Thank goodness my body was in top form. The form of a cream filled donut. However, fear can be a great speed motivator even for us fat folks.

Puffing like a coal train, I gingerly got up to my knees. My lungs were burning. My heart was pounding. My eyes were dilated like a cat's. From the cover of a patch of thorny blackberry bushes, I surveyed the area for my attacker. With Chuck still running, I saw the brute monster finally exit my truck. He was huge. He was hideous. And he was extremely hairy. He gave me one last licking his chops glance before disappearing into a grove of hickory trees.

Some may say I might have over reacted to the attack of this beast. But according to the Animal Kingdom Network, squirrels actually can be quite vicious when cornered in close quarters....and in Chuck's cab the quarters were pretty darn close. Squirrels can bark like Rin

Tin Tin and bite every bit as good as Cujo. I defy anyone to argue the point that a squirrel's nut crackin', chain saw buzzing, diamond tipped, razor sharp buck teeth don't look absolutely ten times bigger when they are six inches from your eyeballs. I'm reasonably sure there were at least a couple of different times that this saber toothed monster had actually sized me up for his perfect nut dinner.

At my age, I'm pretty certain my normal run-of-the-mill good days are most likely numbered. Who knows? Maybe I do need a little more excitement in my life. What would be the fun if every day was exactly the same? Even still.....whether it is a good day or an out-and-out worst day ever, I have absolutely no plans of becoming anybody's nut dinner.

I'M NOBODY'S NUT DINNER

CHAPTER 42

NOT A GOOD IDEA

IN THIS WORLD, THERE are some good ideas and then there are some not so good ideas. It is good to avoid the not so good ideas at all costs. To improve the lives of others, here is my own personal five gallon bucket full of life experienced - not so good ideas.

When I was a kid I always wanted to have a horse so I could be a cowboy. Of course when every mouth full of grass was important during the summer droughts of the 50's, there was no room for a horse on a dairy cow farm. Undeterred from living out my cowboy dream, I talked a milk cow into being my horse. But whenever Hard Faucet got tired of being my trusty steed in the barn lot, she would trot under some low hanging tree branches and rake me off. Using a cow to be a cowboy - not a good idea.

One of the basic criteria for becoming a full-fledged cowboy is to know the correct way to throw a steer catchin' rope. I once made a lariat out of some binder twine to rope a run-away skunk. PePe Le Pew was caught on the second toss of my rope. Roping a skunk is just half the battle. Trying to teach a skunk how to lead....impossible. Definitely - not a good idea. Hiding your skunk fermented clothes under your bed from your mom – an even worse idea.

I tried to recreate an old fashioned Christmas with my kids by finding a real out in the woods living Christmas tree. Christmas trees look smaller in the woods. Since it is hard to fit a 12 foot tall tree into an 8 foot ceiling room, trimming is necessary. Caution! The automatic chain saw oilier can and will splatter oil on carpet and wallpaper. A running chain saw in house - not a good idea.

I had a furnace acting up. Checking it out, I observed a lot of rust and soot covering portions of the burners. I spotted a can of compressed air in my shop and decided it would be great for cleaning up the burners. However, shooting compressed air over a lit pilot light is not only – not a good idea – it is beyond stupid. One eyebrow and the right side of my mustache are now missing.

I tried to pinch pennies by recycling my shower curtain. Washing off the mildew was fine. Drying a plastic shower curtain in the clothes dryer was not. Having to scrape a puddle of molten plastic out of a clothes dryer - not a good idea.

Grandkids chewing gum somehow got into my laundry. A stick of Juicy Fruit got stuck to my favorite Fruit of Looms. Remembering someone mentioning that putting gum stuck clothes into a freezer was an excellent gum removal remedy. Remedy worked, but having a guest spot your boxer shorts lying on a bag of frozen chicken nuggets – not a good idea. Just too difficult to explain.

I received a call at work from someone calling himself Dick Weed. Thinking it was a buddy playing a practical joke I gave myself a fun name and played a long with the prank. When in truth there actually was an out of state landowner with the name of (what are the odds) Dick Weede, calling yourself Pussy Willow turned out to be - not a good idea.

I have never been in danger of getting a headache from lugging around too many gold stars on my crown. In other words, I have a sick and twisted sense of humor. My friend and I once went to a mall at Christmas time for some last minute shopping for the wives. Sometimes we would break the shopping monotony by mess-ing around with the vendors stationed in the center aisle between mall stores. I would pretend to be a deaf mute and he would explain function of items and their prices to me through our own make believe sign language. It was all in fun. But stopping at a kitchen knife booth, with an oriental vendor that actually knew sign language along with a variety of martial arts meat cleaver skills – not a good idea. Chop!! Chop!!

I cooked an old family goulash dish for supper that called for hamburger, macaroni, onions and tomatoes. I had everything except the tomatoes. I substituted cherry juice for the tomatoes to at least have a red color. Serving pink stained macaroni - not a good idea.

I was having company over and decided to spruce up the place. Hand dusted the house from top to bottom. Before running my brand new dirt suckin' Hoover sweeper, I sprinkled a generous amount of smell goody powder all over the carpet to get rid of any objectionable man smells. Not checking to see if the new sweeper actually had a bag in it – not a good idea. The family room looked like a London fog had settled in. I could finger write my name on every piece of furniture.

I lived in town for a short time. One night I accidentally locked my keys in the house and had to break in a bedroom window to get them. Pried open a storm window and was halfway through when the wood frame window fell down across my back. I was pinned. I couldn't go forward or backward. The more I struggled, the further south my wranglers slid. Luckily a spotlight lit up the darkness and I was rescued. But mooning a police officer from the breaking and entering side of a bedroom window – not a good idea.

My youngest son was getting his first chance to start on the varsity football team. Many of the older players had pre-game rituals to physc themselves up before a game. My son decided to copy the ritual of one upper classman by grabbing his football travel bag by the bottom and slinging all of his football gear across the dressing room floor. Out came the shoulder pads, the helmet, the shoes, the jersey followed by his mother's lacy underwear. Washing mom's lacy unmentionables with son's football uniform – not a good idea.....ever.

I went to a Wal-Mart Pharmacy to get a prescription filled. While killing time in the pickup line, I decided to take a seat in the "do it yourself take your own" blood pressure chair. I slid my arm in the cuff and pushed the air compressor button and waited for numbers. When the machine never stopped pumping and my head turned two shades of eggplant purple, a pharmacist and two assistants had to cut the power to get me released. Doing self medical treatments in public – not a good idea.

There was excitement as well as anxiety in my first solo attempt at entertaining guests with a five star cook out meal. Placed four potatoes on the gas grill to bake for an hour. At the 30-minute mark, an exploding grill sent everyone diving for cover. I remembered almost the entire recipe. But forgetting to poke holes in the taters– not a good idea.

One of the curses of old age is the loss of hair in wanted places and the new growth of hair in unwanted spaces. Getting rid of unsightly nose hair, calls for special equipment. However, there is a big difference between trimming and twisting unwanted hair. Inserting the torpedo shaped trimmer in the nostril before turning it on ....Yeow!!! - Tears in your eyes painful -- not a good idea.

I went to execute my patriotic right to vote at a small rural township election. An older woman election judge made an off-handed remark about my age. "Your 52," she announced. She was right. I had just turned 52. Knowing that she had attended school with my mother, I jokingly shot back, "Well you got to be pushing 75 yourself." When an older female election judge is letting you know how many previous 51 voters have already voted before you, kidding her about her age – for sure not a good idea.

A windstorm ruffed up some shingles on the house roof. The

next morning was cold but decided to hop up on the house top and make the repairs. I climbed up the ladder, nailed on some new shingles and quickly glued down some old ones. But before I could exit the roof, the wind blew my ladder down leaving me stranded. Three different neighbors gave me a friendly wave as they drove by while I did jumping jacks trying to flag them down as well as to stay warm. Not securing the ladder or carrying a cell phone for emergencies – not a good idea.

We were on a family vacation and was cruising the main drag of a small Texas town looking for a place to eat supper. Located what looked to be a local favorite family restaurant. There was a long waiting line, but just as we entered the door, a hostess motioned for our family to head towards a newly opened room with just an absolutely superb looking buffet. What a spread. There were three different meats, several veggies and deserts to die for. Half way through the meal a very nice gentleman introduced himself and asked which side of the family we were from. Missourians crashing a Texas wedding rehearsal dinner – not a good idea....but the food was great.

I tried my hand at making brownies. Put all the ingredients in a mixing bowl. The ingredients were mixed with a high-speed hand held mixer for one minute. Used finger to taste and check texture for lumps. I restarted the mixer before getting it quite all the way back into the bowl. Splattering walls, appliances, kitchen cabinets, ceiling and face with brownie mix. – not a good idea

I needed to attend an unexpected out of town meeting. I left town with a full tank of gas and a billfold full of cash. Made the three-hour drive and met a group of friends for dinner. We had a great meal and good story telling conversations. A first day on the job waiter brought the check during one of my last stories. We all grabbed our billfolds and purses to chip in our appropriate meal amounts. Continuing with my story telling, I didn't notice I had absent-mindedly left my billfold on the restaurant booth seat. I made it all the way to our hotel before discovering my billfold was absent. I immediately drove the three miles back to claim my cleaned out billfold. Leaving a $750 tip – not a good idea…but a great motivator for a first day on the job waiter.

I really do understand that our world is made of many various and diverse cultures. I try to be respectful of their religious faiths, their political beliefs, and their inherited family values. However, recently in my local grocery store, I accidentally stumbled upon a food aisle, which specialized in unrecognizable third world foreign cuisine. As I strolled down the aisle, observing jar after jar containing slimy unrecognizable chunks in them, I began getting an eerie creeped out sensation. In my simple way of thinking, when you look at food and all of a sudden you notice the food is actually looking back at you, eating it – probably not such a good idea.

My seven year old granddaughter spent the weekend with me. Her favorite glittery pants got wet so I tossed them in the clothes dryer. I did my own laundry late Sunday evening. Didn't find out that the glittery sparkles had come off in the dryer until my Monday morning doctor's appointment. Glittery BVD's on a guy in a doctor's office – absolutely not a good idea.

The older I get the more aches and pains that seem to show up. One particular pain begins in my shoulder, then seems to shoot up the back of my neck and ends up with a nasty migraine headache. One weekend I watched a TV infra-mercial about a new drug that might be the cure I have been hoping for. However, taking a pill that might cure a headache, but could also offer side effects of dry mouth, sore gums, dizziness, internal bleeding, boils, puffy eyes, darkening stools, dry heaves, heart palpations, stiffening of the joints, shingles, liver damage, anal leakage, loss of motor skills, erratic blood pressure, mood behavior swings, nausea, cold sweats, post nasal drip, eye twitches, long and short term memory loss, foul mouth, and increased suicidal tendencies – maybe not be such a good idea.

THE END